COMPARISON AND HISTORY

COMPARISON AND HISTORY

EUROPE IN CROSS-NATIONAL PERSPECTIVE

EDITED BY
**DEBORAH COHEN &
MAURA O'CONNOR**

Routledge
New York • London

Published in 2004 by
Routledge
270 Madison Avenue
New York, NY 10016
www.routledge-ny.com

Published in Great Britain by
Routledge
2 Park Square
Milton Park, Abingdon
Oxon OX14 4RN U.K.
www.routledge.co.uk

Routledge is an imprint of the Taylor & Francis Group.
Printed in the United States of America on acid-free paper.

10 9 8 7 6 5 4 3 2 1

Library of Congress Cataloging-in-Publication Data for this book is available from the
Library of Congress

ISBN 0-415-94442-2
ISBN 0-415-94443-0 (pbk.)

CIP data TK

CONTENTS

ACKNOWLEDGMENTS

We wish to thank the institutions that made this book possible: the German Historical Institute (Washington, D.C.) and the Charles Phelps Taft Memorial Fund of the University of Cincinnati. Christof Mauch of the German Historical Institute encouraged this project from its earliest days. The Taft Foundation and the German Historical Institute made possible the workshop we convened in April, 2001 at the University of Cincinnati, where the idea of this book developed. David Lazar, editor at the German Historical Institute, made this collection a much better book. We want to thank, too, the editorial staff at Routledge: Karen Wolny, who contracted this volume and Andrea Demby, who saw it through production. Farid Azfar helped to compile the bibliography, Katharina Gerstenberger aided us in translation, and Natasha Margulis ensured that the original Cincinnati workshop ran smoothly. And Maura thanks Rory O'Connor–Mark for his curiosity about her work, his fondness for history, and for the pleasant distractions that come from sharing her study with him.

Deborah Cohen and Maura O'Connor
April 2004

INTRODUCTION: COMPARATIVE HISTORY, CROSS-NATIONAL HISTORY, TRANSNATIONAL HISTORY—DEFINITIONS

Deborah Cohen and Maura O'Connor

Viewed from the long perspective of European history, studies that cross national boundaries are neither new nor necessarily revolutionary. Although historical comparisons may be as ancient as Plutarch's *Parallel Lives*, it was the philosophers of the European Enlightenment who first set out to distinguish various areas of the world based upon customs, laws, and religions. If the nineteenth century saw the beginnings of national history to accompany nation-making projects, it also fed an unprecedented boom in comparisons, bolstered by the emerging disciplines of ethnology, anthropology, philology, and law.[1] Even the systematic practice of comparative history, as pioneered by Marc Bloch, Henri Pirenne, and Otto Hintze in the era that followed the Great War, can now boast a venerable pedigree.[2]

What is new today is the pervasive skepticism about national history itself. In an era of globalization—we are told—the traditional "national" approach to history no longer suffices. Critics have registered a number of objections: the claims of empire are pressing, regions cannot be ignored, the old exceptionalisms no longer persuade.[3] To take the nation as the focal point, it has been argued, overly restricts the view. Enthroned in most subfields since at least the Second World War, national history, especially of Europe, seems increasingly under siege. To these challenges, historians have sought a solution in the realms of cross-national and comparative work. As conferences advertise for comparative panels and foundations solicit cross-national proposals, the virtues of venturing beyond national history are often extolled.

But what is largely missing in this enthusiastic rush beyond the nation is any sense of how to tackle comparative and cross-national work. There are, of course, rafts of theoretical, often hortatory, essays on the subject of comparison. We have classificatory typologies galore, most of them bequeathed to us by sociologists in the late 1970s and early 1980s, the years in which comparative historical sociology reached its apogee. Whether the practitioner's aim is the general demonstration of a theory or the illumination of a specific historical context, comparisons have been sorted by genus and phylum down to a dizzying variety of types.[4] The now-classic typologies developed by Theda Skocpol and Margaret Somers, on the one hand, and Charles Tilly, on the other, help to distinguish the ambitions of the historian from those of the sociologist, a subject that Peter Baldwin takes up in his essay in this volume; however, they shed little light on how one should proceed.

For all of the encomiums to histories that cross national boundaries, practical advice for the would-be practitioner is in short supply.[5] How to formulate a topic that illuminates both the specific national history and the larger phenomenon, how to address the problem of sources that may reveal more about a particular country's archival practices than the subject at hand, how to craft arguments that impress specialists without doing violence to the historical context—all have been left to the skill (and luck) of the individual historian. The wheel has been reinvented a number of times, usually in isolation. Only very infrequently do cross-national or comparative historians openly discuss the disadvantages and pitfalls of what they do. There are few realistic appraisals of the problems and costs. Basic questions remain not simply unanswered, but even unasked. What sorts of studies are most likely to succeed? What kinds of work should be avoided? What are the benefits of cross-national versus comparative work? When should one approach be chosen over another? What sorts of findings and conclusions should we expect of these types of studies?

Comparison and History brings together scholars who have worked either cross-nationally or comparatively to reflect upon their own research. In chapters that engage practical, methodological, and theoretical questions, our contributors assess the gains—but also the obstacles and perils—of histories that traverse national boundaries. These are essays to persuade, to criticize, to warn, but above all, to advise. Our aim is to provide a much-needed assessment of these approaches for scholars who are considering embarking upon projects that lead them beyond their national area of expertise. We hope, too, that this book will be of use to students whose historical training is likely to range to several national, even continental, fields. This book, as its title makes clear, is written by, and chiefly for, historians, although some of its chapters may be of interest to other disciplines that have made comparison a stock in trade, especially sociology, political science, anthropology, and literature.

Although many of the essays will appeal to a broader audience, we have chosen to focus our book on Europe. In part, this reflects an effort at coherence. By choosing a geographical center, we hoped to provoke the sorts of practical exchanges generally lacking in discussions of comparative and cross-national work. Our focus is an acknowledgment, too, of the relative abundance of both comparative and cross-national research in the European fields, as practiced in the United States, and in certain European countries, especially Germany and France.[6] As nations that share a number of common experiences, the European countries lend themselves to cross-national scrutiny. European regions demonstrate the persistence of local ties even as nation-states consolidated their hold. The borrowings and exchanges among European states have been as profound as their antagonisms. With the coming of unification, Europe's commonalities and shared heritage, as well as each individual country's distinctiveness, have become subjects of public debate.

***

Comparison and History explores two crucial alternatives to standard national monographs: comparative history and cross-national history. Of the two genres, comparative history is seemingly the more easily defined. Comparative history is concerned with similarities and differences; in explaining a given phenomenon, it asks which conditions, or factors, were broadly shared, and which were distinctive—a variant on J.S. Mill's classic formulation of the methods of agreement and difference.[7] The comparisons drawn are most often between nations, although other units of comparison are possible, even (as some of the contributors to this volume argue) desirable. The methodological reference points for comparative history have been the social scientific disciplines, especially sociology and political science, although historians have rarely aspired to the sorts of universal explanations associated with the social sciences. Comparative history has often been characterized by an interest in causation. However, explaining *why* need not be its principal ambition, as Susan Grayzel and Maura O'Connor discuss in their respective essays.

If the preceding serves as an adequate description of comparative history, it falls short of a definition. For all of the term's ubiquity, there is little consensus about precisely what comparison means for the historian. Marc Bloch termed it a "method," capable, like other scientific methods, of yielding results for verification and falsification. However, those who have followed Bloch have been less certain. If a method requires faithful adherence to a well-defined set of practices, most comparative histories seem too unsystematic to qualify, the "method" itself either too inchoate or, as Raymond Grew has noted, no different from standard historical practice more generally.[8] Rather than a method or a distinct historical genre, writes Thomas Welskopp, comparison offers "a way of considering" a problem, closer to a mode of analysis.[9] On similar grounds, others have preferred to think of comparison more modestly, as a tool to provoke thought, or, more lyrically, as George Fredrickson puts it, as an "imagination."[10] For Louis Hartz, impatient with the narrow horizons of American historiography, comparative history served as the "intellectual expression of the new cosmopolitanism" afoot in the early 1960s—less, in other words, a method than a liberation.[11]

Cross-national history, by contrast, has largely been defined by the researcher's range of inquiry. Whether the subject is the culture of celebrity or the transatlantic slave trade, cross-national histories follow topics beyond national boundaries. They seek to understand reciprocal influences, as well as the ways in which the act of transplantation itself changes the topic under study. As a consequence, scholars who work cross-nationally are often more interested in crossings—whether real or imaginary—than they are in the specific national settings. Their focus is upon the historical contingency that movement itself introduces; the subjects of their studies can be as influenced by events abroad as they are by those at home. Understood broadly, cross-national history includes the history of colonialism and imperialism, which have illuminated both the crucial importance of empire to the European nations, and the European states' often malevolent influences abroad. It also encompasses what American historians have called the "new transnational history," a historiographical project that seeks to transcend a narrow focus upon the nation-state in the pursuit of (to quote Ian Tyrrell) "the international context of national action in all of its manifestations."[12]

As David Armitage points out in this volume's final chapter, the term "transnational" first took root in legal scholarship during the 1950s to indicate "actions or events that transcend national frontiers."[13] It has since migrated to the social sciences and humanities, defining a realm of interdependence or relation that, by definition, supercedes national sovereignty and boundaries; in this way, it differs from the purely descriptive term "international." For Glenda Sluga, transnational history has helped to conceptualize "an alternative spatial framework to the nation," calling into question, as she puts it, "the units out of which histories are made."[14] In the United States, as in France and Germany, "transnational" history has taken up many of the concerns of imperial history, prospering, too, in the subfields of immigration, environmental, and social movement history. And yet, as a number of critics have charged, the term "transnational" itself involves an analytic limitation: it presumes the extranational quality of the given subject.[15] The cautions that Armitage offers about the teleological character of globalization hold true for the category of the transnational as well; far from inevitable, global interconnectedness was, as Armitage demonstrates, notoriously contingent: "Globalization's histories are multiple and its pre-histories just as various. It would be fallacious to seek a single pre-history of globalization, both because it has had many paths and because none of those paths has been unbroken."[16]

If transnational analysis presupposes a skeptical stance towards the nation as the chief organizing category of history, we intend "cross-national," by contrast, as a more neutral term to describe the scope of an historian's investigation. Under the rubric of the cross-national, we include the genres of *Transfergeschichte* and *histoire croisée*, as they have been developed in France and Germany. *Transfergeschichte*, the history of transfers between nations, owes its origins to the work of scholars such as Michel Espagne, who have sought to demonstrate how knowledge, broadly defined, has traveled across national boundaries.[17] Topics for *Transfergeschichte* have included, among others, the reciprocal influences of French and German educational systems and the reception accorded Hegel in France. The focus is upon processes, and especially upon cultures; historians of transfer have argued that purportedly "national" cultures instead reflect a wide array of external influences. *Histoire croisée*, as delineated by Bénédicte Zimmermann and Michael Werner, has taken the historian's own positionality as its methodological starting-point.[18] *Histoire croisée* (an imperfect English translation from the French is "entangled history" or connected and shared history) emphasizes the cultural and social connections between nation-states. *Histoire croisée* demands a self-reflective practice among historians: it asks that historians understand their categories of analysis, as well as their objects of study, as "entangled" products of national crossings; thus methodological approaches, historical evidence, and categories of analysis inherited from the past need to be historicized. Rather than proceeding on the basis of established categories of "nation," "state," or "society," *histoire croisée* orients itself around problems, particularly the "entangled" historical relationships between Germany and France in the nineteenth and twentieth centuries.[19] In demonstrating the *longue durée* of European integration, *histoire croisée* can be understood as a scholarly homage to the European Union. Indeed, the first edited volume on the subject of *histoire croisée* carried a preface by Jacques Delors, former president of the European Commission.[20] But perhaps because of the narrow focus of much *histoire croisée*, in the United States and Great Britain, transnational history has all but upstaged its debut.[21]

We have chosen to include essays both about comparison and cross-national research within the covers of one book because, as a number of the chapters make clear, these two types of studies have often been considered as alternatives to each other and in opposition.[22] Scholars who practice *Transfergeschichte* and transnational history have criticized the static conceptions of the nation and emphasis upon national differences that (they claim) plague comparative history.[23] Comparativists have answered, as Heinz-Gerhard Haupt and Jürgen Kocka do in this volume, that without some comparative starting point, how can one really understand the nature of a given transfer? For their part, historians who endorse the genre of *histoire croisée* have maintained (among other criticisms) that comparative history too often verges upon tautology; the argument that a given study wishes to prove is already implicitly embedded in its construction. However, as the essays in this volume demonstrate, the line between cross-national history and comparative history is not necessarily a bright one. Many studies can, and should, accommodate a range of different approaches.

***

Represented within this book are a variety of different points of view. We have not attempted to harmonize our contributors' opinions, viewing their differences as a fruitful guide to the sorts of questions and decisions that confront the historian. The points of difference about comparative history, the reader will see, are more sharply drawn than those about cross-national analysis. There are, of course, disagreements among cross-national historians. However, at least as reflected in these essays, they tend to center upon the place of comparison in the analysis. Perhaps because the systematic practice of comparative history can call upon a much longer period of development, the problems have come into clearer focus. Three main points of contention on the subject of comparison run through the essays: its aims, its costs, and its prospects.

Comparison is rarely a goal in itself, but a means to a larger end. So what is its purpose? For Peter Baldwin and Michael Miller, comparative history is fundamentally concerned with causation, particularly with explaining differences and divergences. Comparison's unique contribution, writes Baldwin, is its ability to expose causes: "Comparative history serves primarily to separate the important from the incidental and thus to point the way towards causal explanations."[24] This is a widely shared view. Whereas Marc Bloch's contemporaries tended to assume that comparison had "no other purpose than hunting out resemblances," historians for the past five decades have instead (like Bloch himself) underscored the quest for differences and, ultimately, explanations.[25] "It is only when the job of explaining differences is undertaken," observed Carl Degler, "that comparative history begins."[26]

And yet, as Nancy Green and Susan Grayzel argue, causality need not be the comparativist's principal aim. Studies that focus upon similarities among nations will, as Green observes, necessarily subordinate the search for explanations to other objectives. In Grayzel's work on women and the First World War, for instance, causality is peripheral; her central pursuit is to identify what elements were shared, while also recognizing local variations. "Comparative cultural history," writes Grayzel, "sets itself the task of identifying elements of culture that are wider than the nation." Hers is an effort to understand not simply how France and Britain dealt with the problems of mobilization and mass death, but the overarching and unprecedented experiences of the First World War itself.

Although Baldwin and Grayzel stake out the two most forceful positions on the issue of causation, essays by Petrusewicz, Pedersen, and Cohen call attention to the other uses of comparison. For Marta Petrusewicz, the aim of comparison is not so much to explain a given phenomenon as it is to lead the researcher to new ways of posing questions. At work on a history of modernization in Poland, Ireland, and the Kingdom of the Two Sicilies, Petrusewicz proceeds by transferring key terms used in one national context to another. Thus she finds that the Polish concept of "organic labor" well describes the work of Daniel O'Connell, whose work in the Irish context is generally seen in terms of the Catholic–Protestant divide; proceeding in the other direction, the Irish term, "Bog-mania"—applied to Poland—reveals a similar drive to create large infrastructural works. Viewed in this way, comparison serves as a means of unlocking attitudes, meanings, or developments that would otherwise remain unnamed, and hence closed.

If Petrusewicz envisions comparison as a heuristic tool, for Cohen and for Pedersen, comparison is important because it casts into relief facets of national experiences that specialists have taken for granted. These are, Cohen argues, rarely the spectacular discoveries heralded in theoretical essays, but the more modest harvest that comes from revealing juxtapositions. According to Pedersen, comparison "performs a crucial 'de-normalizing' function." Comparison unsettles, for instance, the perceived naturalness of gender identities and relations. It also, she observes, provides a basis for accurate evaluations and for formulating relative judgments. Comparative analysis allows historians to "identify and determine the salience ('more' or 'less') of a variety of different factors, and to show how such factors combine to produce often unexpected and singular results." Causation is not absent from either of these chapters, but it is understood as a risky proposition. It is something, writes Pedersen, to be "ventured."

Closely allied to the question of comparison's purpose is the second subject of contention: the costs of comparative history. What are the disadvantages of comparative history? That comparison takes longer, offers more room for mistakes, may be poorly received by specialists in the field: all are, for this volume's contributors (unspectacularly) uncontentious. However, even beyond these perils, or so some of the essayists have it, lurk others. In his essay, Michael Miller charges that comparative history almost inevitably sacrifices depth for breadth: "what is gained in scope is most likely surrendered in depth." Comparative history substitutes static categories for an accurate depiction of time and place, it misses the movement that takes place beyond borders, it relies upon "orthodox versions" of national histories, and hence cannot challenge the conventional wisdom. Miller does not deny that comparative history pays dividends: he lauds those practitioners who manage to combine a mastery of two fields with in-depth archival research. Given the difficulties in execution, however, such work will, Miller contends, remain a rarity.

Although many of the volume's contributors criticize comparative history as it was practiced in the heyday of structuralism, Miller offers among the more pessimistic appraisals of its intrinsic shortcomings. In his essay, he explains how he came to write a cross-national history rather than one that was strictly comparative, arguing that comparison presented obdurate problems, such as the very different character of source materials in each country and the difficulty of fully incorporating the specific local context into a comparative study. Susan Pedersen agrees; as she became interested in Britain for its own sake (not as a "case" for comparison), "the more I doubted that I would ever be able to comprehend a second culture that deeply." Other authors contend that the problems that Miller cites are not inherent in comparative history per se, but a consequence of research choices. Comparative history, in other words, need not sacrifice depth; it depends on the subjects chosen and the questions asked. Miller's chosen topic, port cities, may require knowledge of the local that is beyond the reach of a nationally oriented study, but other subjects—say, for example—an inquiry into social insurance, do not. Moreover, depth in itself is not, as Peter Baldwin charges, necessarily desirable: comparativists believe that they avoid the dangers of irrelevant details while capturing broader patterns.

If comparison entails risks, it also offers (or so claim those in the book who defend it) opportunities. Comparison's oft-vaunted short-comings may even translate into strengths. In her essay, Nancy Green responds to those critics who argue that comparative history takes national difference as its starting point, thus reifying the nation-state and obliterating regional and local variations. Comparisons need not be confined to the national level, she points out, nor, for that matter, should they ignore the similarities between nations. For Green, comparisons offer a powerful means of breaking down the monolithic, blindered national narratives that historians often take for granted; they help us, in her words, to "relativize their rigidities and understand their constructed nature....Comparisons...can highlight the borrow-ings and the divergences that have gone into the making of those states." Susan Pedersen comes to a similar conclusion for different reasons: she sees virtues in comparative history's focus upon the nation-state. As scholars move beyond the nation, they are in danger of neglecting the crucial role that states have played in structuring the life-chances of their citizens; in seeking life outside the national paradigm they run the risk of forgetting how much of people's existence was determined by it. It is for this reason that Pedersen asks whether comparative history's nation-centered bias, in fact, serves as a "useful check in an age of globalization."[27]

Differences over comparison's aims and purpose result in very different appraisals of its future. What are the prospects for comparative history? Where some of the essayists, like Nancy Green, envision a rosy future, others view the situation with more caution. If not extinct, comparative history is, according to Pedersen, at the very least endangered. In the field of women's history, post-structuralist and post-colonial analyses have challenged the basis on which a generation of comparisons rested. The relative decline in comparative women's history, Pedersen argues, reflects larger disciplinary trends. As historians' romance with social science has dwindled, historians have, in the last decade, found the methods of anthropologists and literary scholars more persuasive. And yet, as Marta Petrusewicz notes, it is precisely these fields that have developed innovative strategies for comparison. Maura O'Connor agrees: whereas post-structuralist analysis and comparative history have often been seen as incompatible, O'Connor suggests that they should instead be practiced in tandem. Critiquing her own book, O'Connor demonstrates how comparisons can serve as an important counterweight to an account based upon representations. Petrusewicz and O'Connor call for the historian to develop new analytical techniques so that the inevitable asymmetries (whether of sources or of phenomena) serve to inspire, rather than to foil, comparative reflections.

What emerges from these essays is not the demise of comparative history as such, but a redefinition of its aims and practices. The diversity of opinions here represented signals a shift from the overweening influence of the social sciences to a more flexible understanding of the benefits of multicountry analysis. Where Ian Tyrrell once characterized comparative history as a genre too rigid to permit cross-national connections ("The connections between the units considered for testing cannot be admitted or brought to the center of concern..."), this volume's contributors recognize that comparison and cross-national work, rather than being opposed, should be seen as complementary approaches.[28] O'Connor's essay demonstrates why those who work cross-nationally cannot afford to ignore comparative history. Sluga's piece, conversely, indicates the value of a cross-national framework for comparativists. In the modern era, she explains, nations were made in a transnational arena, and constructed, at least in part, by comparisons. Drawing upon her work on the port city of Trieste, Sluga demonstrates that the nations which resulted from the ruins of the Habsburg empire owed their form, if not their very existence, to American and British conceptions about the proper composition of a nation. Because such comparisons lie at the heart of our very conceptions of the nation, there is "no untainted past that we can pare back to in order to arrive at an originary point." Thus, Sluga argues: "Comparative histories which disregard the ideological function of comparisons in the constitution of national differences are liable to take as self-evident what has been constructed and further entrench those distinctions rather than analyzing them."[29]

***

Comparison and History's contributors reflect upon their own experiences to offer advice. Many decisions await the historian who sets out to work beyond national boundaries. Although comparative and cross-national study should ideally be joined, the historian needs to decide which—or what combination of the two—will suit. If comparative history is the goal, a careful consideration of study design and framing is necessary even before research begins. What one compares is, of course, a fundamental question, with profound implications for the ultimate results. Germany, as Peter Baldwin notes, looks very different when compared to Russia than when it is compared to Britain. The contributors to this volume offer suggestions about the sorts of comparisons that work best. As Marta Petrusewicz argues, by comparing the incomparable (as Marcel Detienne has suggested), the historian may best be able to challenge common verities: "moving the object of comparison beyond the similar and the parallel towards the different and divergent can get us out of the predictability of the dogmatic application."[30] George Fredrickson has even suggested that the term comparative history be limited to "scholarship that has as its main objective the systematic comparison of some process or institution in two or more societies that are not usually conjoined within one of the traditional geographical areas of historical specialization."[31]

And yet, these are the kinds of comparisons most likely to raise the hackles of national specialists, who feel that the particular history has been violated in search of the "case"—that the stories are not, as Frederick Cooper puts it in a critical review of Fredrickson's work, "told better because they are told together." [32] It is here, according to Jürgen Kocka and Heinz-Gerhard Haupt, that the tensions between comparison and the basic principles of historical scholarship become evident. If comparative history necessarily involves "selection, abstraction, a detachment of the case from its context," studies of widely divergent societies, even diachronic analysis can be justified as long as the "actual intent" of the comparison is clearly defined in advance.[33] Even the maligned comparison of apples and oranges is legitimate if the larger quest is for the essence of fruit. But if the ambition is to understand the appleness of apples, comparisons between places remote in time or space will not yield the desired results. For Deborah Cohen, the issue is one of risk. The gains of apple–apple comparisons may be more modest, but so, too, is the chance of failure.

How one compares is at least as important as what one compares. It is crucial, as Peter Baldwin demonstrates, that the historian get the level of generalization right: that is, the study should both address national specificities and shed some light on the broader phenomenon at issue. That hinges on the sorts of questions asked. The comparativist must be sensitive to the issue of national context. In different countries, seemingly similar phenomena can mean very different things, as Kocka and Haupt caution: "modern German society differs from that of the United States or Great Britain not only in its legal forms, but also in the relative significance of the law."[34] Furthermore, it is important, as a number of contributors stress, to consider both similarities and differences. If differences focus attention on where paths diverge, similarities point the way to patterns that may be broader than the nation itself. However, whether one finds differences or similarities depends, at least in part, upon the ways in which the topic is framed; as Nancy Green points out, a study of "immigration" is likely to yield similarities, whereas a survey of Jewish or Polish immigrants may well tend to differences.[35]

Treated in these essays are questions central to the process of research: whether the comparative historian can rely principally upon secondary sources (the contributors largely come down in favor of primary materials, and therefore studies confined to two, at the most, three cases); what to do with incomparable sources; how to avoid what Bloch called homonyms, terms that seem to mean the same thing but are in fact different. As the reader will see, there are no easy answers to these problems, although the contributors do suggest a number of solutions. To some extent, too (as is so often the case with comparative history), these are simply a magnification of the normal obstacles that await the historian in the archives.

Writing poses a different set of challenges. The essays that follow ask, and attempt to answer, how much of the context a comparativist needs to convey; they consider, too, whether the stories should be told in parallel, or explicitly juxtaposed. Some practitioners have defined only the latter as comparative history. According to Peter Kolchin, those who alternate chapters "take the easy way out."[36] Only systematic comparison and intertwined narratives count; all else is mere juxtaposition. However, the contributors to this volume are not dogmatic on the question. There are, as they demonstrate, good reasons to devote separate chapters to each national case, not the least of which are the preferences of readers. If interwoven stories may in some ideal sense be preferable, they are not necessary. Setting the bar so high requires acrobatics that few can sustain, and fewer still master.

Historians who work cross-nationally face some of the same kinds of problems as comparativists: they, too, are dependent upon the vagaries of archives and required to master historiographies in several different national fields; they, too, run the risk of sundering their particular topic from its broader national context. Some elements of the cross-national historians' job seem to be easier; the dilemmas of writing and chapter organization, for instance, seem less acute than for comparativists. However, cross-national historians arguably trade in one set of difficulties for another. Above all, they have to grapple with the place of the nation in their studies. Where comparativists tend to assume as a matter of course that their contribution ultimately lies at the level of the nation-state, for those who work cross-nationally, the aim is less clear. Is the object to illuminate realms that extend beyond the purview of individual nation-states? If so, to what extent, asks Sluga, should cross-national studies seek to "recast our knowledge of individual national histories?" If the ambition is to explore crossings, points of contact and exchange, movement and trade, the answers that result may be tangential to the central concerns of the individual national historiographies.

In cross-national history, too, there is a danger of focusing upon one national story to the detriment of another. Both sides of a given interaction require attention, no easy task for an historian trained in a single national field. Just as imperial history has, under the influence of post-colonialism, been re-cast to take account of the perspectives of the colonized, so, too, do the essays in this volume underscore the importance of moving beyond representations of the other (whether Russian views of the Tatars or English images of Italy) to account for the dialectical nature of such exchanges. In revisiting her own book, a history of the role of English travelers in the making of the Italian nation, O'Connor asks how her work would have been different had she fully considered the part that Italians themselves played in this encounter. Systematic comparison between Italian and English views of the nation would, she argues, have granted to the Italians an autonomy that an overwhelmingly English focus inadvertently denied them. However, such an enterprise requires, if anything, more work. Cross-national history, in O'Connor's telling, is no less time-consuming or taxing than comparison.

***

Taken together, there is much that these essays share. They indicate the benefits to be gained from a closer relationship between comparative and cross-national analysis. They seek a middle ground between those who would organize history according to national boundaries and those who wish to unseat the nation as the center of historical study. Above all else, however, the contributors to this volume aim to shift the discussion from abstract praise to self-reflective evaluation so that studies which venture beyond national borders become more likely, not less.

REFERENCES

1. See, for example, Peter Mandler, *History and National Life* (London: Profile Books, 2002).
2. Marc Bloch is often hailed as the father of comparative history. Although the term was in wide use before his famous 1928 lecture to the Sixth International Congress of Historical Sciences, the range of practices it described were more extensive (and less systematic) than would be recognized today under the rubric. On the history of "comparative history," see Heinz-Gerhard Haupt, "Comparative History." *International Encylopedia of the Social & Behavioral Sciences*, Neil J. Smelser and Paul B. Baltes, eds. (Amsterdam: Elsevier, 2001). See, too, Fritz Redlich, "Toward Comparative History," *Kyklos* XI (1958): 365-376; Otto Hintze, "Soziologische und geschichtliche Staatsauffassung," in Hintze, *Soziologie und Geschichte: Gesammelte Abhandlungen*, G. Oestreich, ed., vol. 2 (Göttingen, 1964); Sylvia Thrupp, "The Role of Comparison in the Development of Economic Theory," *Journal of Economic History* 17: 4 (December 1957), 556.
3. Among others, AHR Forum "Bringing Regionalism Back to History," *American Historical Review* 104: 4 (October 1999), 1156–1220; Thomas Bender, ed., *Rethinking American History in a Global Age* (Berkeley: University of California Press, 2002); Jürgen Osterhammel, "Transnationale Gesellschaftsgeschichte: Erweiterung oder Alternative?" *Geschichte und Gesellschaft* 27: 3 (2001), 464–479; Sebastian Conrad, "Doppelte Marginalisierung. Plädoyer für eine transnationale Perspektive auf die deutsche Geschichte," *Geschichte und Gesellschaft* 28 (2002), 145–169; "The Nation and Beyond: A Special Issue. Transnational Perspectives on United States History," *Journal of American History* 86: 3 (December 1999); Ann L. Stoler, "Tense and Tender Ties: The Politics of Comparison in North American History and (Post)Colonial Studies," *Journal of American History* (December 2001), 831–864; Albert Wirz, "Für eine transnationale Gesellschaftsgeschichte." *Geschichte und Gesellschaft* 27: 3 (2001), 489-498; Antoinette Burton, "When was Britain? Nostalgia for the Nation at the End of the 'American Century'" *Journal of Modern History* 75: 2 (June 2003), 359–376; Antoinette Burton, "Who Needs the Nation? Interrogating 'British' History," *Journal of Historical Sociology* 10: 3 (September 1997), 227–249; Anthony Hopkins, "Back to the Future: From National History to Imperial History," *Past and Present* 164 (August 1999), 198–243.

4. Theda Skocpol and Margaret Somers, "The Uses of Comparative History," *Comparative Studies in Society and History* 22 (1978), 174–197; Charles Tilly, *Big Structures, Large Processes, Huge Comparisons* (New York, 1984); A.A. van den Brambussche, "Historical Explanation and Comparative Method: Towards a Theory of the History of Society," *History and Theory* 28 (1989), 1–24. According to Margaret Somers and Theda Skocpol, there are comparisons in the service of a general theory (parallel type), those whose principal purpose is to shed light upon a particular historical context (the contrasting type), and the macro-causal brand, which takes into account both parallels and differences in the pursuit of hypothesis-testing.

5. See Heinz-Gerhard Haupt and Jürgen Kocka, "Historischer Vergleich: Methoden, Aufgaben, Probleme," in *Geschichte und Vergleich: Ansätze und Ergebnisse international vergleichender Geschichtsschreibung* (Frankfurt; New York: Campus, 1996), pp. 9–45; Hartmut Kaelble, *Der historische Vergleich : Eine Einführung zum 19. und 20. Jahrhundert* (Frankfurt.a.M.: Campus, 1999), pp. 114–150; Karen Marrero, "Finding the Space Between: The Means and Methods of Comparative History," *Canadian Review of American Studies* 33 (2003), 147–152.

6. See, among others, Haupt and Kocka, *Geschichte und Vergleich; Geschichte und Gesellschaft* 27: 3 (2001); Michael Werner and Bénédicte Zimmermann, "Vergleich, Transfer, Verflechtung. Der Ansatz der Histoire croisée und die Herausforderung des Transnationalen," *Geschichte und Gesellschaft* 28: 4 (2002), 607–636; Michael Werner and Bénédicte Zimmermann, "Penser l'histoire croisée: entre empirie et réflexivité," *Annales HSS* (January–February 2003), 7–36.

7. For criticisms of Mill, see Morris Cohen and Ernest Nagel, *An Introduction to Logic and Scientific Method* (New York: Harcourt, Brace, 1934), pp. 251–261.

8. Grew, "The Case for Comparing Histories," pp. 776–777; Raymond Grew, "The Comparative Weakness of American History, *Journal of Interdisciplinary History*, XVI: I (Summer 1985), 94–95.

9. Thomas Welskopp, "Stolpersteine auf dem Königsweg: Methodenkritische Anmerkungen zum internationalen Vergleich in der Gesellschaftsgeschichte," *Archiv für Sozialgeschichte* 35 (1995), 339–367.

10. George Fredrickson, *The Comparative Imagination: On the History of Racism, Nationalism, and Social Movements* (Berkeley: University of California Press, 1997).

11. Louis Hartz, "American Historiography and Comparative Analysis: Further Reflections," *Comparative Studies in Society and History* 5: 4 (July 1963), 365.

12. Ian Tyrrell, "American Exceptionalism in an Age of International History," *American Historical Review* 96: 4 (October 1991), 1053.

13. See Armitage's essay in this volume.

14. See Sluga's essay in this volume.

15. For a trenchant critique of Tyrell, see Michael McGerr, "The Price of The 'New Transnational History,'" *American Historical Review* 96: 4 (October 1991).

16. Armitage, "Is There a Pre-History of Globalization," in this volume.

17. See, for example, Michel Espagne and Michael Werner, eds., *Transferts. Les Relations interculturelles dans l'espace franco-allemand (XVIIIe et XIXe siècle)* (Paris: Editions Recherches sur les Civilisations, 1988); Michel Espagne and Werner Greiling, eds., *Frankreichfreunde. Mittler des französisch-deutschen Kulturtransfers (1750–1850)* (Leipzig, 1996); Michel Espagne, *Bordeaux Baltique. La présence culturelle allemande à Bordeaux aux XVIII et XIX siècles* (Paris: : Editions de la maison des sciences de l'homme, 1991); Michel Espagne, *Les transferts culturels franco-allemands, perspectives germaniques* (Paris: Presses universitaires de France, 1999); Michel Espagne and Matthias Middell, eds., *Von der Elbe bis an die Seine: Kulturtransfer zwischen Sachsen und Frankreich im 18. und 19. Jahrhundert* (Leipzig: Universitätsverlag, 1993); Marc Schalenberg, ed., *Kulturtransfer im 19. Jahrhundert* (Berlin: Centre Marc Bloch, 1998);

Matthias Middell, "Kulturtransfer und historische Komparistik. Thesen zu ihrem Verhältnis," *Comparativ* 10 (2000), 7–41.

18. Werner and Zimmermann, "Vergleich, Transfer, Verflechtung"; Werner and Zimmermann, "Penser l'histoire croisée"; Bénédicte Zimmermann, Claude Didry, and Peter Wagner, eds., *Le travail et la nation: histoire croisée de la France et de l'Allemagne* (Paris: Maison des sciences de l'homme, 1999).

19. See Werner and Zimmermann, "Penser l'histoire croisée: entre empirie et réflexivité," *Annales HSS*, 1 (January–February 2003), 1–36.

20. *Le Travail et la nation*, pp. xiii–xvii.

21. A.G. Hopkins, ed., *Globalization in World History* (New York: Norton, 2002).

22. Richard White, "Nationalization of Nature," p. 981; Tyrrell, pp. 1031–1038; on the different merits of each, Frederick Cooper, "Race, Ideology, and the Perils of Comparative History," *American Historical Review* 101: 4 (October 1996), 1135.

23. Michel Espagne, "Sur les limites du comparatisme en histoire culturelle," *Genèses* 17 (September 1994), 112–121; Tyrrell, "American Exceptionalism," pp. 1031–1038.

24. Baldwin's essay in this volume.

25. Bloch, "Toward a Comparative History," p. 507.

26. Carl Degler, "Comparative History: An Essay Review," *Journal of Southern History*, p. 426. Degler was here objecting to what he viewed as C. Vann Woodward's too-broad definition in the introduction to *The Comparative Approach to American History*. In a review article on comparative history published in 1980, George Fredrickson objected to Robert Kelley's *Transatlantic Persuasion* (1969) in the following fashion: "But Kelley's pursuit of uniformities and his conviction that he was really dealing with a single transatlantic phenomenon inhibited his use of comparative analysis. Another kind of comparativist would have been more alert to differences that would require explanation." George Frederickson, "Comparative History" in *The Past Before Us*, Michael Kamman, ed. (Ithaca, NY: Cornell University Press, 1980).

27. See Gary Gerstle, "The Power of Nations," *Journal of American History* 84: 2 (September 1997), esp. 579–580.

28. Tyrrell, "American Exceptionalism," p. 1038, fn. 24.

29. Sluga in this volume.

30. Petrusewicz in this volume.

31. Frederickson, "Comparative History" in *The Past Before Us*, Michael Kammen, ed., p. 458; see also Grew, "Comparative Weakness," p. 95: "There may even be a general law that the comparison of cases distant in cultural context is more likely than other comparisons to produce a fresh perspective and thus new questions to explore; the comparison of very similar cases more likely to identify one or two critical variables." Robert Kelley, "Comparing the Incomparable: Politics and Ideas in the United States and the Soviet Union," *Comparative Studies in Society and History* XXVI (1984), 672–708.

32. Cooper, "Race, Ideology," p. 1134.

33. Kocka and Haupt in this volume.

34. Kocka and Haupt in this volume.

35. See Nancy Green, "The Comparative Method and Poststructural Structuralism—New Perspectives for Migration Studies," *Journal of American Ethnic History* 13: 4 (Summer 1994), 3–22; "L'histoire comparative et le champ des etudes migratoires," *Annales, ESC* 6 (November December 1990), 1335–1350.

36. Peter Kolchin, "Comparing American History," *Reviews in American History* 10: 4 (December 1982), 77.

1

COMPARING AND GENERALIZING: WHY ALL HISTORY IS COMPARATIVE, YET NO HISTORY IS SOCIOLOGY

Peter Baldwin

Historians are notoriously resistant to comparisons. Despite nods in the direction of comparison, the profession remains organized by national field. Historical methodology emphasizes the uniqueness of its subjects, explaining their development by presenting a narrative of their evolution. It implicitly assumes that by saying what, step by step, we have also accounted for why. Experts in particular areas, the products of the study it took to master a field in all its glorious singularity, historians traditionally have preferred being specialists, as the joke has it, who eventually knew everything about nothing, rather than generalists, knowing nothing about everything. Comparative studies, as Sylvia Thrupp noted apologetically in 1958, introducing the then fledgling journal, *Comparative Studies in Society and History*, threatened to undermine the historian's craft skills and to turn historians into jacks of all trades.[1] Comparative historians commonly find that they are read much more appreciatively by sociologists and political scientists than by their more immediate colleagues.

Comparisons are often seen as but one step from generalizations and generalizations, in turn, as the province of the hard social sciences, not of particularizing historians. Outfitting the historian's toolbox with

1

generalizations, it is feared, would be to accept the challenge thrown out by the philosopher Carl Hempel as he sought to clasp history in the embrace of the hard sciences based on covering-law models. In his view, explanation and prediction were logically equivalent acts, merely extending in different directions temporally. The singular could never be understood except as an instance of a generality.[2] History, the historian will argue in rejecting such approaches, deals not with reproducible results nor with laws that hold true of all societies at all times, but with the temporally unique, the particular context, the unprecedented confluence of circumstances.

Of course, the same could be said of literature, or law, or religion, all of which are the subjects of flourishing comparative studies. If anything, indeed, the claim of uniqueness could be made more validly in these cases than for much of what the historian studies. Most nations, after all, have developed a tax system, most have had a peasantry, and most an industrial proletariat, but not every culture, to stick with literature for the moment, writes sonnets or haiku or essays. So why should the former be incomparable while the latter are? Why should scholars of literature have embraced the idea of comparison so fervently that there are now departments of comparative literature—often the most prestigious and methodologically sophisticated of such endeavors— while individual students of comparative history still suffer under the prejudices of their colleagues? (Let us, in contrast, not stop to ask why there are Departments of Romance, Germanic, Slavic, etc. literature, but no similar subdivisions of history. That way lies madness. Is it the insularity of traditional literary studies that forces the need for separate institutionalization of comparisons, while historians have built at least the possibility, if not the reality, of comparison into their nationally mongrel departments?)

Indeed, the only good stories about comparison come from the literary scholars. Renato Poggioli, for many years a professor of comparative literature at Harvard and author of *The Theory of the Avant-Garde* and other books, was once at a party with a society dame of Cambridge. Upon being introduced, she gushed to him, "Professor Poggioli, I understand that you study comparative literature. Tell me, please, to what do you compare literature." His response, so the story, is unprintable.[3] Another comes from a dream once had by the noted professor of English literature, Hugh Kenner: the bell rings early on a bright morning, his wife descends the stairs, opens the door. There before her stand René Wellek, professor of comparative literature at Yale, and Harry Levin, professor of comparative literature at Harvard.

She turns and calls up to her husband, still in bed, "Wake up dear, the men are here to compare literature." We historians do not have any stories because we hardly have comparisons yet, not to mention the fun and jollity that comes with them.

We resist generalizations because we regard them as inherently untrue to the particularity of the past. We reject Occam's principle of parsimoniousness, basic to the harder sciences and their forms of explanation, and welcome multiplicity, overdetermination, and complexity. We are inherently postmodern, and were so long before that concept was ever invented, in rejecting master narratives and universality, the one-size-fits-all of Enlightenment dogma. We are by profession historicist in Ranke's sense, seeing the past as unique and inexplicable except by particularist understanding. We reject overly dogmatic applications of universal principles to explain the past, whether Gibbon's Enlightenment attempts to see Romans as Englishmen in togas, and both as exemplars of abstract humanity, gussied up with a bit of historical trapping for temporally local color, or the dogmatic Marxist attempt to find class struggle in every altercation. Rational choice theory is perhaps one of the last few remaining hopes of finding an underlying logic of historical development that in theory applies everywhere at all times. With only a few lonely and (curiously) largely Scandinavian practitioners, however, this is hardly a booming business.[4]

And yet comparisons, or at least the claim that they ought to be practiced, remain stubbornly with us, however much more they are honored in the breach than the practice. Why? For one thing, national histories are going the way of nationalism and nations. As the constructed nature of national identity becomes an increasingly accepted dogma, it is obvious that the historical aspect of nationalist ideology, the primacy of national histories, must also fall by the wayside. Just because Bismarck was *kleindeutsch*, must modern-day historians also be? Merrily treating Bavaria and Prussia as part of the same thing, but excluding Austria? Content with a reference to Schnabel's Badenese approach to Germany, but otherwise treating it as a largely undiversified *Brei*? Why should Scandinavia be treated as separate national histories, as it remains to this day, with national rivalries as fierce and unforgiving as anywhere, if Britain is often not? The focus has gradually shifted from nations, with clearly delineated boundaries and allegedly homogeneous interiors, to the tense interactions between them, the borderlands and their peculiar dynamics.[5] Or to the gradually emerging study of regions in preference to nations.[6] Now that the individual as a unified, coherent, isolated subject has been dispatched, should it prove hard to drive a stake through the heart of the nation?

But such an enlargement and enfuzzification of historical focus, however welcome, does not necessarily imply an interest in comparison. Indeed, quite the opposite may be true. By enlarging the scope, taking the region and not the nation as the given to be studied, comparisons that were earlier possible—in theory at least—are now subsumed in a larger and higher entity and thus undercut. If general statements are made about Central Europe, then comparisons between, say, Prussia and Austria are either undermined or at best turned into internal juxtapositions between entities no longer regarded as the primary objects of attention. We get big and bigger history, but not necessarily comparative history. On the other hand, if the regions are subnational, then comparisons are possible within what was formerly regarded as a monolithic country. Much recent German historiography has broken loose of Prussian domination in this respect. Reunification has focused attention both on past regional divisions and on more recently created ones. The notorious reluctance of American historians to regard their country in internationally comparative perspective is to some degree counterbalanced, at least in terms of gaining methodological experience, by an increasing willingness to undertake regionally based comparisons within the nation.[7]

Embraced in theory, shunned in practice, comparative history leads a shadowy existence. Few deny at least some of its virtues, but even fewer set them in practice.

Comparisons have helped undermine the smug assumptions made by national histories. At least the non-French will smirk when recalling the way that R.R. Palmer was damned forty years ago for having dared to dilute the uniqueness of the French Revolution into the western brew of the Democratic Revolution.[8] Today, it is Mona Ozouf who goes to great lengths to defend the uniqueness of French feminism against the comparativists, especially those who draw unflattering conclusions about its development.[9] In certain cases, comparisons have opened up whole fields of investigation. The study of slavery and racial difference was rejuvenated by examinations of Latin and South America and the sharp differences they uncovered between the southern and northern (both European and American) approaches to ethnic intermixture, definitions of race and slavery.[10] The Sonderweg debate has offered a bracing tonic that raises basic questions of whether national uniqueness exists at all.[11]

The peculiarities of X argument is increasingly, and justly, seen as a cheap escape, a desire to avoid reading the wider literature, a penchant for eternally reinventing the wheel, a sign of intellectual laziness. Yet, while the peculiarities of German history may be moribund, exceptionalism still thrives among historians of Scandinavia, allergic as they are to comparisons with that obvious example, Germany—culturally so closely related, politically so damnable. Peculiarity arguments also remain healthy among American historians. Daniel Rodgers, for example, can enlighten with a massive tome demonstrating how policy makers in the United States participated in a larger transatlantic reformist discussion—surprising perhaps to American historians in their splendid insularity, but rather thinner beer to others.[12] Though in all fairness, exceptions are becoming more common and the oft-remarked uncomparative nature of American historiography must be put in the perspective of an immense nation with regional variations as wide as those found within the European subcontinent.[13] Moreover, as mentioned, some of the comparative impetus within American history has found fulfillment in inter-American studies.

Few things are as annoying to the comparative imagination as the national history that invokes general causes as though they explain particular national outcomes. Jill Harsin's book on prostitution in France, for example, argues that the French stood out by imposing a draconian system of regulations on the merchants of venery because women had but low status there.[14] Her assumption that women were worse off than in nations—Switzerland or England, say—less inclined to regulate, may, of course, be true. But without a comparative argument to that effect, this cause cannot possibly account for the particular outcome it is invoked to explain. Ann La Berge claims that the French lagged behind the British in terms of public health because of factors that include the vested interests of garbage collectors, ragpickers, and the like in the sanitary old regime, the huge cost of investments in infrastructure, and the conviction that there was money to be made supplying solid waste as fertilizer. All of these were, no doubt, concerns, but ones that, as far as the argument is presented, held equally in England, or other nations, and thus explain nothing about the peculiarities of the French case. A comparative question is posed, but answered in an uncomparative manner.[15]

Such comparisons call into question the basic premises of any national history, showing that none can be isolated from others in glorious solitude, that comparison is inevitably part of any *Fragestellung*, however blinkeredly national. Is X peculiar? Compared to what? The assertion of singularity obviously and trivially poses a comparative question. Sociologists, as Hinze put it in an overly neat juxtaposition, compare to find the general features shared by the matters studied, historians, in contrast, to discover what it is that makes their topic singular.[16]

Comparisons are often used in political battles. The Comintern theory of fascism as the highest stage of capitalism sought to blame by association. Tit for tat, the theory of totalitarianism returned the comparative innuendo, lumping fascism and communism together as essentially similar despite their pretensions to ideological opposition. The controversies provoked by the *Historikerstreit*, the debate over whether Hitler's attack on the Soviet Union was preventive, and the *Black Book of Communism* were all extensions of this campaign of reciprocal smear by comparison.[17] Less obviously, but nonetheless politically driven, the assertion of Scandinavian peculiarity stems from assumptions of Nordic moral superiority commonly drawn in these nations. The revelations of forced sterilization and other eugenic barbarities inflicted during the interwar years posed a special dilemma, not because what took place was out of the ordinary compared to other nations, but precisely because, in this case, the Swedes mistakenly regarded themselves as superior and blameless in such respects.[18] To take a less charged example, the highly developed welfare state of Sweden is the base of that nation's claim to pride of place at the pinnacle of social policy development. In the welfare whiggery of a Social Democratic reading of history, Sweden ranks at the summit, other nations being relegated to less heady altitudes along this Marshallian progression towards the embodiment of social rights. But if, instead of taking only western — indeed northwestern — Europe (with occasional allusions to North America thrown in for salutary lessons on the price of straying from the narrow path of virtue), the scope is broadened globally, matters Scandinavian appear in a different light. They now seem less as the precocious attainment of an inevitable ideal towards which all others are striving and more as the peculiar, insular, and localized development of a small niche, happy in its well-upholstered obscurity, but hardly indicative (as Richard Rose has argued) of the possibilities or indeed even ambitions of the rest of the globe.[19]

All history, however hermetically limited to one nation, is comparative in this inherent sense that the very implication of uniqueness presupposes a measuring stick formed from the experiences of other countries. But there is more. Most contemporary historiography takes as its starting point the radical otherness and difference of the past.

History has reemphasized its historicist roots by treating the past as a different country, highlighting the discontinuities and breaks between us and our predecessors. It no longer assumes that they were much like us, set perhaps against a backdrop of technologically less evolved circumstances. History is, in this sense, temporally comparative, between the present and the past. This is a less trivial point than it may seem at first inspection. The older social science paradigms of history, with roots in the Enlightenment's Cartesian belief in the universality and invariability of human nature, along with their continuation in rational choice theory applied to the past, assume that there are broad constants that hold across time: that humans are rational interest maximizers, that differential position in the productive system leads to conflicts between groups, and so forth.

The cultural turn in history, and the radical neohistoricism it has helped foster as the profession's fundamental methodological dogma, in contrast, tends to emphasize the uniqueness and difference of each era, seeking to understand it on its own terms. The basic assumption is that things change dramatically; the weakness of this approach has come in explaining why things change at all. Hence the rather tepid conclusion that studies written in this vein often come to, namely that the past is different, *tout court*. This temporal comparison is not the usual way the word is used, but it does introduce a note of comparison into history that otherwise seems to reject such premises. The battle of interpretation between Norbert Elias and Hans Peter Duerr, for example, over whether or not human nature changed radically during the early modern period, turns on the conclusions drawn from such a temporally comparative argument.[20]

Many comparisons attempt to dismantle a formerly accepted standard. The *Sonderweg* debate questions why the experience of France and Britain should be seen as normative and deviations from this high road therefore explained. Historians of Britain have for long wondered whether the reason political histories took France, with its revolution, as the standard was simply that spectacle is spectacular as quiet reformist change is not. When Behrens posed the same question in her comparison of Prussia and France, the answer must have seemed perverse to the French point of view. According to her, the Prussians managed successfully most of the changes in administrative and governmental prowess required to avoid revolution while the French failed miserably.[21] The Revolution, so the implication, was not the glorious culmination of strivings for change and betterment, but the expression of a developmental pathology. The standard had been reversed.

Similarly, one could take the development of the American labor movement as the baseline against which the violence and confrontation of similar developments in Continental Europe should be judged. Or one could, as Sombart did, take the German case as the standard against which the lack of socialism in the United States must be explained. The choice makes, of course, for quite different *Fragestellungen*. In examining the comparative development of welfare states, Rose's deliberate provocation (mentioned earlier) poses the question in reverse of its usual formulation: not why did the United States and most of the world not follow the example of well-developed social policy blazed in northern Europe, but conversely, why should this obscure nook of the world be considered the standard against which the geopolitically more important nations of the new world and Asia are to be measured? Who's the deviant here?

Fundamental to the fear of comparison lies the question of generalizations, covering laws and their relationship to historical explanation. Must comparison involve generalization and must it therefore raise the hackles of historians who fear the incursion of inapplicable explanatory paradigms? In the first place, studying the history of more than one nation does not necessarily involve comparison, much less generalization. Some histories are broad rather than comparative. When Arno Mayer set out to investigate the persistence of the aristocracy into the modern world, he could have limited himself to one nation or the other. Instead he ran through the same scenario across a broad gamut of countries and could thus claim to be speaking about the old regime in Europe as a whole.[22] But rather than comparing, he added and accreted layers of pigment one on top of the other, giving a deeper luster than one coat, but not fundamentally changing the hue. This is repetitive, not comparative, history, the argument inflated but not extended by the comparisons. Main Currents of X is a broad, but not necessarily comparative topic. Broad history is best practiced in certain fields. The history of medicine, for example, sports especially well-executed examples. Its topic typically concerns an activity that is clearly delineated, with manageable materials and relatively few subjects, where broad, international contacts were common. Hence expansive surveys of a particular theme across a wide range of nations can be accomplished more easily than were the subject, say, the labor movement.[23]

Most often, historical comparisons pause along the path leading from one national history to abstract sociological generalizations, arrested by what we may call the typologizing temptation: X countries, X number of variations on a theme, paths to a particular goal, varieties of a phenomenon. Barrington Moore gave us three routes to modernity and thus showed that the inherited unilinear highway of modernization was not the only one that could be followed. Thomas Ertman gave us a multiplicity of paths to statehood, Louis Hartz various means of new world settlement, Charles Maier and Gregory Luebbert approaches to the crises of the interwar years, Rogers Brubaker conceptions of citizenship, and so it goes.[24] Studies of the evolution of the welfare state are rife, some would say overripe, with typologies. Careers have been made by trying to become the Linnaeus of social policy.[25]

Similarly, scholars of fascism have spent disproportionate energy on categorizations and typologies. On the other side of the political spectrum we are content to have *Main Currents of Marxism* and could equally well have main currents of socialism, communism, or any permutation thereof. Partly, this has to do with variations on a theme in an ideology with common touchstones to which all, at whatever removes, refer back. Equally, it concerns the self-professed internationalism of the movement(s). With fascism, in contrast, there is a fundamental contradiction at the heart of any comparison of antagonistic nationalisms, each seeking to distinguish itself from others, indeed to fight them with all possible means. What could be the common denominator here, other than the fact of difference? Hence we have attempts either to soar into the stratosphere, as with Nolte's fascist essentialism as resistance to transcendence, or Sternhell's hope of getting to the core of the movement in his argument that it partook of both left and right, Enlightenment and reaction. Or, we get shopping lists of characteristics, as with Payne's fascist minimum. This is a sort of mix-and-match approach that argues, much as when ordering at a Chinese restaurant, that since it's all fascism on the menu, so long as you've been through enough from the various possibilities to be satiated, you've had a meal.[26]

Such typological approaches seek to lay out the different ways a topic could be and was dealt with, without necessarily insisting on inducing broad laws that hold in all cases. The difference between Barrington Moore, on the one hand, and Theda Skocpol or Jack Goldstone, on the other, lies at the point where typologies strain to become generalizations. Moore rests content with having destroyed the unilinear approach to political and social modernization with a more variegated set of alternative routes. His sociological colleagues, in contrast, seek to uncover the general laws governing the breakdown of states and the outbreak of revolutions. Social scientists, at their most ambitious, search, like the hard scientists of their emulatory ambitions, to uncover general laws hiding in the fragments of particularity. Even

Goldstone, who claims to be seeking "robust processes" rather than Hempelian laws, phrases his results in terms that are all but indistinguishable from generalizations: that "revolution is likely to occur" when a society simultaneously experiences three sorts of crises whose details need not detain us here.[27]

It is at this point, when comparisons strive for generalization in their ambition to extrapolate allegedly universal laws, that historians bristle. Generalizations based on a limited number of cases often are just conclusions about those, convinced that they are arrayed in the finery of universality, yet traipsing about, like Hans Christian Andersen's emperor, in their underwear. From a historian's point of view, they do not add anything substantive by being phrased in generalities. Indeed, if anything, they lose by dilution. Juan Linz developed the insight that the ideological polymorphousness of fascist ideology stems from its tactical positioning as a latecomer ideology. It was required to seek support where it could find it and thus to appeal, often in mutually contradictory fashion, to various and variegated social groups. This is the sort of fruit of a broad study of several European nations that comparativists aspire to. But his more specific conclusion, phrased needlessly in the terminology of social science, that "wherever a communist or soviet type revolutionary attempt was made and wherever the socialist parties embraced a maximalist ideology rather than a social democratic one, fascism in one or another version was more likely to emerge" does not recognizably tell us much that a potted summary of events in Germany and Italy would fail to.[28]

Ted Robert Gurr, in a classic case of social science run amok, analyzes political violence, including revolutions, guerrilla wars, coups d'état, rebellions, and riots, at a high level of abstraction and comes to conclusions such as these: that "the greater the frustration, the greater the quantity of aggression against the source of frustration," or that the more the deprivation, the more people are likely to act against it.[29] It was an approach of such generality that it prompted Philip Abrams to remark that it blurred the distinction between idiocy and analysis.[30] In a similar way, do we need world-renowned social scientists to tell us that diseases affecting all are likely to attract more funding in hopes of a solution than those that afflict only (despised) minorities?[31] Or what does a historian make of Charles Tilly's worry whether the influence of the Reformation on distinguishing Spain from Prussia was merely a "minor distinction" or an "idiosyncratic" characteristic of Western European development that hindered hopes of drawing general lessons on the development of the modern state from the European past?[32] A salutary warning of the perils of generalization is offered by what is clearly intended as praise, but which no historian could accept as other than intellectual interment by trivialization. As Mary Douglas, Richard Mohr blithely assures us, sums up the main finding of her lifework, "Solidarity is only gesturing when it involves no sacrifice."[33] A lifetime of scholarship and you end up sounding like a fortune cookie. In defense of such lofty altitudes, however, it must be said that a book on Newtonian gravity entitled *Why Things Fall Down* would take a similar approach and that, if aiming to uncover the most fundamental processes, we must be prepared to tackle issues at a level that, while mysterious until discovered, will seem trivial once apparent to all. The question remains whether historians should or can have ambitions to be Newtonian.

But comparison does not necessarily mean generalization. Indeed, in the hands of historians, it should never do so. One of the most common operations of comparative history is to test and — usually — to undercut the validity of generalizations formulated by the harder social sciences. Jürgen Kocka's book on the political inclinations of white-collar employees in Germany and the United States was written to test the generalization, put forth most famously by Seymour Martin Lipset, that, as an ideology of appeal to such groups, fascism was an "extremism of the middle." Since American *Angestellten* did not fall for the siren song of the far right that so enchanted their German colleagues, there must (so Kocka's conclusion) have been something other than white-collar status that explains this outcome.[34] May not historians ask, however, why it should be their task to spend long years disproving ideas thought up by sociologists in their baths? Do historians want to be the empirical foot soldiers commanded about by a bunch of sociological colonels?

The most effective comparative histories are those which, eschewing generalizations, formulate arguments at a middle range about differences and similarities among a range of cases that allow us to understand the general issue at hand (World War One, say, but not necessarily in this or that nation) better than had we limited our scope to one country only. At a minimum, good comparative histories should give insights into each particular case that would have remained unrevealed had they been studied in isolation. They juxtapose in order to isolate what is crucial, which is to say causal, and distinguish it from what may be only incidental in any given national context. My own work on the political and social origins of the European welfare state argued that the emphasis on the working class and its political representatives that derived from a Scandinavian focus did not hold up when subjected to comparative scrutiny. Social policy of a solidaristic bent was supported also by parties of the center and right in the Nordic countries, as well as in other nations, Germany and France above all. The broader the geographic perspective, the looser is the couplet between the working class and solidaristic social policy.[35]

Methodologically similar was my attempt to isolate the factors determining the style of public health adopted across European nations during the nineteenth century. It was not so much the political culture of a nation that was reflected in its public health tactics, since nations quite different in this respect shared similar approaches to disease. Rather, so the conclusion, it was the geographic positioning that countries found themselves in during the crucially formative period of the early nineteenth century vis-à-vis epidemic disease that dictated which preventive tactics made sense. Geography, not politics, was the motor.[36] Morillo's comparison between the early modern military revolution in Europe and Japan allowed him to argue that the historically important factor was not technical changes as such (gunpowder weaponry and the shift of power to the infantry), but the broader social developments that allowed such novelties to have an effect. Only through a comparison with Japan, where the purely technological changes did not have the effect supposed for them in Europe, could the argument that in Europe, too, technology was not destiny, be sustained.[37]

The pitch and level of the comparison is crucial in this respect. Comparisons that deal with a broad variety of nations are most likely to arrive at universal conclusions or to formulate ones of such a generality and vagueness that their value will strike most historians as dubious, trivial, or both. Plethora is the mother of platitude, as Barrington Moore observed in gist.[38] Where Quincy Wright, in his massive transnational study of war, felt obliged to classify collisions of stars as one form of war and to begin with a discussion of fighting between animals, historians will be tempted to think that while a running start is needed, to begin so far before the starting line calls into question the stamina needed to arrive at the finish.[39] Where Orlando Patterson approached slavery around the globe for its entire recorded history and concluded that the only thing shared by all forms (some with no racial or color differences, some with no necessary connection to forced labor, some not deprived of legal personality, and so forth) was the violent domination of natally alienated and generally dishonored persons who thus suffer social death, historians interested in empirical muck might justifiably conclude that at this level of abstraction the air is simply too rarified.[40] When Ernst Nolte sought to define the core and essence of fascism everywhere always, the answer was a resistance to transcendence. He thus turned what most would regard as a political movement, possibly with significant cultural overtones, into something bordering on theology. At such ethereal levels, what are the questions to be answered?

Much of what bothers historians about generalizations at this altitude is what exactly they are after. Generalizations that seek the essence of the matter *in vitro*, such as Nolte's definition of fascism or Patterson's of slavery, attempt Platonically to construct an ideal form of what exists only in imperfect fragments on Earth. If so, then what is the relationship between the ideal form—generic fascism, say—and the really existing fascisms of history? The real ones will only partly embody the essential attributes identified in the ideal form, becoming thus examples of something "higher." Generic fascism has never existed and the question is what purpose such a construct serves. What more do we know about any actual fascism by constructing an ideal type? In the case of Nazi Germany or Italy under Mussolini, probably very little. But perhaps we do, in fact, gain knowledge through an analysis which argues that, compared to the generic measuring rod, Franco was not a fascist but Idi Amin was. It is conceivable that the generic concept would allow us to detect regularities among current political movements that might otherwise escape notice.[41] While not actually gaining more empirical knowledge of any individual cases, we would know more about them in a conceptual sense, to the extent that we now recognized them as members of a larger class of events.

On the other hand, the relationship between the individual cases and the general one is problematic. What is there about fascism, to stick with a difficult example, that makes formulation of a generic version so difficult? Are Italy and Germany during the interwar years simply too different to fit into the same definition? If fascism is defined as an economically modernizing movement, some have claimed that Nazi Germany would have to be cut. But, conversely, if fascism is modernizing, then Italy fits, and so, in this view of seeing things, do Cuba, Vietnam, Nasser's Egypt, and a slew of other nations that no one but a political scientist with a stepmotherly approach to the past would want to lump together as fascist. Focusing overly sharply on economic modernization thus gives us a general category that includes the wrong nations. The task at hand is to settle on common criteria that apply to both interwar Italy and Germany. But, if so, then have we not inverted cart and horse? How do we know that

Germany and Italy are the fascist nations whose core and essential commonalities are those we wish to alembicate?

If the social sciences are Platonic in their search for essences and ideal forms that explain the commonality of phenomena that in other respects are different, historians are Wittgensteinians. They are content to point out family resemblances among phenomena that are related, without thereby invoking any particular Smithness to account for that charmingly lopsided grin sported by so many of the really existing Smiths, while also not denying family membership to those with straight mouths.[42] Comparative historical arguments, at their best, are made in the interstices of their empirical foundations; they emerge from the interplay of different national or other cases. This is what distinguishes a comparative argument from Arno Mayer's. His is additive: there is no interplay between the cases, there is no reason to read the others once you have read one, since they add nothing new, only repeating the same argument for each subsequent national case. Imagine standard uncomparative historical narratives as like the Washington Monument: monolithic, unipedestal. Let us think of comparative arguments as like the Eiffel Tower, resting on multiple feet without which it could not stand, but with the tower as something other than the sum of its foundations.

Take, as an example, the difference between the standard-issue *Sonderweg* view of German historical development, phrased classically by Ralf Dahrendorf, and the attempts to dethrone it, given a major boost twenty years ago in the salutary provocations of Eley and Blackbourn. In the former, Germany is amalgamated to a standard case, the evolution of liberal bourgeois industrial democracy. This occurred either peacefully, as in Britain, or with a revolution thrown in, as in France. Ultimately, however, it rests on a social science view of modernization, its allegedly inevitable stages and coherences. Having failed to achieve a bourgeois revolution, Germany is classified as a failed or at best belated development, Bloch's ponderous *Gleichzeitigkeit des Ungleichzeitigen*. The generalization renounces its bastard child.

In the hands of the anti-*Sonderweg*ians, in contrast, the generalized verities have dissipated. No implicit standard of development exemplified in the trajectory of any one or two nations lies at the heart of comparative judgments. Each nation is seen as moving in its own direction at its own pace, with the similarities among them banished to the realm of far greater abstraction: industrialization, but in very different ways and timing; the gradual assertion of preeminence by the bourgeoisie, but often in ways that to the old view would appear covert, subterranean, or even examples of false consciousness. Formal political democracy, formerly the crux of the matter, now becomes an optional appurtenance whose presence or absence can equally be reconciled with bourgeois interests and their achievement. We have a bouquet of flowers, all of the same genus, though perhaps not phylum, dazzling in their complementarity rather than their similarity. We have a bouquet and no longer — stretching the horticultural analogies — a tree, with its singular trunk and massed branches.

Here are a few examples of comparative mid-level historical arguments that fall shy of any ambitions to generalize. These are good arguments, not necessarily in the sense that they are accurate or right, but in that they compare and juxtapose different cases in an attempt to isolate what it is that is unique, crucial and therefore causal to some of them. Why did the German, Austrian, and British medical research communities contribute more to a scientific understanding of homosexuality than the French during the nineteenth century, even though the French were the nation of Pasteur and the proud inheritors of a venerable and distinguished tradition of scientific prowess in matters medical? The northern movements in favor of homosexual rights arose as ones concerned to prove their scientific mettle in part because homosexuality remained criminalized in these nations, where in France the Napoleonic Code had no penalties for sodomy. The hope was, by invoking the appropriate academic credentials, to lend an air of respectability to a political cause that, to the south, did not need to be fought.[43]

Similar is the argument that emerges from Richard Evans's comparison of the evolution of feminist movements across a broad range of nations: that the delay of the Australasian women's movement may be explained in that many of the reforms, around whose achievement organizations were formed in other nations, had already been granted here.[44] Both of these arguments harken back to the structure of the argument presented in Sombart's classic explanation of why the socialist dog did not bark in the United States. In all these cases, such conclusions, telling us both something of the dynamics of political organization across nations and the particular trajectory of developments in specific instances, would not have been apparent from a study of individual circumstances. They emerge precisely from the juxtaposition with others, both similar and different in various respects. Seymour Martin Lipset's comparison between the United States and Canada also comes close to this ideal, using the two as equally posed counterpoints to illustrate what it is in American developments that cannot be attributed to new worldishness, expansive geography or other features that are equally shared with Canada.[45]

Or take one of the best examples of comparative history, Peter Kolchin's study of American slavery and Russian serfdom.[46] There are general conclusions in the book, mainly in the form of confirmation or negation of generalizations advanced by others: that race was not a biological given, but socially constructed, as seen in the way that serfs were eventually treated as a race apart on the basis of their legal status; that forced labor systems arose in response to the demand for agricultural goods in Europe and a shortage of labor in the peripheral food-producing nations; that egalitarian societies generally had a harder time emancipating slaves than did stratified, authoritarian ones. And yet, the genius of the book lies in the juxtaposition of its two cases and the way that each is illuminated and enriched by the comparison, fruits whose juice cannot be squeezed in a sentence or two. Tellingly, there is no concluding chapter where the results of induction are served up; the nuggets are embedded along the way in the narrative empirical chapters.

One such mini-conclusion deals with why revolts in Russia tended to be large-scale violent uprisings (huge units, absentee landlords, majority of the population serfs, largely autonomous daily serf life) while in the United States they were smaller (the opposite of the factors mentioned in the other case). This allows Kolchin to dispute accounts of the relative paucity of slave revolts in the United States that rely on factors like an alleged Sambo mentality among slaves that encouraged docility. While it would, in principle, have been possible to account accurately for, say, the unrebellious nature of American slaves without a comparison to Russia, in practice the likelihood of being able to iden-tify which factors set the American situation apart from another where, in fact, rebellions were frequent and large, would seem almost impossi-ble—much like searching the proverbial haystack without even know-ing whether we were looking for needles or toothpicks or matches. The Russian case with its obverse set of circumstances is what allows identi-fication of the possible causes in the American situation, a classic instance of Mill's method of difference.

The contrast of this sort of mid-level, historical, empirically based comparison with the supersonic altitude of Patterson's approach is striking. Where Patterson would scarcely have registered the differences between serfdom and slavery, except to note perhaps that these two examples showed the extent to which, *sub specie aeternitas*, race has little if anything to do with slavery, it is precisely the differences that are important for Kolchin. A similar, although less successful, attempt at such national juxtapositions to get at what is crucially causal is found in Jonathan Steinberg's ambition to explain why the Holocaust did not take place in Italy and thus, by extension, why it did in Germany.[47]

This also raises the issue of which comparison. The very choice of the nations, or whatever the unit of analysis may be, to be compared often determines the answers drawn. This is clearly the case in terms of the content of the analysis, as when Germany looks quite different, more or less *sonderbar*, when compared either eastwards or westwards. It looks perhaps exceptional and, in certain respects, unwestern when compared to France or England. But if the focus is shifted eastwards, suddenly the nation looks like a cousin, and perhaps even a sibling, of its western neighbors.[48] In a more methodological sense, the level of comparison helps determine the nature of the arrived-at conclusions. Skocpol insists on the role of states and their respective (in)abilities to deal with international crises as causal factors in the outbreak of revolutions. Clearly, much of this focus on the state is determined precisely by her comparison among France, Russia, and China. State apparatuses are one of the few and obvious things that these nations shared in common, however different and perhaps incomparable other aspects of their internal domestic arrangements were. Similar in its methodological determination is her dismissal of urban revolts, in favor of a focus on peasant insurrections, since not all of these nations had politically active city dwellers.[49] One could make a similar argument concerning Barrington Moore's focus on the role of peasants and agriculture.

When Goldstone is interested in the broad sweep of crises in the early modern world across a range of nations, including Europe, the Ottoman Empire, and China, it is clear that he will not conclude that political factors, nor even economic ones, were their cause.[50] Rather, the level of generality in his *Fragestellung* will lead on to factors all his nations had in common. In his case, that means ecological and demographic crises, and their intersection with other sorts of problems. Ertman's arguments against geopolitical explanations for the divergent development of constitutional versus absolutist states in Europe (above all France, Prussia, and England), hinge in large measure on including in his remarkably expansive scope nations formerly considered peripheral and not studied comparatively. By incorporating also Hungary and Poland, for example, he can show that the geopolitical arguments, by which both should have been absolutist and bureaucratic states, fail in that, in fact, they were constitutional and nonbureaucratic.[51]

But, if comparative history does not necessarily mean a concern with generalization and universal laws, it does signify one with cause. There is no history that is not, ultimately and at least implicitly, comparative. It is not just that we need comparisons to know whether a national case is unique and singular, since the very formulation here presupposes at least an implied juxtaposition. It is also that, in order to know what is causal and what merely trivially connected, we must juxtapose to other, related yet different instances in order to isolate the important from the incidental, following the technique laid out so lucidly by Mill.[52] Comparative history serves primarily to separate the important from the incidental and thus to point the way towards causal explanations. It does not necessarily accept the Hempelian claim that the particular must always be understood as an instance of a larger regularity.

But neither does it embrace the idea, put forth by Oakeshott, that, unlike the sciences, history explains by filling in the interstices ever more finely in a chain of narrative that, by being continuous, explains how one thing led to another. History, as he says, accounts *for* change by means of a full account *of* change.[53] Explanation and narrative become the same thing. Comparative history accepts that the methods of difference and agreement are the closest history can come to laboratory conditions and falsifiability and that comparison is the historical experiment.[54] It rejects as superficial the fashionable claim that the return of narrative to historical writing is more than an aesthetic fashion, concerned as it is with elevating palatability over plausibility. It sees the antinomy thus implied between narration and analysis as deeply misleading.

History has, in recent decades, drifted away from a concern with causality. One of the reasons has been not only the linguistic turn and the priority recently granted cultural history. Causality has come to be seen as part of a fixation on monocausal, reductionist, or at least overly parsimonious explanations rooted in an older and increasingly outmoded social-scientific paradigm. Cultural history is perfectly capable of comparisons. But generally speaking it is fair to say that history after the linguistic turn, and cultural history in particular, has been more concerned with what than with why, more focused on complexity than causation. To the extent that various coalitions of young fogies and Old Turks swing the pendulum slowly away from its predominating cultural focus, comparative history stands to play a crucial role. It will aim history at a goal short of the generalizing tendencies of the harder social sciences, yet still concerned with causality. It should refuse to allow our cousins in the social sciences to corner that market.

REFERENCES

1. *Comparative Studies in Society and History*, 1 (1958), pp. 1–2.
2. Carl G. Hempel, "The Function of General Laws in History," *Journal of Philosophy*, 39: 2 (1942).
3. I owe this story to that master of Cantabridgiana, Mark Pinson.
4. Leif Lewin, *Ideology and Strategy: A Century of Swedish Politics* (Cambridge, 1988). Some of the most lucid and brilliant rational choice analysis, applied to sex and love, which would otherwise seem a field least susceptible to an economistic approach, and of great potential interest to historians, is in Richard A. Posner, *Sex and Reason* (Cambridge, MA, 1992).
5. Peter Sahlins, *Boundaries: The Making of France and Spain in the Pyrenees* (Berkeley, 1989); William W. Hagen, *Germans, Poles and Jews: The Nationality Conflict in the Prussian East 1772–1914* (Chicago, 1980).
6. "Bringing Regionalism Back to History," *American Historical Review*, 104: 4 (October, 1999).
7. Philip D. Morgan, *Slave Counterpoint: Black Culture in the Eighteenth-Century Chesapeake and Lowcountry* (Chapel Hill, 1998); E. Digby Baltzell, *Puritan Boston and Quaker Philadelphia: Two Protestant Ethics and the Spirit of Class Authority and Leadership* (Boston, 1979).
8. R.R. Palmer, *The Age of the Democratic Revolution: A Political History of Europe and America, 1760–1800*, 2 vols. (Princeton, 1959–1964).
9. Mona Ozouf, *Women's Words: Essay on French Singularity* (Chicago, 1997).
10. Frank Tannenbaum, *Slave and Citizen* (New York, 1946); Herbert S. Klein, *Slavery in the Americas: A Comparative Study of Virginia and Cuba* (Chicago, 1967); Carl N. Degler, *Neither Black Nor White: Slavery and Race Relations in Brazil and the United States* (New York, 1971). Overviews in Frederick Cooper, "Race, Ideology, and the Perils of Comparative History," *American Historical Review*, 101: 4 (October 1996) and George M. Fredrickson, *The Comparative Imagination: On the History of Racism, Nationalism, and Social Movements* (Berkeley, 2000), pp. 30–35.
11. David Blackbourn and Geoff Eley, *The Peculiarities of German History* (Oxford, 1984).
12. Daniel T. Rodgers, *Atlantic Crossings: Social Politics in a Progressive Age* (Cambridge, MA, 1998).
13. Ian Tyrell, "American Exceptionalism in an Age of International History," *American Historical Review*, 96: 4 (1991); Shearer Davis Bowman, *Masters and Lords: Mid-Nineteenth Century U.S. Planters and Prussian Junkers* (New York, 1993); George M. Frederickson, *White Supremacy: A Comparative Study in American and South African History* (New York, 1981); Colleen A. Dunlavy, *Politics and Industrialization: Early Railroads in the United States and Prussia* (Princeton, 1994).
14. Jill Harsin, *Policing Prostitution in Nineteenth-Century Paris* (Princeton, NJ, 1985), pp. xvi–xix.
15. Ann F. La Berge, *Mission and Method: The Early Nineteenth-Century French Public Health Movement* (Cambridge, 1992), pp. 238–239. A similar invocation of factors not particular to France to explain a particularly French outcome, in this case why physicians played such an unusually important role in the politics of the III Republic: Jack D. Ellis, *The Physician-Legislators of France: Medicine and Politics in the Early Third Republic, 1870-1914* (Cambridge, 1990), p. 6. Similar is the case with Paul Farmer, *AIDS and Accusation: Haiti and the Geography of Blame* (Berkeley, 1992), pp. 184–190 or David A. Moss, *When All Else Fails: Government as the Ultimate Risk Manager* (Cambridge, MA, 2002), pp. 300–301.
16. F. Gilbert, ed. *The Historical Essays of Otto Hinze*, (New York, 1975), p. 23

17. Peter Baldwin, ed., *Reworking the Past: Hitler, the Holocaust and the Historians' Debate* (Boston, 1990).

18. Gunnar Broberg and Mattias Tydén, *Oönskade i folkhemmet: Rashygien och sterilisering i Sverige* (Stockholm, 1991); Maija Runcis, *Steriliseringar i folkhemmet* (Stockholm, 1998); Maciej Zaremba, *De rena och de andra: Om tvångssteriliseringar, rashygien och arvsynd* (n.p., 1999); Gunnar Broberg and Nils Roll-Hansen, eds., *Eugenics and the Welfare State* (East Lansing, 1996).

19. Richard Rose, "Is American Public Policy Exceptional?" in Byron E. Shafer, ed., *Is America Different? A New Look at American Exceptionalism* (Oxford, 1991).

20. Norbert Elias, *The History of Manners* (New York, 1982); Hans Peter Duerr, *Der Mythos vom Zivilisationsprozess*, 4 vols. (Frankfurt, 1988).

21. C.B.A. Behrens, *Society, Government and the Enlightenment: The Experiences of Eighteenth-Century France and Prussia* (New York, 1985).

22. Arno J. Mayer, *The Persistence of the Old Regime: Europe to the Great War* (New York, 1981).

23. Examples: James C. Riley, *The Eighteenth-Century Campaign to Avoid Disease* (New York, 1987); Richard Harrison Shryock, *The Development of Modern Medicine* (New York, 1947). A study with similar advantages and accomplishments: Elliott A. Krause, *Death of the Guilds: Professions, States, and the Advance of Capitalism, 1930 to the Present* (New Haven, 1996).

24. Barrington Moore, Jr., *Social Origins of Dictatorship and Democracy* (Boston, 1966); Thomas Ertman, *Birth of the Leviathan: Building States and Regimes in Medieval and Early Modern Europe* (Cambridge, 1997); Louis Hartz, *The Founding of New Societies* (New York, 1964); Charles S. Maier, *Recasting Bourgeois Europe: Stabilization in France, Germany and Italy in the Decade After World War I* (Princeton, 1975); Gregory M. Luebbert, *Liberalism, Fascism or Social Democracy: Social Classes and the Political Origins of Regimes in Interwar Europe* (New York, 1991); Rogers Brubaker, *Citizenship and Nationhood in France and Germany* (Cambridge, MA, 1992).

25. Peter Baldwin, "Can We Define a European Welfare State Model?" in Bent Greve, ed., *Comparative Welfare Systems: The Scandinavian Model in a Period of Change* (London, 1996); P. Abrahamson, "The Welfare Modelling Business," *Social Policy and Administration*, 33: 4 (1999).

26. Ernst Nolte, *Three Faces of Fascism* (New York, 1965); Zeev Sternhell, *Neither Right Nor Left: Fascist Ideology in France* (Berkeley, 1986); Stanley G. Payne, *Fascism: Comparison and Definition* (Madison, 1980).

27. Jack A. Goldstone, *Revolution and Rebellion in the Early Modern World* (Berkeley, 1991), p. xxiii.

28. Juan J. Linz, "Political Space and Fascism as a Late-Comer," in Stein Ugelvik Larsen et al., eds., *Who Were the Fascists? Social Roots of European Fascism* (Bergen, 1980), p. 160.

29. Ted Robert Gurr, *Why Men Rebel* (Princeton, 1970), p. 9.

30. Philip Abrams, *Historical Sociology* (Ithaca, 1982), p. 222.

31. Mary Douglas and Marcel Calvez, "The Self as Risk Taker: A Cultural Theory of Contagion in Relation to AIDS," *Sociological Review* (1990), 463.

32. Charles Tilly, "Reflections on the History of European State-Making," in Tilly, ed., *The Formation of National States in Western Europe* (Princeton, 1975), p. 12.

33. Richard D. Mohr, *Gays/Justice: A Study of Ethics, Society and Law* (New York, 1988), p. 251.

34. Jürgen Kocka, *White Collar Workers in America 1890–1940* (London, 1980).

35. Peter Baldwin, *The Politics of Social Solidarity: Class Bases of the European Welfare State* (Cambridge, 1990).

36. Peter Baldwin, *Contagion and the State in Europe, 1830–1930* (Cambridge, 1999).

37. Stephen Morillo, "Guns and Government: A Comparative Study of Europe and Japan," *Journal of World History*, 6: 1 (1995), 75–106.
38. Moore, Jr., *Social Origins of Dictatorship and Democracy*, p. xiii.
39. Quincy Wright, *A Study of War*, 2nd ed. (Chicago, 1965), pp. 8, 42ff.
40. Orlando Patterson, *Slavery and Social Death* (Cambridge, MA, 1982), p. 13.
41. Anthony James Joes, *Fascism in the Contemporary World* (Boulder, 1978); A. James Gregor, *Phoenix: Fascism in Our Time* (New Brunswick, 1999).
42. "Consider for example the proceedings that we call 'games.' I mean board-games, card-games, ball-games, Olympic games, and so on. What is common to them all? — Don't say: 'There *must* be something common, or they would not be called "games" — but *look and see* whether there is anything common to all. For if you look at them you will not see something that is common to *all*, but similarities, relationships, and a whole series of them at that. To repeat: don't think, but look! Look for example at board-games, with their multifarious relationships. Now pass to card-games; here you find many correspondences with the first group, but many common features drop out, and others appear. When we pass next to ball-games, much that is common is retained, but much is lost... And the result of this examination is: we see a complicated network of similarities overlapping and criss-crossing: sometimes overall similarities, sometimes similarities of detail. I can think of no better expression to characterize these similarities than 'family resemblances'; for the various resemblances between members of a family: build, features, color of eyes, gait, temperament, etc. etc. overlap and criss-cross in the same way. — And I shall say: 'games' form a family." Ludwig Wittgenstein, *Philosophical Investigations*, §§ 66–67.
43. Robert A. Nye, *Masculinity and Male Codes of Honor in Modern France* (New York, 1993), Ch. 6; Michael Dreyer, "Minorities, Civil Rights and Political Culture: Homosexuality in Germany and the United States," in Manfred Berg and Martin H. Geyer, eds., *Two Cultures of Rights: The Quest for Inclusion and Participation in Modern America and Germany* (Cambridge, 2002).
44. Richard J. Evans, *The Feminists: Women's Emancipation Movements in Europe, America and Australasia 1840–1920* (London, 1977), p. 63.
45. Seymour Martin Lipset, *Continental Divide: The Values and Institutions of the United States and Canada* (New York, 1990).
46. Peter Kolchin, *Free and Unfree Labor: American Slavery and Russian Serfdom* (Cambridge, MA, 1987). Again the proviso all too familiar to comparative historians must be stated here. The book has been criticized, especially by Russian historians, for its portrayal of serfdom, while generally lauded by the other side. I am in no position to evaluate the empirical foundations of the two aspects of the argument and, although obviously not denying that this has bearing on the merit of the work as history, my interest here lies with the formulation of the argument as a comparison. For criticism, see especially Michael Confino, "Servage russe, esclavage américain," *Annales ESC*, 5 (1990), 1119–1141. I am indebted to Richard Wortman for this caution.
47. Jonathan Steinberg, *All or Nothing: The Axis and the Holocaust 1941–43* (London, 1990).
48. Heinz-Gerhard Haupt and Jürgen Kocka, Historischer Vergleich: Methoden, Aufgaben, Probleme," in Haupt and Kocka, eds., *Geschichte und Vergleich: Ansätze und Ergebnisse international vergleichender Geschichtsschreibung* (Frankfurt, 1996), p. 13; see also their essay in this collection.
49. Theda Skocpol, *States and Social Revolutions: A Comparative Analysis of France, Russia and China* (Cambridge, 1979), p. 113.
50. Goldstone, *Revolution and Rebellion in the Early Modern World*, pp. 1–2.
51. Ertman, *Birth of the Leviathan*, p. 15.

52. *John Stuart Mill's Philosophy of Scientific Method*, Ernest Nagel, ed. (New York, 1950), Book III, Ch. 8, pp. 211–227.
53. Michael Oakeshott, *Experience and Its Modes* (Cambridge, 1933), p. 143.
54. For consideration of the limitations of Mill's method for comparative studies, see Ira Katznelson, "Structure and Configuration in Comparative Politics," in Mark Irving Lichbach and Alan S. Zukerman, eds., *Comparative Politics: Rationality, Culture, and Structure* (Cambridge, 1997), pp. 98–102.

2

COMPARATIVE HISTORY: METHODS, AIMS, PROBLEMS

Heinz-Gerhard Haupt and Jürgen Kocka

The relative significance of comparative history depends very much upon an individual nation's historiographic traditions. Comparative history is more common in Germany than in France or Italy, where historians have instead tended to devote far greater attention to regional studies and to interactions across borders. Across all nations, however, particular subjects seem to have lent themselves more readily to comparative inquiry. Comparative history is more frequently practiced by historians of antiquity, the modern era, and the recent past than by medievalists or early modernists. Economic, social, and political historians, as well as historical demographers, are more likely to employ comparisons at the level of the nation-state than are researchers into cultural history, the history of everyday life, or the history of ideas.[1]

Historians are notoriously less willing to compare than are political scientists or sociologists. This chapter then begins with a simple question. What, if anything, distinguishes comparison when it is practiced by historians? We argue that there are important differences between the comparative method in historical scholarship and the systematic social sciences. However, these differences are not, to our minds, fundamental, but rather differences of degree. We begin with the assumption that historical studies generally share certain basic properties. Our essay asks about the expectations, possibilities, and challenges that historians face when they seek to compare.

THE BASICS OF COMPARATIVE HISTORY

Since the latter part of the Enlightenment, professional historians have come to agree that their research and findings, if they are to have validity, must proceed from primary sources. Primary sources confer at least the hope of authenticity. Historians proceed from the principle of reading closely the sources upon which they rely. They have developed, as a consequence, a critical skepticism with regard to hasty generalization. And yet, even if one subscribes to this cardinal principle of professional scholarly history — which we do — one must nevertheless acknowledge that the chances of its actual realization vary wildly from case to case. For example, the primary-source principle lends itself well to monographic studies, but quite poorly to grand syntheses. Its importance should not be overemphasized to the detriment of other basic principles of scholarly history, such as the goal of discovering more profound historical connections.

Similarly, historians generally also attempt to understand change over time. As a rule, our interests in understanding, explaining, and portraying (even if they are not primarily narrative, but argumentative) are bound up with the structure of "before" and "after." That is true even if one takes only a snapshot or a cross-section of a particular moment in time. Indeed, our discipline is marked very fundamentally by its peculiar relationship to time. Since its rise as a modern scholarly discipline, history has, by definition, attempted to comprehend changes over time as a form of development. Put differently, as new phenomena arise over the course of time, the new necessarily proceeds from the old, but not merely as repetition. The old, then, contains the potential of the subsequently new. Empirical findings must be viewed rigorously within their diachronic context. Thus history is not merely a sum or a series of cases useful for exemplifying general laws. Historians, in other words, attach great significance to the principle of uniqueness.

Historians assume narrow limits on our ability to understand any given part of the past in isolation from its wider context. Understanding the parts requires a broader view of a subtly interpreted whole. At the same time, an accurate sense of the whole depends upon a reconstruction of the parts. Historical findings gain meaning from their relations in both synchronous and diachronic context. Historical scholarship therefore sets much narrower strictures upon the procedure of isolating and dealing with variables than is the case in political economy or in the empirical social sciences.[2]

The comparative approach is thus always partly at odds with these basic principles of historical scholarship. The more cases we employ for a comparison, the less possible it is to work closely with primary sources, and hence the greater our dependence upon the secondary literature. Moreover, comparisons presume that the objects of comparison can be isolated, that their developmental contexts can be usefully dissected into separate parts. The relation of two or more units of comparison to each other cannot usually be conceived as a relation between stages of a development or moments of mutual causation, but only as independent cases related by the device of a general question and measured in terms of "similarities" and "differences." Those who compare do not view their objects of study exclusively as particularities, but as examples of a general case that are in some ways similar or identical, in other ways different. Comparison breaks continuities and interrupts the flow of narrative. Comparison is not necessarily associated with change over time, but with similarities and differences.

One cannot compare phenomena in their multilayered totality. Rather, we select aspects. Comparison requires selection, abstraction, detaching of the case from its context. Comparisons that involve many cases make the need for abstraction obvious. Comparing, say, industrialization in twenty countries or slavery in sixty requires that the object of comparison be abstracted and removed from its synchronic and diachronic contexts. Historians, however, are reluctant to work in this way. But although the problem may be less pronounced when we choose to compare only two or three cases, it does not entirely disappear. Put simply, comparison always necessitates abstraction.

This need for abstraction goes a long way towards explaining why historians, ever since the days of historicism, have regarded comparative history with reserve. It explains, too, the relative paucity of comparisons among historians of everyday life, who generally take a micro-historical approach in their efforts to reconstruct past ways of life in their totality and who tend to be skeptical of analytic concepts.[3] Comparison is the province of a more theoretically oriented, analytic type of history, more explicit in its concepts, with a certain distance from historical tradition. As a consequence, comparative history has been the concern of a minority.

Ideally, comparative history should be pursued in a way that minimizes its contradictions with the basic principles of historical scholarship. Comparative history will differ, if only subtly for the most part, from the types of comparison employed in the systematic social sciences. Historians who take the comparative route tend to restrict themselves to a small number of cases, often just two. They usually employ a moderate level of abstraction and follow a rule that might be summed up as follows: the minimum necessary abstraction, and the maximum possible detail and context. They value contrasts over generalizations, and they tend to be more interested in the differences than in the similarities between their cases. They strive to include transformations over time and historical dynamics, often by choosing processes as their objects of comparison. Especially frequent is the combination of arguments drawn from comparative and cross-national history. Historians who strike out on a comparative path tend to combine analyses of structures and processes with the reconstruction of experience and patterns of behavior.

One can, of course, overstate the conflicts between the comparative approach and the principles of historical scholarship. There are also important affinities. As historical scholarship has grown beyond its own traditions, especially during the last few decades, it has become more open to comparative history and increasingly dependent on it in turn.[4] There is a close and mutually reinforcing relationship between comparison and the analytic orientation in historical scholarship. Properly understood, historical scholarship is always dependent in its methods on emphasis, and always selective and (re)constructive. Comparative history merely tends to make these unavoidable properties all the more obvious. Historians always need to define their units of study very carefully, so as to avoid misunderstandings and achieve clarity. Comparative history makes us all the more aware of our selections. If we are to remain intellectually honest and self-reflective, we need to consider both our choice of concepts and their relation to the wider world. Comparison, then, ultimately helps us because it forces us to acknowledge the fact of selection.

Comparative history is theoretically challenging to its practitioners, who are forced to reflect constantly on their own methods. Among the issues they must consider are the following:

(a) What are the appropriate units of comparison: nations, regions, cultures, epochs, crisis situations, institutions? Surely the choice depends upon the availability of sources, but above all on the questions to be posed.

(b) What and whom are we to compare? It is said that we cannot compare apples and oranges. That means that we should never try to compare the incomparable. The comparability of two or more objects is primarily determined through the questions posed. In this regard, the objects of comparison must show a minimum similarity so as to allow comparison, which of course always means that they can be studied with regard to their differences. We cannot compare apples and oranges if we want to understand the advantages or disadvantages of different kinds of apples. But we may and should compare apples and oranges if our intent is to study fruit. The historian must define in advance what the actual intent of the comparison is, and whether the questions that one pursues are relevant to that intent, and whether the choice of cases for comparison can be therefore justified.

(c) But even given a solution to the problem of apples and oranges, the question of appropriate cases for comparison remains. For instance, should we contrast the German bourgeoisie of the nineteenth century with a Western European or an Eastern European case? The results will differ according to the perspective we adopt.[5] Our own presumptions, experiences, and values will often play a role in the choice of a case. This cannot always be avoided, nor perhaps should it be avoided. But reflection upon this point is crucial.

(d) Often a diachronic comparison is necessary. In this regard, as well, the choice of comparative cases depends upon the research question and certain systematic prerequisites. Imagine a comparison of trade union history in Germany and England that focuses on the connection between industrialization and the workers' movements. The historian who wishes to examine the origins of unions in each country will have to take account of the differing chronologies and epochs of English and German industrialization. A diachronic comparison, or one in "delayed time," is necessary.[6]

Comparative historians know that they construct, not in a vacuum, of course, but with due regard for the importance of the particular truth they seek. They construct, then, not in the sense of invention, but nevertheless aware that their findings are not mere depictions of past realities. Their conclusions are strongly influenced by the choice of emphasis and of subject and, of course, by the researcher's own analysis. If these (re)constructions are not to differ too greatly from the reality of each actual case, the historian must engage in a thorough consideration of the terms and conceptual particularities of each of the cases in the comparison.

The affinity between historical analysis and historical comparison serves to explain the special strengths, attractions, and also the difficulties of comparative history. At present, the historical subfields are characterized by extreme specialization, gradualism, and a primary orientation to national history, all the more true in Germany. In that context, the danger of a sudden flood of comparisons that violate the basic principles of historical scholarship is low. The danger is not too much comparative history, but too little. In the cause of reducing national bias, of raising the level of theoretical and analytical rigor, and of making history more open and innovative, comparative history deserves a higher status within the discipline.

COMPARATIVE HISTORY: RESULTS AND PROSPECTS

Although the comparative approach was once rare among European and American historians, there has been an abundance of successful comparative studies in recent years. In the following section, we review methods and results, asking above all: What are the units and realms of comparison? What are comparative history's prospects?

THE WHOLE AND THE PARTS

In his 1999 treatise *Der historische Vergleich,* Hartmut Kaelble, the distinguished social historian of Europe, unreservedly advocates global comparisons. These are, according to his definition, "explicit and systematic comparisons of two or more historical societies, so as to explore commonalities and differences as well as processes of differentiation and/or convergence."[7] Many studies have followed Kaelble's approach, although they have increasingly included not just the macro- but also the meso- and micro-levels. Indeed, those who have shifted in their own projects towards greater detail have often been critical of structural history, accusing it of focusing too much on social histories of complete societies and structures, thereby sacrificing the perspectives of those who actually experienced and took part in events.[8]

A typical example of the global structures approach is the classic work of the historical sociologist Barrington Moore. While earlier agrarian historians tended to see a variety of differing conditions among those who lived from the land, Moore set out to compare whole societies and to consider the effects of different types of rural social structures on the process of democratization. Similarly, Kaelble's stimulating sketch takes as its unit of analysis entire societies, in his case to explore the social and historical underpinnings of the process of political unification in twentieth-century Western Europe.[9] On the basis of quantitative evidence, Kaelble sees the incipient similarities of Western European societies in areas such as urbanization, family, and employment structures, which he then contrasts with structures in the United States.

Comparative historians portray global structures mainly by using developmental models or general theories. Comparisons among European and non-European societies often hinge upon the economic, cultural, or political characterizations assigned to each system.[10] Here comparison serves to distinguish identifying properties or ideal types for individual case studies.[11] The comparative historian might look at bourgeois revolutions and perhaps compare a selection of revolutionary uprisings, employing categories such as feudalism or bourgeois society, or processes such as modernization, urbanization, and industrialization. The more such models of critique and empirical revision are relativized and opened up, the greater the chance that the historical comparison can yield precision, needed revisions, and valid reformulations. But when the fundamental theoretical assumptions are too closed and neat, there is a danger that comparison will, at best, present illustrations of near-uniform cases.

Of course, comparisons based on global terms and overarching social structures play an important role. They can help us in crafting hypotheses, without which many a case study ends up running unsystematically aground. The successful global comparisons offered, for example, by Barrington Moore and Reinhard Bendix have provided useful paradigms for different fields of historical practice, and have served as generators of grand hypotheses. But the work of the historian, in contrast to the more systematic social sciences, is bound by clear limits. Global comparison carries the risk of becoming an attempt to illustrate a prior theoretical conclusion, with the result that empirical findings will be considered only if they confirm the validity of the initial premise. Furthermore, although a macro-level view of societies or social structures ensures the coherence of a particular study, it too easily tramples upon the fine details of historical process and structure that are often relevant to the actual actors and events of history. Especially in comparisons that take on "Europe" as a whole, there is a great danger of exaggerating the uniformity of the continent.[12]

Unlike their cousins in the systematic social sciences, then, historians more often concentrate on parts of the big picture, accepting clear thematic, geographical, and chronological boundaries. The importance of confessional loyalties in local elections, the contrast between villages from different areas of a nation-state, or agrarian movements in the initial phase of the European revolution of 1848 are legitimate units for comparison taken from a single society or from multiple countries.[13] This middle level offers a wealth of potentially meaningful perspectives. Social practices, like the mechanisms of cooptation, structures of association, and marriage and social mobility patterns can all be fruitfully compared to each other, both in time and between localities.[14] The whole and its parts are, of course, intimately related. Their relation can be defined through analysis, if interpreted as factor, result, or as emblem of the social totality, as Pierre Vilar trenchantly put it in his contribution to the debate on industrialization.[15] We must attempt, therefore, to view each case study in proper relation to the general processes and structures, whether it is dependent upon them, analogous to them, or even a factor that affects this larger context in turn. This systematic orientation is useful even in local studies, inasmuch as it helps to dispel the naive assumption that everything local has exclusively local causes.[16]

If particular phenomena or parts of various societies are to be compared, we must remember that the very same phenomenon can have different meanings in different contexts. This applies, *mutatis mutandis*, to comparisons of units within a society. For example, modern German society differs from that of the United States or Great Britain not only in its legal forms, but also in the relative significance of the law. Similarly, to note merely that nobles held important positions in pre-1914 Central and Western European countries neglects the differences in the significance of the nobility in Galicia or Hungary as opposed to descendants of nobles in no-longer aristocratic France or the strong influence wielded by noble ideals and models in Germany. The "persistence of the Ancien Regime" postulated by Arno Mayer conceals thoroughly diverse lifestyles and strategies, channels of influence, and developmental processes.[17] As discussions of the problem of "nominalism" have revealed, phenomena that look identical can actually mean very different things, depending upon the wider context.

As the genre of *histoire croisée* championed by Bénédicte Zimmermann and Michael Werner has demonstrated, micro-, meso-, and macro-levels are not disconnected from one another. This tangle of connections can be variously examined through exploration of particular objects or as a group of societal processes.[18] Contrary to the doctrines of *histoire croisée*, however, either approach can be combined with the comparative method. Comparison allows for the perspectives developed by the social sciences, as well as for the elucidation of interconnections between individual regions.[19] For example, the question of whether the members of the national parliaments of Germany, France, and Italy in the nineteenth century were primarily seen as "brokers" or as representatives of the common good offers an interesting illustration of this problem.[20] Even by the strict standards of *histoire croisée*, a comparison can relate either to an entire society or its parts. In the process, as we show, transfer history and *histoire croisée* become forms of comparative history.

TRANSFER HISTORY AND *HISTOIRE CROISÉE*

Comparisons are, in essence, tied neither to particular regions nor to particular units of time. For Marc Bloch, this quality was part of comparison's appeal: "Those who wish finally to drop the burden of artificial separations must find the appropriate geographic context for every aspect of European social life and for different periods; one that is defined not from the outside, but from the inside."[21] That context might be the nation, the region, or even some larger geographic entity, such as a continent. At the same time, however, historical research has tended to privilege the comparison between nation-states, at least as far as the nineteenth and twentieth centuries are concerned. This national orientation reflects not only the fact that important historical processes took place within the boundaries of nation-states, but also that historians were themselves bound up in national discussions and languages.[22] Depending upon their opinions about the French Revolution's consequences, for instance, French historians largely concentrated their research on particular problems that they debated within a national context. Historians in the Federal Republic of Germany rarely reached beyond German history and its particularities to explain Nazi extermination policies. With few exceptions, they did not, for instance, address a general crisis of modernity or the "European civil war" that Ernst Nolte postulated.[23]

In recent years, however, the national perspective has come increasingly under fire: it has been regionalized and localized as well as globalized. In continental Europe, historians have sought to overcome the national standpoint by means of two approaches: transfer history, as advocated in particular by Michel Espagne and Michael Werner, and *histoire croisée*, or "entangled history."[24] Transfer history looks at the interrelationships between two entities, whether nations, regions, towns, or institutions. It underscores the significance of given intermediaries, such as booksellers, publishers, and universities; the weight of various media, above all cultural media; and the specific co-optation process of the transfer. Like *histoire croisée*, it aims to relativize the meaning of the nation-state; it seeks to demonstrate, for example, that what we know as "French" culture incorporates a variety of foreign influences. Technologies, types of sport, even models of the social state: all of these are phenomena that were disseminated across borders and, as such, constitute appropriate subjects of cross-national study.[25]

Exponents of transfer history and *histoire croisée* accuse comparative history of privileging the nation-state, and thus of always confirming the nation's significance. Comparativists, they further charge, tend to accept nations' own self-representations without critical examination. Above all, comparative history's focus upon national differences tends to minimize the overlap and similarity among countries. And yet, as we have discussed, comparative history need not restrict itself to the nation as the sole unit of examination, and by no means must it follow blindly the history of national self-description. Moreover, comparative history does not rule out relations of interdependence or cross-national influence simply because it considers two or more cases alongside each other. Indeed, the conventional methods of source analysis in comparative historical work explicitly take such transfers into account.

Transfer history, for its part, can go too far in assuming completed transfers or obligations that cause both sides to define themselves in new ways. Too often, such studies fail to reflect upon what constitutes a successful transfer and tend, therefore, to neglect the significance of resistance in territories or among social elements that are subjected to outside influences. Transfer history also tends to document cultural transfer as a history of success and to demonstrate its range chiefly within cultural history and the histories of ideas and science.[26] That is why one most often speaks of "intercultural transfer." But as is the case with *histoire croisée*, transfer history does not fundamentally contradict the principles of historical comparison. To the contrary, as Johannes Paulmann has convincingly demonstrated, transfer history in fact requires a comparative starting point:

> To recognize what happens in an intercultural transfer the historian is forced to compare, at the very least to look at the old state of the examined object in contrast to its new context, to compare the social origins of the disseminators and affected populations in one land with those in another, to consider the terms of one language alongside that of another, and finally to interpret a phenomenon as it exists in the national culture from which it originates to the same phenomenon as introduced within a different culture.[27]

Histoire croisée distinguishes itself both from comparative history and from transfer history. It proceeds not from fixed quantities or terms, but from "problems and questions that can only be defined in the course of the analysis." It privileges concrete objects such as "institutions, legal systems, works, disciplines," while retreating from global constructions such as nations and societies. It proceeds from ways and means, conflicts and strategies. "Entanglement" is its magic word, not only as a general condition, but as an historical process; "entanglement" binds together the macro and the micro and underlines the self-reflexivity of both actors and historians, as well as the plurality of perspectives among observers.[28]

Histoire croisée and transfer history remind us of the importance of reflecting upon our categories of analysis and the perspectives we employ. The choice of nation-states as units for comparison must be undertaken carefully, with the caveats these two genres have offered clearly in mind. But even when we proceed from the questions that *histoire croisée* prefers — questions not bounded by the category of the nation-state — we must first decide upon the unit of study. How many comparative historians have begun with a national study only to land in a regional comparison! Even *histoire croisée* needs, at least theoretically, to limit the unit and the problems subject to analysis, in order to provide for comparative starting-points. In the final analysis, only actual empirical work can demonstrate whether the choice of different objects of study helps in achieving a greater methodological accuracy or an improved reconstruction of a given historical reality. Most important, "entangled connections" and comparative history are not mutually exclusive forms; the study of entanglements, whether on the supranational or regional level, can profit from comparative history's methods.

Insofar as historians are interested in such current-day problems as migration, borders, and expulsions, the national frame does not decline in significance, but requires instead an expanded view that includes the international picture. As the world globalizes, financial crises that arise outside Europe affect Europe, the exploitation of natural resources in European cities has a global impact; and regional military conflicts have consequences for all of Europe, indeed for the world. The history of the German nation-state necessarily includes the history of the countries once occupied by German troops as well as the history of emigration from or to Germany. Similarly, there are excellent reasons to study parts of northern France, Belgium, and the Rhineland in the nineteenth century together, since these regions were not only joined by similar economic and social structures, but also developed under the influence of the Catholic Church.[29] Research on mountain ranges, on the regions bounding seas, on border areas that, in the same way as coastlines, cannot simply be assigned to one national society further proves the salience of a broader international frame.[30]

Transnational historical scholarship has been reinforced by the contributions of post-colonialism, in which colonies are no longer viewed as appendages, but rather in complex relation to the motherland. Analogously, the once neatly national attribution of phenomena has been replaced by a stress on the "hybrid."[31] Those who study migrant groups no longer tend to view them simply as arrivals or departures from a given national society, but rather in terms of their own role, language, and social self-definitions as they seek to find a home in different national societies.[32] Post-colonial history concentrates on exchanges and the forms of domination, taking topics such as migration and the interactions between the member states of an empire as its subject matter. The impact of this research has been felt in a number of different areas. Historians of science have demonstrated that the very categories of scientific knowledge and the structures of academic fields have been influenced by colonial experiences. To take one example: the separation of sociology from anthropology in nineteenth-century Germany had much to do with the view of the colonies as entirely other.[33] Similarly, we now better understand how the urban, social, and military experiments carried out in the European colonies affected later developments in the mother countries, especially in the period beginning in the 1880s. Colonies were in part perceived as testing areas for the metropole.[34] Whether this pattern was equally strong in all European societies or only in those with longer histories of colonization remains an open question.

Although national comparisons dominated research in the past, the future will undoubtedly see more variations — both local and global — as we consider what units of comparison are most appropriate for each area of research. Smaller geographic units may well play a larger role in the comparative histories of the future. In the study of family size, for example, regional comparisons have proven more meaningful than national ones. This is also true of the history of religious practices and mentalities. In studies of given professions, forms of association and cultural practices such as celebrations, ceremonies, processions, and exhibitions, local comparisons have been found more illuminating than national ones.[35] By the same token, research on industrialization has emphasized regions as the territorial units within which industrial growth and the transformation of economic and social relations took place.[36] A comparison of identification patterns among nineteenth-century citizens must take into account their regional connections and hometown loyalties, which were by no means always in harmony with emergent national identities.[37] At the same time, the national framework remains indispensable in discussions of lawmaking processes or legal systems. But even in that realm, the unit of analysis changes when we consider the actual application of laws.

✳✳✳

If we ask in conclusion what problems are likely to be especially interesting to comparative history in the future, the following areas (at the least) present themselves.

First, the comparative study of European modernity remains of central concern: the question of when, if, and how equality before the law, economic innovation, cultural autonomy, and rationalized lifestyles took hold across Europe. We have yet to determine how to analyze comprehensively the various modernization projects that accompanied bourgeois emancipation movements. We need studies that neither concentrate solely upon one leading nation nor narrow down the question to one national history. The comparative study of modernity includes both economic as well as cultural history; it cannot be restricted to a teleology or a history of success. Let us not forget that analyses of war and oppression, exclusion, and extermination also belong in this context of modernity. These phenomena should be examined to determine whether they contradict the principles of modernity or simply represent its most inhumane extremes. In the expansion of this research to the eastern, southern, and northern regions of Europe (all of which have often been ignored in comparative studies), we may gain substantial new insights into modernity, the principles and effects of which have generally been seen as originating in Western Europe. The examination of civil society's function has been expanded to include the political structure of modernity. In comparisons of the more-developed with the less-developed states, it is useful to assess the structures of civil society and their influence.[38]

Second, there is much to recommend both a globalization as well as a stricter delineation of comparison. A global approach acknowledges the very general and evident expansion of the political arena, something that historical scholarship has not sufficiently examined to date. The point is not just to promote insights into the many variations of the processes observed in Europe by looking beyond the European continent, but also to relativize the European perspective itself. The mere insight that various macro-processes take place under various cultural conditions, in differing contexts and with differing consequences, can enrich the historian's perspective and add to the range of our terms and theories. Through the inclusion of non-European cultures and structures, we can, as Clifford Geertz wrote, expand the human "universe of discourse." At the same time, geographic expansion also helps to cast constructive doubts upon how historians view reality itself. Although some may view the comparison of European with non-European developments with suspicion, comparisons between widely separated societies can, as Marc Bloch noted, reveal intriguing commonalities that "cannot be attributed either to mutual influence or to some kind of common origin."[39] Carlo Ginzburg's *Ecstasies* is an inspiring example.[40] This form of comparison can proceed from preliminary research on intensive contact zones between different cultures and the problem of border areas, or from comparisons between individual non-European societies, as Jürgen Osterhammel has proposed.

Third, the regional and the local, as well as the realms of culture and ideas, will play an increasingly important role in comparative research. A limitation of comparative history to structural analysis within a national framework is clearly inappropriate. Comparative history has already expanded to incorporate the subjects of meanings and behaviors. Such work has provided an opportunity to test combinations of arguments taken from structural, social, and cultural histories, which can also prove useful in the analysis of other interpretative models. Whether we consider the symbolic language of national monuments, consumption patterns of the bourgeoisie, the journalistic work ethic, or particular discourses on modernity — values, standards, and symbols are legitimate objects of historical comparison and gain even richer meaning when viewed in relation to social practices, their carriers, and conditions of behavior. Defined broadly in this fashion, the comparative approach allows valid insights into specific societies. But comparative history is not necessarily restricted to the national framework; it can also analyze social mechanisms and effects in regions and localities.

Today, Europe remains just as relevant as the focal point of historical comparison as it was to the fathers of the method. Henri Pirenne and Marc Bloch formulated their concept of comparative historical scholarship in order to overcome the European crisis after the First World War. They, too, hoped to transcend Europe's nationally oriented historical disciplines. Today, European histories can rely, for their strength, on the existing comparative literature; conversely, where comparisons are lacking, there is weakness. Comparisons that take on two or three cases with methodological discipline and a good theoretical grounding can help us avoid seeing Europe as a homogeneous or uniform space, but as a diverse and various one.[41] They can help in deriving typologies of developments, structures, definitions of reality, contradictions, and similarities, and in naming the conditions of mutual causation from which, in the great variety of contexts, European perspectives writ large can emerge.

REFERENCES

An earlier version of this essay appeared as "Historischer Vergleich: Methoden, Aufgaben, Probleme" in *Geschichte und Vergleich*, Heinz-Gerhard Haupt and Jürgen Kocka, eds. (Frankfurt, 1996).

1. On the Italian research, see Mariuccia Salvati, "Storia contemporanea e storia comparata oggi: il caso dell Italia," in *Rivista di storia contemporanea*, 2–3 (1992); and the overview on international research in *Passato e Presente*, 28 (1993); also essays by Geoffrey Crossick, Heinz-Gerhard Haupt, and Jürgen Kocka in *Geschichte und Vergleich* (Frankfurt, 1996). On comparison in gender history, which automatically has a strong comparative element through the comparison of feminine as opposed to masculine roles, see (among others) Ida Blom, *Geschichte und Vergleich*, 315–338; and the excellent comparison of political history in Gisela Bock and Pat Thane, *Maternity and Gender Politics* (London, 1991).

2. See Jörn Rüsen, *Historische Vernunft. Grundzüge einer Historik I: Die Grundlagen der Geschichtswissenschaft* (Göttingen, 1983) and Jörn Rüsen, *Rekonstruktion der Vergangenheit. Grundzüge einer Historik II: Die Prinzipien der historischen Forschung* (Göttingen, 1986).

3. Among others, Alf Lüdtke, ed., *Alltagsgeschichte. Zur Rekonstruktion historischer Erfahrungen und Lebensweisen* (Frankfurt a.M., 1989).

4. Georg G. Iggers, *New Directions in European Historiography* (Middletown, CT, 1984).

5. Jürgen Kocka, "Das europäische Muster und der deutsche Fall," in Kocka, ed., *Bürgertum im 19.Jahrhundert*, Vol. 1 (Göttingen, 1995), pp. 41–55.

6. This problem is posed and solved by Christiane Eisenberg, *Deutsche und englische Gewerkschaften: Entstehung und Entwicklung bis 1878 im Vergleich* (Göttingen, 1986).

7. Hartmut Kaelble, *Der Historischer Vergleich* (Frankfurt, 1999), 12.

8. Thomas Welskopp, "Die Sozialgeschichte der Väter. Grenzen und Perspektiven der Historischen Sozialwissenschaft," *Geschichte und Gesellschaft* 24 (1998): 173-198.

9. Kaelble, *Auf dem Weg zu einer europäischen Gesellschaft. Eine Sozialgeschichte Westeuropas, 1880–1980* (Munich, 1987).

10. Reinhard Bendix, *Kings or People: Power and the Mandate to Rule* (Berkeley and Los Angeles, 1978); Bendix, *Nation-Building and Citizenship* (Berkeley and Los Angeles, 1977).

11. Theda Skocpol and Margaret Somers, "The Use of Comparative History in Macrosocial Inquiry," *Comparative Studies in Society and History* 23 (1980), 174–197.

12. S.N.Serneri, ed., "L'Europa: identita e storia di un continente," *Contemporanea* 2 (1999), 79–102.

13. Deborah Cohen, "Comparative History: Buyer Beware," in *Bulletin of the German Historical Institute* 29 (2001): 23–33; also J.L.McClain, J.M. Merriman, and Ugawa Kaoru, eds., *Edo and Paris. Urban Life and the State in the Early Modern Era* (London, 1994); Detlev Lehnert, *Kommunale Politik: Parteiensystem und Interessenkonflikte in Berlin und Wien 1919–1932* (Berlin, 1991).

14. Heinz-Gerhard Haupt, ed., "Les mobilités dans la petite bourgeoisie du XIXe siècle," Special Issue, Bulletin du Centre Pierre Léon d'Histoire économique et sociale, 1993.

15. Pierre Vilar, "Croissance économique et analyse historique," in *Première Conférence internationale d'Histoire économique* (Stockholm, 1960), vol. 1, pp. 35–82.

16. Marc Bloch, "Pour une histoire comparée des sociétés européennes," [1928] in *Mélanges historiques*, vol. 1 (Paris, 1963), p. 26; Carol Fumian, "Le virtù della comparazione," *Meridiana* 4 (1988), 197–221.

17. Arno Mayer, *Persistence of the Old Regime: Europe to the Great War* (New York, 1981).

18. Michael Werner and Bénédicte Zimmermann, "Vergleich, Transfer, Verflechtung. Der Ansatz der Histoire croisée und der Herausforderung des Transnationalen," *Geschichte und Gesellschaft* 28 (2002), 607–636.

19. Peter Wagner, *Sozialwissenschaften und Staat: Frankreich, Italien, Deutschland 1870–1980* (Frankfurt a.M and New York, 1990); V. Dimier, "Enjeux institutionnels autour d'une science politique des colonies en France et en Grande-Bretagne, 1930–1950," *Genèses* 37 (1999), 70–92.

20. See Heinrich Best, *Die Männer von Bildung und Besitz. Struktur und Handeln parlamentarischer Führungsgruppen in Deutschland und Frankreich 1848/49* (Düsseldorf, 1990); G. Gribaudi, "Klientelismus im Parteiensystem. Staat und Bürger in einer süditalienischen Stadt, 1945–1994," *Historische Anthropologie* 3 (1995), 1–33; see also the theoretical work of Robert Putnam, *Making Democracy Work: Civic traditions in Modern Italy* (Princeton, NJ, 1993).

21. Bloch, "Pour une histoire," 37.

22. See Glenda Sluga's essay in this volume.

23. Kocka, "German History Before Hitler: The Debate about the German 'Sonderweg,'" *Journal of Contemporary History* 23 (1988), 3–16.

24. On Transfergeschichte, see Michel Espagne and Michael Werner, eds., *Transfers culturels. Les relations interculturelles dans l'espace franco-allemand (XVII-XXe siècles)* (Paris, 1988); Michel Espagne, *Les transfers culturels franco-allemands* (Paris, 1999); Hans-Jürgen Lüsebrink and Rolf Reichardt, eds., *Kulturtransfer im Epochenumbruch Frankreich-Deutschland 1770 bis 1815* (Leipzig, 1997); Lothar Jordan and Bernd Kortländer, eds., *Nationale Grenzen und internationaler Austausch. Studien zum Kultur- und Wissenschaftstransfer in Westeuropa* (Tübingen, 1995). Michel Espagne, "Sur les limites du comparatisme en histoire culturelle," *Genèses* 17 (1994), 112–121.

25. See Rudolf Muhs, Johannes Paulmann, and Willibald Steinmetz, eds., *Aneignung und Abwehr. Interkultureller Transfer zwischen Deutschland und Großbritannien im 19. Jahrhundert* (Bodenheim, 1998); also Johannes Paulmann, "Internationaler Vergleich und interkultureller Transfer. Zwei Forschungsansätze zur europäischen Geschichte des 18. bis 20. Jahrhunderts," *Historische Zeitschrift* 267 (1998), 649–685.

26. Bloch, "Pour une histoire."

27. Paulmann, "Internationaler Vergleich," 681.

28. Werner and Zimmermann, 617 ff., see also Bénédicte Zimmermann, Claude Didry, and Peter Wagner, eds., *Le travail et la nation: Histoire croisée de la France et de l'Allemagne* (Paris, 1999).

29. Gabriel Motzkin, "Säkularisierung, Bürgertum und Intellektuelle in Frankreich und Deutschland während des 19. Jahrhunderts," in Jürgen Kocka and U.Frevert, eds., *Bürgertum im 19.Jahrhundert*, vol. 3 (Munich, 1988), pp. 141–174.; Joel Michel, *Le mouvement ouvrier chez les mineurs d'Europe occidentale. Etude comparée des années 1880-1914*, 7 vols., (Lille, 1987).

30. Michael Geyer, "Historical Fictions of Autonomy and the Europeanization of National History," *Central European History* 22 (1989), 316–342; Alain Corbin, *The Lure of the Sea: The Discovery of the Seaside in the Western World, 1750–1840*, trans. Jocelyn Phelps (Berkeley, 1994); Peter Sahlins, *The Making of France and Spain in the Pyrenees* (Berkeley, 1989).

31. R.J.C.Young, *Postcolonialism. An Historical Introduction* (Oxford, 2001); Ann Stoler and Frederick Cooper, "Between Metropole and Colony. Rethinking a Research Agenda," in Stoler and Cooper, eds., *Tensions of Empire* (Berkeley, 1997); Homi Bhaba, *The Location of Culture* (London, 1994); Jürgen Osterhammel, "Transnationale Gesellschaftsgeschichte: Erweiterung oder Alternative?" *Geschichte und Gesellschaft* 27 (2001), 464–479.

32. Susanne-Sophia Spiliotis, "Wo findet Geschichte statt? oder Das Konzept der Transterritorialität," *Geschichte und Gesellschaft* 27 (2001), 480 ff.

33. Sebastian Conrad, "Doppelte Marginalisierung. Plädoyer für eine transnationale Perspektive auf die deutsche Geschichte," *Geschichte und Gesellschaft* 28 (2002), 145–169.

34. Stoler and Cooper, "Between Metropole," 5. This interesting problem is not taken up in Christophe Charle, *La crise des sociétés impériales: Allemagne, France, Grande-Bretagne, 1900–1940* (Paris, 2001).

35. Arno Mayer, *The Furies: Violence and Terror in the French and Russian Revolutions* (Princeton, NJ, 2000).

36. See Carlo Ginzburg, "Traces: racines d'un paradigme indiciaire," in Ginzburg, *Mythes, emblèmes, traces, morphologie et histoire* (Paris 1989), p. 177.

37. See the debate in the journal *Histoire et Mesure* as well as J.Y.Grenier, "L'histoire quantitative est-elle encore nécessaire?" in Jean Boutier and Dominique Julia, eds., *Passés recomposés. Champs et chantiers de l'histoire* (Paris, 1995), pp. 173–183.

38. Manfred Hildermeier, Jürgen Kocka, and Christoph Conrad, eds., *Europäische Zivilgesellschaft in Ost und West. Begriff, Geschichte, Chancen* (Frankfurt a.M. and New York, 2000).

39. Bloch, "Pour une histoire," 18.

40. Carlo Ginzburg, *Ectasies: Deciphering the Witches' Sabbath*, trans. Raymond Rosenthal (New York, 1991).

41. S.Woolf, "L'europa e le sue storie" *Passato e presente* 50 (2000), 5–13; Heinz-Gerhard Haupt, "Erfahrungen mit Europa. Ansätze zu einer Geschichte Europas im langen 19. Jahrhundert," Heinz Duchhardt and Andreas Kunz, eds., *"Europäische Geschichte" als historiographisches Problem* (Mainz, 1987), pp. 87–103.

3

FORMS OF COMPARISON

Nancy L. Green

Comparisons come in different shapes and sizes, large and small, implicit and explicit, heuristic and hierarchical. There are "spontaneous" comparisons which arrive at judgments between things in relation to each other but without any particular analytical project. There are reciprocal visions, or the view of the Other: Americans fawn over or fear ("impossible to wear") Paris fashions while the French rush to see American films while rising up against McDonald's. Arthur Young's view of France or Chateaubriand's image of America are all based on the comparative gaze, as are experts' investigations abroad. What I examine here, however, are the constructed comparisons of scholars, who may indeed study the ways in which historical actors exchange information and compare each other, but who may also create their own subjects of comparison.

Some have argued that only actual historical exchange (cultural transfers or *histoire croisée*) is the proper domain of comparative study.[1] Others have maintained that it suffices to test a concept against a historical practice in order to come under the comparative rubric. My own definition is both larger and narrower. One does not have to "find" comparison in cross-cultural encounters in order to "apply" the comparative method, heuristically, to two or more periods, places, or subjects. On the other hand, the broadest definition, that which considers the comparison of historical practices to sociological concepts as "comparative history," seems too wide to be pertinent here.[2] But, regardless of one's definition, two important questions remain: why and how. Why should we be interested in a comparative perspective and how can we adopt one?

A decade ago, simply to argue for the importance of a comparative imperative for historians seemed a major proposition in and of itself.[3] For over a century now, historians have periodically called for a comparative perspective for a variety of reasons: to render the historical discipline more scientific (François Simiand), to seek the origins of historical phenomena (Marc Bloch), and to transcend nationalisms (from Henri Pirenne after World War One to Geoffrey Barraclough after World War Two). All of these reasons remain valid, but two seem particularly pertinent today. The first, to which I return, has to do with the current political and historiographic contestation of the nation-state. Applying the comparative method to countries as categories is a powerful way of questioning the absoluteness of their boundaries, both legally and metaphorically. Second, and even more fundamentally, a comparative approach helps render the invisible visible; it aids us in questioning our own generalizations. As Marc Bloch put it over half a century ago: "By considering only a single series, in a single social system, the historian risks attributing an exaggerated explanatory value to certain facts which are in reality of mediocre importance."[4]

Comparative history is a manner of testing our conclusions and of putting them in another perspective. No single perspective is "right," but a comparative approach changes the angle of vision and helps test our conclusions.[5] Today, as comparative topics abound, we can move beyond "the call" to comparison in order to examine the ways in which that call can be heeded.[6]

OF SIMILARITY AND DIFFERENCE

One of the greatest difficulties in defining or understanding the comparative method has to do with the word "compare" and its use. Etymologically, the verb "compare" means to couple like things, whereas the word "contrast" (from the Middle French to oppose) emphasizes difference. However, if the first Webster's definition of compare is "to represent as similar: liken," the second definition widens the scope: "to examine the character or qualities of, esp. to discover resemblances or differences."[7] At the word contrast, compare is given as the synonym. Clearly, similarity and difference have become melded in the term and concept "to compare."

Nevertheless, in practice, the word is often used to suggest either resemblance or difference. Two common phrases illustrate this point. "Comparisons are odious" implies that comparisons of difference create an invidious hierarchy. On the other hand, to say that "you can't compare apples and oranges" enjoins the comparativist to postulate a certain level of similarity as the basis for a pertinent comparison. A debate about the comparative method that has raged in France and Germany hinges on the question of whether comparison's purpose is to seek differences or similarities. Michel Espagne, Michaël Werner, and Bénédicte Zimmermann have rejected comparison per se as a mode of understanding Franco–German relations, warning (understandably) that comparisons may reify differences. Perhaps they assume, not unrealistically, that a comparison of difference between France and Germany (as seen from France) could create a hierarchy critical of Germany, tainted by the World War Two experience. Yet other historians, such as Jürgen Kocka or Heinz-Gerhard Haupt, have argued for a comparative method that seems more interested in similarity.[8] Depending on the emphasis, comparisons may indeed emphasize either similarity or difference. John Stuart Mill identified the two approaches as distinct—a method of difference and a method of agreement—and most comparative projects seem motivated by one approach or the other.[9]

The level of analysis may in and of itself tend toward perceiving sameness or focusing on particularities. As I argued over a decade ago, the subject and level of analysis are important preliminary choices that determine much of the way in which a comparative project is structured. Continents, societies, nations, regions, cities, or groups all require different types of inquiry and different assumptions about similarity and difference.[10] Macro-level studies often seem both to postulate and uncover greater levels of generality. An analysis of "immigration," for example, can be writ broadly and approached globally, as a category concerning a certain common form of human movement across the world. Yet to choose a subject such as Jewish immigrants in the modern diaspora or Italians around the world is already to choose another level of analysis, one in which certain particularities — Jewish, Italian — are postulated. To refine the subject, Jewish immigrants in France or Italians in America, reduces the level of generality further and the possibility of comparison within the chosen topic.[11] Indeed, studies of individual experience can celebrate the specific in a way that makes comparison difficult. Rudolf Vecoli well described for migration studies what I would call a dilemma of levels.

He suggested that separate ethnic case studies may ignore those aspects of the migration experience that are common to all groups.[12] It is only through a broader comparative approach that commonality can be found. In this respect, microscopic or macroscopic viewpoints may in themselves structure the search for the specific or the general.

Do macro-oriented studies therefore necessarily imply similarity, and micro-studies highlight difference? I would be less categorical today than I was in my original *Annales* article as to a necessary linkage between the level of analysis and an emphasis upon similarity or difference.[13] Samuel Huntington's "clash of civilizations" thesis serves as a reminder of the fact that macro-level analysis does not necessarily lead to a search for similarity. Such comparisons can also structure and emphasize difference while ignoring the complexities of each unit. On the other hand, certain micro-historians (especially those of the first generation, such as Carlo Ginzburg or Emmanuel Le Roy Ladurie) used very specific studies not to emphasize difference but to discuss broader similarities within local early modern mentalities.[14] The choice of level does not therefore always coincide with a choice between similarity and difference.

The choice of an analytical level and the Millsian distinction between difference and agreement are crucial issues when constructing a comparative project. The choice of similarity or difference, perhaps even more so than that of level of analysis, is key to understanding comparative history. Here, too, one approach or the other does not necessarily imply a single interpretive framework. An emphasis on similarities may lead to a (stifling?) structuralism just as it may mean a (more humanistic) project of search for sameness. Underlining differences may result in an invidious comparative hierarchy or it may be a way of celebrating diversity. That is, a comparative project that elides difference may result in a structuralist similarity that ignores specificity, whereas a contrastive comparison that emphasizes difference may minimize that which more generally joins people around the world. The point, however, is that comparative projects are most often undergirded by choices about emphases on similarity or difference that should be more carefully and consciously weighed.

Ultimately, the most ambitious comparisons combine both aspects of the term's definition, joining both the comparisons and contrasts in a method that engages both the specific and the structural. In my own study of immigrant garment workers, I needed to understand both change and agency on the part of Jews, Italians, Chinese, labor organizers, and rank-and-file workers at the same time as I recognized immigrant garment workers as an identifiable and usable category within an industrial structure whose exacerbated flexibility and subcontracting implies constraints that cannot be ignored.[15] Comparative history in this respect helps identify both the agency of difference and the structures of similarity that together comprise the parameters of human action.

As the French sociologist Pierre Bouvier has put it (in an analysis of "ethnocentrism and differentiation"), "the comparative approach reveals the contradictory processes of unification and diversification."[16] This, it seems to me, is the veritable creativity at the heart of comparative research. Comparisons can serve to highlight that which joins human experience while exploring that which remains specific to individuals or groups. Historians are perhaps particularly well placed to integrate research into the particular with general questions. But each is knowable only in relation to the other.

BEYOND THE NATION-STATE

The recent thrust toward globalization has widened the historian's horizon,[17] and the most common forms that comparative history projects have taken are those that compare two or more nations. However, two critiques emerging from France have questioned the validity of comparing nation-states. In their edited volume, Bénédicte Zimmermann, Claude Didry, and Peter Wagner argue that "the simple comparison" is dangerous because it reifies cultural difference.[18] The purpose of the collected articles is explicitly to highlight similarities within a more global discussion of European integration. Their collection of essays explicitly highlights *histoires croisées,* that is, actual interactions between and among historical agents. Although one could argue that this focus limits the possibilities of historical comparison, the more general point is well taken: the choice of any comparison can reify the categories under study and blind us to the historical process of their emergence. Comparative history, linked as it is to the nation-state itself, is rooted in nineteenth-century historiographic traditions. By the same token, national comparisons tend to freeze nations as—essentially unchanging—comparative entities.[19]

Marcel Detienne has gone much further than Zimmermann and her co-editors. In his broadside, *Comparer l'incomparable,* Detienne criticizes historians as dangerous nationalists and argues that the only comparisons worth doing are of an anthropological nature and of widely different societies. This implies greatly widening one's expertise or, as he has done, working collaboratively with different specialists, especially anthropologists.[20] He argues passionately for collaboration between historians and anthropologists (seemingly ignoring historical anthropology as an already constituted interdisciplinary subfield).[21]

Nations are under attack today, from above (the European Union, globalization) and from below (regions). Indeed, we are perhaps living at the end of the nation-state paradigm. Europeanists, transnational-ists, post-modernists, and those engaged in the emerging field of borderland studies argue for the declining importance of the state. At the same time, however, recent studies of citizenship and work on legal history have reinforced notions of the state's importance.

Comparative history offers a means of reconciling those who wish to transcend the nation-state and those who insist upon its importance. Several points are crucial. First, nation-states are very much a part of the nineteenth- and twentieth-century past. To herald their coming demise may encourage new questions about their "invention" over the past two centuries. But to dismiss them as outdated sites of historical inquiry seems, at the very least, ahistorical. However, comparing historical nation-states can help relativize their rigidities and aid us in understanding their constructed nature. Comparisons, by scholars today, through *histoires croisées*, or the reciprocal visions of historical actors in the past, can highlight the borrowings and the divergences that have gone into the making of those states. Comparative cross-national history may itself be a partial antidote to nation-centered histories.

Second, even if the nation-state can still be useful as a unit of inquiry, we should still explore other levels of comparison. The *mezzo* level of comparison holds promise for fruitful inquiry.[22] Regions, cities, or industries provide an intermediary level of analysis where the variables may be more closely defined. The industrialization of France and England was a central preoccupation of many (comparativist) economic historians; however, that process appears in an entirely different light when the shipping industry is studied around the world or the garment industry examined in two cities.[23] Mid-level comparisons are often linked to national-level comparisons, but they have the advantage of allowing closer views of variety within individual nation-states as well. For instance, garment making in Rochester or Argenton-sur-Creuse is not the same as in New York City or Paris, yet it is still part of the American and French garment industries more generally conceived.

Third, critics of comparison often use the term lopsidedly, forgetting that comparison implies both similarity and difference. The assumption that national comparisons will only reify difference is incorrect in that it reduces the comparative project to but a portion of itself. That nation-state comparisons have, in fact, often been used to emphasize difference and, indeed, may sometimes be tautological—postulating difference and finding it—is not inherent to the comparative method. National comparisons may underscore similarities just as they can aid in understanding difference. The comparative inquiry should be as interested in the one as in the other. The challenge, in other words, for constructed comparisons is to choose a unit, level, and subject that can be used to ask creative questions about the similarity of human experience as well as about its singularities.

TYPES OF COMPARISONS

The challenges of comparative history are thus epistemological and research-related. They also have to do with the particular problems of writing the comparative story. Comparative history seems to come in at least two sorts: the implicit and the explicit. Explicitly comparative projects can in turn be subdivided into the juxtapositional and the constructed.

Like Monsieur Jourdain, many historians have been doing comparative history all along; there is the implicit comparison that does not know itself. It can range from the banal (the tourist's gaze) to the expert's study abroad, to reciprocal visions inherent in all forms of cross-cultural contact.[24] All of these are subjects that historians can elucidate. Entire fields of historical inquiry have been based upon comparative logics without explicating them as such. The question of assimilation within the field of migration history, for example, has rarely been recognized as a fundamentally comparative issue. Yet immigrants have been compared, along a timeline of adaptation, both to the ways and manners of the new country and to their distance from the old. One could even argue more generally that most historical research is implicitly comparative to the extent that the study of the past is often linked, explicitly or not, to questions of the present. This temporal comparison is rarely made clear. At its most general level, historical contextualization is in itself an implicitly comparative reflex. The point here is not to shift from a pessimistic view about the lack of comparative history to an overly optimistic image of its pervasiveness: from comparisons nowhere to comparisons everywhere. It is rather to urge us to re-examine historical practice in order to understand the ways in which questions and projects are often informed by comparative assumptions.

Perhaps the most prevalent form of explicit comparison today is juxtapositional: a conference panel or a book structured around a theme, with the individual speakers or contributors addressing the same issue from the perspective of their own fields. The unifying comparative vision is provided by conference commentators or the book's introductory chapter. Historians have applied this method in studies ranging across the social spectrum.[25] Comparative research seminars, in which researchers present individual projects (that are not explicitly comparative), can also combine a juxtapositional approach with explicitly comparative discussions. However, juxtaposed comparisons are often unsatisfactory (especially in their conference panel format); specialists tend toward monologue rather than dialogue.

There are those who have attempted comparative studies on their own,[26] tackling two (or more) countries, languages, cultures, industries, or cities. In exploring the women's wear trade in Paris and New York from the late nineteenth to the late twentieth century, I explicitly chose a mid-level comparison where two cities, rather than two countries, formed the background for an industrial study. The combined temporal and spatial comparison allowed patterns of production and labor to emerge in a way that a more monographic approach could only partially suggest. I will admit that I became in the process ever more struck by the similarities while remaining fascinated by the complexities of each case. Yet this tension between sameness and difference had another consequence: it rendered the research and writing particularly difficult. If the task of the historical comparativist is not only to make the implicit explicit but also to structure and better integrate the juxtaposed, all comparisons are, nevertheless, not alike. We can take a closer look at the practices and ways in which the lone scholar's comparisons can be constructed.

FEAR OF FLATTENING: RESEARCH AND WRITING

If one criticism of the comparative method has to do with the fear of exaggerating difference, another set of problems may be called the fear of flattening. There is a risk inherent in Detienne's suggestion of wide-ranging comparisons based on collaboration or secondary sources: the farther one moves from archival research, the more one is dependent on the findings and conclusions of others. An imbalance of sources and proof occurs when one part of a comparative study relies on personal research and another depends on others' findings. Combining one's own primary research with the fruits of a secondary source creates more food for thought, but the risk is loss of depth and a flattening of detail. For this reason, comparative history may well be the luxury of the second book. With one set of archival notes in the filing cabinet or on disk, an historian can assemble a second set, or more, in order to broaden the scope of the questions she asks with the answers she proposes.

More generally, Raymond Grew once warned against the too-static nature of many comparisons.[27] The overly systematic search for parallels or divergence may be a pitfall of certain research projects. Preconceived categories, too neatly constructed criteria, and tables of results may homogenize the data and detract from the richness of the inquiry. A table comparing, for instance, voting patterns or employment data requires that a single set of terms be used, but harmonizing terminology carries the risk of obscuring changes that occurred over time. Although pertinent categories for the purpose of comparison are necessarily constructed from the sources and by historians, each nation or group, like each time period, needs to be rendered as far as possible in all of its complexity. Thus Werner and Zimmermann wisely underscore the importance of rich contextualization in *histoire croisée*.[28]

One of the major difficulties of comparative history generally is the different nature of the available sources. This was particularly apparent to me when I began my study of immigrant workers in Paris and New York. The archives of the Préfecture de Police (police department) are one of the richest sources for the social history of Paris. Informers seem to have known about even the smallest of meetings when they felt there was reason to follow suspicious characters. Beat cops filed local reports, higher-ups sent more summary analyses to the Ministry of the Interior. The ensemble gives a fascinating view of strikes, labor conditions, and city life. In New York, by contrast, no police archives are available. Union archives, however, are. The International Ladies' Garment Workers' Union set up its own extremely well-organized archive, which provides detailed information on decision making, on the economic and political activities of the union, and on its interaction with other organizations. There is no comparable body of sources in Paris. Most of the garment unions' papers there seem to have been misplaced, lost, or destroyed during the war, and the archives that have been preserved are scattered among various sites, with access often restricted.[29]

It is rare that the same types of sources exist for both sides of a comparative study. This is but a particular case of a more general problem. All historians know that most archives rarely hold that "perfect box" which answers all of one's questions. The comparative project multiplies the problem because of a presumably added exigency, that of symmetry, or sameness in the archives. Comparative archival research is necessarily in itself a creative process of inquiry, where one has to do the best with that which is available.

Dealing with difference in the archives is perhaps one of the first lessons for the comparative historian. Indeed, one might suggest that the notion of symmetry in the archives is in itself a fallacy of the comparative method when the latter is only taken to mean the possibility of confronting things that are similar. Asymmetrical archives should, in fact, be an integral part of a reflection on similarity and difference itself.

Even when similar types of sources may be found, the categories of inquiry, from catalogue entries to statistics, are most often quite different. Counting is done differently around the world, and terminology varies over time and space. In the New York industrial statistics for 1900, for example, "apparel" included dressmakers, tailors, and factory garment workers. Only in 1920 were factory garment workers listed apart, signaling, by the very appearance of the separate category, the increased importance of their numbers and of the shifting mode of production; the women's wear custom-made trade had begun its inexorable decline.[30] In French statistics, the garment industry was for decades named not after the workers but after the labor transformation of the raw material: *travail des étoffes* (literally, work on cloth). It was not until 1946 that increasing standardization in the industry, along with other factors (most notably the war), led to a new counting system and a new mode of dividing labor categories.[31] I ultimately argued that garment workers in Paris and New York are both very much alike (and yet have particular identities at different times), however, I recognized that they have been counted differently in each city over time. I finally gave up the idea of presenting one summary statistical table and instead presented more general figures specifying the different terminology involved.

Marc Bloch warned years ago about what could be called a differential nominalism.[32] Homonyms can trick us into believing that the same word means the same thing; or, as Bloch put it, "How many different notions are hiding under the word nobility!" Heteronyms are equally surreptitious. How often have we looked for a concept under one name only to find it hiding under another, sending us scurrying back to the sources to rethink the use of the second term.

Indeed, we are prisoners of the order of our research. Knowledge is a continual process, and comparative knowledge has the added problem of running us in circles. Everyone starts somewhere, with one set of hypotheses, one set of sources, one language, one set of categories or area of expertise. The questions we ask are framed by our prior knowledge. After first studying Jewish immigrant garment workers in the French archives, I necessarily brought my original "Parisian" knowledge with me when I turned to other immigrants and other archives. The secondary and primary sources in New York were by far more abundant than those in Paris, but often, just when I thought I had come upon a significant similarity or an important difference, I would have second thoughts. What if the similarity was of my own making? What if the difference simply meant I had overlooked another concept, another word in the Paris case? How similar were the language locals (immigrant sections within the unions) in each city? Is it just pure coincidence that they were largely disbanded on both sides of the Atlantic in the 1930s? How did the very different roles of the Communist Party in both countries affect the forms of labor organizing within the garment industry?

All research is necessarily informed by this back-and-forth process of conceptualization and research. Once my early research on Jews in one city evolved into a larger inquiry into the function of immigrant labor within the garment industries of Paris and New York,[33] I was able to delve into the New York archives from the basis of an understanding of the industry in general. But although certain similarities stood out, the specificity of the New York story also emerged powerfully, leading me to re-examine the Paris data, which in turn brought up new questions about the New York industry, and so on. Comparative history, more than other more monographic studies, requires that answers be constantly refined and new questions asked; it necessitates shuttle research and an incessant shuffling between one set of data and another. That liability can, however, be one of comparative history's greatest strengths.

Although we all know that archives may be bottomless and that there can always be one more detail to verify, comparative history runs a final risk of endlessly spiralling inquiry. I initially thought that my study of immigrants in the garment industry in Paris and New York was a "simple" tale of comparing groups over time in two places. The industry itself was intended to be a nonproblematic constant. In the end, the first half of my study became an examination of the development of the industry itself and how that process created the categories with which the immigrant workers would interact: manufacturer, jobber, homeworker, flexibility, subcontracting. A comparative history of immigration became a comparative history of light industrialization along with comparative queries about the impact of immigration legislation, social legislation in France and New York,[34] unionization, and even fashion, all of which could be and are independent topics in and of themselves. The initial question led to concentric circles of queries, and each bit of research in itself intersected with others. Part of the difficulty is in deciding just where to stop. Time and money often provide the key impetus here. But sociologists have spoken of "saturation." When the interviews or archives begin to seem repetitious, when the marginal value of new questions decreases, it's fair to say that we know it's time to turn, at last, to the keyboard.

For the comparativist, writing poses an organizational nightmare. Here, too, the headache is perhaps just a variant on the general difficulties of creating a reasonable narrative. In this case, however, the complexity of the organizational task may, at times, seem overwhelming. The problem of those floating paragraphs that, even in single-case studies, seem to roam frustratingly from one chapter to another until they find their best home, is multiplied by as many cases and variables in the comparative study.

And what about the fear of sameness? How to avoid turning a comparative history into repetitive history? The most important organizational question is separation or integration. Should each case get its own chapter or should the exposition be thoroughly thematic, integrating examples throughout? The organizational answer may in itself be a reflection of the hypotheses and conclusions, of an emphasis on either similarity or difference. Integrated thematic chapters may best emphasize resemblance, whereas chapter by chapter case studies may best highlight difference. Yet, much depends on the writing itself, and both of these strategies can serve either purpose.

Regardless of the approach chosen, the danger of repetition lurks. Rewriting the same story with different actors, different place names, or a somewhat different chronology may be fascinating to the comparativist but not necessarily for the reader. Thematic chapters may solve the problem with judicious use of examples, but repetition is always a latent threat. A mixed format may work the best: an introductory chapter outlining the generic form of the question, case studies allowing each story to be told on its own, with its own language and its own chronology, and then both thematic and case chapters as needed. Comparative questions may be interspersed throughout, as well as gathered in a conclusion. There is no single model for presenting variations on a theme. A motif needs to be present, but choosing the emphasis of theme or variations in the writing is ultimately a result of the analysis itself.

***

Jewish immigrants build synagogues; Catholic immigrants build parishes. Both are worthy topics of study. But to choose to compare immigrants who set up religious institutions implies another level of analysis that broadens the horizon of inquiry and asks different questions about similarity and difference among immigrant groups. To study Sicilians in New York in relation to their home roots is not the same, methodologically, as studying Genovese and Sicilians in Chicago, Italians and Jews in New York, or, even more generally, immigrants in two countries. The questions and levels of analysis are necessarily different. An intraethnic comparison highlights differences within a group, whereas an interethnic study looks at more general characteristics of "Jews" or "Italians" for the purpose of asking other questions. It is not that one category, whether nation or group, is better or worse. Rather, to structure the questions asked, the issue is which level of study is chosen and how it is understood.

The forms of comparative study are many. Carl Guarneri has suggested that a flexible definition of comparative history should include international connections, national comparisons, and macro-social categories of analysis, as well as the larger context.[35] I and others have also argued for the importance of mid-level studies of cities, groups, and industries. Whether implicit or juxtaposed, we need to examine the comparative logic and the choices inherent in any comparative project in order to analyze the ways in which they affect our research and writing. Research beyond one's usual frontiers can provide the frisson of discovery. The "oohs" of difference and the "ahs" of similarity surely raise as many questions as they answer. The comparative method helps us question given categories of framework and reference, not the least of which is the nation itself.

REFERENCES

1. Bénédicte Zimmermann, roundtable, "De la comparaison entre les nations," May 28, 1999, and, in general, the research seminar of the Centre de recherches interdisciplinaires sur l'Allemagne (EHESS-CNRS, Paris), directed by Michaël Werner. See Michaël Werner and Bénédicte Zimmermann, "Vergleich, Transfer, Verflechtung, Der Ansatz der *Histoire croisée* und die Herausforderung des Transnationalien," *Geschichte und Gesellschaft* 28:4 (2002), 607–636; and Michel Espagne, "Sur les limites du comparatisme en histoire culturelle," *Genèses,* 17 (September 1994), 112–121. On Young and Chateaubriand, see Nancy L. Green, "Modes comparatifs dans le regard de l'Autre: Récits de voyages chez Chateaubriand et Arthur Young," in *De Russie et d'ailleurs: Mélanges Marc Ferro,* Martine Godet, ed. (Paris, 1995), pp. 405–416.
2. Raymond Grew, "The Case for Comparing Histories," in *American Historical Review,* 85:4 (October 1980), 763–778.
3. Nancy L. Green, "L'histoire comparative et le champ des études migratoires," *Annales, E.S.C.,* 6 (November–December 1990), 1335–1350; idem, "The Comparative Method and Poststructural Structuralism—New Perspectives for Migration Studies," *Journal of American Ethnic Studies* 13:4 (Summer, 1994), 3–22. Other disciplines have been using the method for years. See, for example, Claude Lévi-Strauss, *Anthropologie structurale* [1958] (Paris, 1974); Adam Przeworski and Henry Teune, *The Logic of Comparative Social Inquiry* (New York, 1970); Amitai Etzioni and Frederick L. Du Bow, eds., *Comparative Perspectives: Theories and Methods* (Boston, 1970); Theda Skocpol and Margaret Somers, "The Uses of Comparative History in Macrosocial Inquiry," *Comparative Studies in Society and History* 22:2 (April 1980), 174–197; Victoria E. Bonnell, "The Uses of Theory, Concepts and Comparison in Historical Sociology," 156–173; Ivan Vallier, ed., *Comparative Methods in Sociology* (Berkeley, 1971); Neil J. Smelser, ed., *Comparative Methods in the Social Sciences* (Englewood Cliffs, NJ, 1976); S.N. Eisenstadt, "Problems in the Comparative Analysis of Total Societies," *Transactions of the Sixth World Congress of Sociology* 1 (Geneva, 1966); Charles Tilly, *Big Structures, Large Processes, Huge Comparisons* (New York, 1985); Stein Rokkan, ed., *Comparative Research Across Cultures and Nations* (Paris, 1968).
4. Marc Bloch, "Comparaison" [1930], in *Histoire et historiens* (Paris, 1995), p. 93. This was his second article on the subject, published two years after his initial call to comparison: Marc Bloch, "Pour une histoire comparée des sociétés européennes" [1928], *Mélanges historiques* (Paris, 1983), vol. 1, pp. 16–40. See also Hartmut Atsma and André Burguière, eds., *Marc Bloch aujourd'hui. Histoire comparée et sciences sociales* (Paris, 1990).
5. William H. Sewell, Jr., "Marc Bloch and the Logic of Comparative History," *History and Theory* 6 (1967), 208–18; on changing the scale of analysis, see Jacques Revel, ed., *Jeux d'échelles: La micro-analyse à l'expérience* (Paris, 1996).
6. Cf. Heinz-Gérhard Haupt, "La lente émergence d'une histoire comparée," in Jean Boutier and Dominique Julia, dirs., *Passés recomposés: Champs et chantiers de l'Histoire* (Paris, 1995), pp. 196–207.
7. *Webster's Seventh New Collegiate Dictionary.* My emphasis.
8. Werner and Zimmermann, "Vergleich, Transfer, Verflechtung"; Espagne, "Sur les limites"; Haupt, "La lente émergence"; and Jürgen Kocka, ed., *Bürgertum im 19. Jahrhundert: Deutschland im europäischen Vergleich* (Munich, 1988). Note that Espagne and Werner and Zimmermann do not agree on the notion of historical transfers. See also the special issue of *Genèses,* "Le comparatisme en histoire et ses enjeux: l'exemple franco-allemand," 17 (September 1994).
9. John Stuart Mill, "Two Methods of Comparison" (excerpt from *A System of Logic,* 1888), in Etzioni and Du Bow, *Comparative Perspectives,* pp. 205–213.

10. See also Judith E. Vichniac, "Introduction," *The Management of Labor: The British and French Iron and Steel Industries, 1860–1918* (Greenwich, 1990); and Louise A. Tilly and Joan W. Scott, who show how conclusions may change depending on the level of analysis chosen in *Women, Work, and Family* (New York, 1978).

11. See, e.g., Donna Gabaccia, *Italy's Many Diasporas, Elites, Exiles and Workers of the World* (London, 2000); Nancy L. Green, ed., *Jewish Workers in the Modern Diaspora* (Berkeley, 1998). For a global view, see Dirk Hoerder, *Cultures in Contact: World Migrations in the Second Millennium* (Durham, NC, 2002).

12. Rudolph J. Vecoli, "European Americans, from Immigrants to Ethnics," *International Migration Review*, VI:4 (Winter 1972), 418. Or, as Serge Gruzinski has written: "L'intérêt pour la micro-histoire—ou la micro-ethno-histoire—a si bien dressé notre oeil à observer le proche que certains chercheurs ont fini par négliger le lointain." "Les mondes mêlés de la Monarchie Catholique et autres 'connected histories,'" *Annales HSS* 56:1 (January–February 2001), 85–117, 88. See also subsequent issues of *Annales HSS* 57:1 (2002) and 58:1 (2003).

13. See also George Fredrickson, *The Comparative Imagination: On the History of Racism, Nationalism, and Social Movements* (Berkeley, 1997), Introduction and Ch. 3.

14. Emmanuel Le Roy Ladurie, *Montaillou, village occitan, de 1294 à 1324* (Paris, 1975); Carlo Ginzburg, *The Cheese and the Worms: The Cosmos of a 16th-century Miller* (Baltimore, 1980); Samuel P. Huntington, *The Clash of Civilizations and the Remaking of the World Order* (New York, 1996).

15. Not dissimilar to approaches suggested by Pierre Bourdieu, Anthony Giddens, Roger Chartier, and William Sewell, I have called this method a "post-structural structuralism," which incorporates post-structural attentiveness to agency, change, and mutable identities without ignoring a more refined understanding of structures as constraining, albeit challengable, entities. Nancy L. Green, *Ready-to-Wear and Ready-to-Work: A Century of Industry and Immigrants in Paris and New York* (Durham, NC, 1997), pp. 8–11, 282–285 and passim. Fredrickson, *Comparative Imagination,* p. 9, speaks of a "middle ground" that "combines elements of cultural contrast and structural analysis."

16. Pierre Bouvier, "Différences et analogies," in Pierre Bouvier and Olivier Kourchid, eds., *France-U.S.A.: Les crises du travail et de la production* (Paris, 1988), pp. 11–17, 14; see also Olivier Kourchid, "Qualitatif, quantitatif, comparatif," *France-U.S.A.,* 19–31.

17. See, e.g., the titles in the American Historical Association's "Essays on Global and Comparative History" series: e.g., "The Columbian Voyages, the Columbian Exchange, and their Historians" (by Alfred W. Crosby, 1987); "Interpreting the Industrial Revolution" (a comparativist classic topic by Peter N. Stearns, 1991, dealing with Britain, France, Germany, Japan, Russia, the United States, etc.); "Industrialization and Gender Equality" (by Louise Tilly, 1994, examining Britain, China, France, Germany, Japan, and the United States).

18. Bénédicte Zimmermann, Claude Didry, and Peter Wagner, eds., *Le travail et la nation: Histoire croisée de la France et de l'Allemagne* (Paris, 1999), p. 4. The book is prefaced by Jacques Delors, emphasizing similarities in order to overcome past differences and promote European integration. I would like to thank Bénédicte Zimmerman for our ongoing discussions on this matter.

19. See Espagne, "Sur les limites du comparatisme." See also Sanjay Subrahmanyam, "Connected Histories: Notes Towards a Reconfiguration of Early Modern Eurasia," in *Beyond Binary Histories: Reimagining Eurasia to c.1830,* Victor Lieberman, ed. (Ann Arbor, MI, 1997), pp. 289–315.

20. Marcel Detienne, *Comparer l'incomparable* (Paris, 2000).

21. For a particularly good example, see Lucette Valensi, "Retour d'Orient, De quelques usages du comparatisme," in Atsma and Burguière, *Marc Bloch aujourd'hui.*

22. Hervé Le Bras proposed this term during the Ecole des Hautes Etudes en Sciences Sociales conference on "Problèmes et objets," Montrouge, June 12, 1987. On mid-level analyses, see also Grew, "Comparing Histories," p. 773; Fredrickson, "Comparative History," p. 461; Beverly Lozano, "The Andalucia-Hawaii-California Migration, A Study in Macrostructure and Microhistory," *CSSH* XXVI: 2 (April 1984), 305–334; and Jan Lucassen, *Migrant Labour in Europe 1600–1900* (London, 1987), pp. 21–22, 52, 92–94, 211; and Caroline B. Brettell and James F. Hollifield, eds., *Migration Theory* (New York, 2000), pp. 8–11.

23. Michael Miller's paper in this volume; and Green, *Ready-to-Wear.*

24. See, e.g., Nancy L. Green, "The Comparative Gaze: Travelers in France before the Era of Mass Tourism," *French Historical Studies* 25:3 (Summer 2002), 423–440.

25. Ira Katznelson and Aristide Zolberg, eds., *Working-Class Formation: Nineteenth-Century Patterns in Western Europe and the United States* (Princeton, NJ, 1986); Geoffrey Crossick and Heinz-Gerhard Haupt, eds., *Shopkeepers and Master Artisans in Nineteenth-Century Europe* (London, 1984); and Jürgen Kocka, ed., *Bürgertum.*

26. Including the participants in this book.

27. Grew, "The Case for Comparing Histories."

28. Werner and Zimmermann, "Vergleich, Transfer, Verflechtung".

29. The Communist CGT union archives have been in a slow mode for many years now; it has been difficult to tell whether the problems are due to lack of means and personnel or lack of motivation.

30. *Occupations at the 12th Census (1900), Special Reports* (Washington, DC, 1904), pp. 636, 638, 640; *13th Census of the United States, vol.4, Population 1910, Occupation Statistics* (Washington, DC, 1914), p. 574; *14th Census of the United States, vol.4, Population 1920, Occupations* (Washington, DC, 1923), pp. 188 and 192.

31. *Résultats statistiques du recensement général de la population (1921),* tome II (Paris, 1925), pp. 1–5 (for 1906 in recapitulative table); *Résultats statistiques du recensement général de la population (1926),* tome III (Paris, 1929), p. 3; *Résultats statistiques du recensement général de la population (1931),* tome II (Paris, 1935), p. 3; *Résultats statistiques du recensement général de la population (1946),* tome V, *Tableaux pour le département de la Seine* (Paris, 1951), p. 38 (1936 and 1946 in recapitulative table).

32. Marc Bloch, "Comparaison," 93.

33. Nancy L. Green, *The Pletzl of Paris: Jewish Immigrant Workers in the Belle Epoque* (New York, 1986), pp. 199–200.

34. I explained why it was necessary and useful to compare the legislation of two different geographic units in Green, *Ready-to-Wear,* p. 329, note 71.

35. Carl Guarneri, ed., *America Compared* (Boston, 1997), p. viii, plus discussions at the OAH-NYU symposium in Florence in 1998. Correspondence with the author, October 30, 2000.

4

COMPARATIVE HISTORY: BUYER BEWARE

Deborah Cohen

Comparative history has few detractors but even fewer practitioners. In seminars and lectures, historians compare constantly, yet nearly seventy years after Marc Bloch proclaimed the "perfection and general use [of the comparative method] one of the most pressing needs of present-day historical science," the vast majority of historical studies still reside comfortably within the parameters of individual nation-states.[1] Despite paeans to the method and conference sessions devoted to its propagation, comparative history has remained a marginal affair in the United States. Unlike gender history or the new cultural history, it is neither fashionable nor, until recently, a matter for controversy.

Comparative histories owe much to national shame. In European social history, the idea of a German *Sonderweg*, which set Germany apart from other industrialized Western nations, provided the most powerful stimulus to comparative research; more than two-thirds of the comparative studies published by Europeans between 1970 and 1989 focused upon Germany.[2] In the same years, American historians took their own "peculiar institution" as a starting point. Race and slavery furnished the subject matter for most comparative studies, until displaced by the welfare state in projects conceived and executed during the Reagan–Bush era. These concerns — together with the social scientific methods of the 1970s, exemplified by the title of Charles Tilly's surprisingly slim treatise, *Big Structures, Large Processes, Huge Comparisons* — account for the lion's share of comparative work.[3]

Unlike quantitative history, that other darling of the late 1960s and early 1970s, comparative history endures today. However, it is a sparsely populated island in an ocean of agnostics. The handful of comparativists who come readily to mind are the exceptions who prove the rule. Despite the paucity of comparative studies, there are innumerable methodological treatises on the subject, most notably in the field of historical sociology.[4] We have a multiplicity of typologies of comparison. Calls for comparison still issue from all quarters, even as the responses echo back faintly. This siren song of comparison plays in an evangelical key. We comparativists dourly exhort our colleagues to assume ever-larger burdens with the promise of self-improvement in the distant offing. Like the early nineteenth-century British Evangelicals, we hold out the possibility of salvation, after enormous labors and unremitting self-scrutiny, to those who will only "row their boat ashore."

And yet, most historians remain at sea, surrounded everywhere by comparisons but unwilling to commit their craft to the purported island paradise of systematic comparative study. And who can blame them? Practical advice is wanting; there are, as noted in this book's introduction, few coordinates to guide the voyage. Moreover, the would-be adventurer need not look far for evidence that many comparative studies wreck on the rocky shores in sight of a safe harbor. In his 1980 article in the *American Historical Review*, Raymond Grew sounded a dismal note. Of the five hundred manuscripts submitted to the journal *Comparative Studies in Society and History*, founded in 1958 to further comparative research, the ones most *likely* to be rejected were actually the comparative pieces.[5]

With friends such as these, who needs enemies? Perhaps it is significant that the most stinging criticisms of comparative work have come from historians who themselves work across national boundaries but reject comparison. Michel Espagne has characterized comparison as a relic of structural history, incompatible with the new questions raised by cultural historians and post-structuralist analysis. He proposes instead a history of cultural transfer to document points of contact, movements that traveled, and ideas that were exchanged.[6] The Australian historian of the United States, Ian Tyrrell, has criticized the tendency among comparativists to take the nation as the unit of analysis. Comparative history, Tyrrell argues, suffers from a research design "narrowly conceived to test purely national differences rather than convey a more varied sense of the elements that make up the diversity of historical experience."[7] Similarly, Bénédicte Zimmermann and Michael Werner have charged that comparative history reifies the nation and thus obscures the dynamic relations that obtained across national boundaries.[8] For Tyrrell, the solution is "transnational" history; for Zimmermann and Werner, *histoire croisée*, or entangled histories.

Both cross-national and comparative studies stake their claim to legitimacy on the ability, through multicountry analysis, to see something that a focus on one nation obscures. In that sense, they are animated by similar impulses. Both share a restlessness and chafe at the boundaries of single-nation studies. But comparative and cross-national approaches also have different motivations and can yield very different types of findings. After all, comparative history is concerned fundamentally with differences and similarities, often with questions of causality. Cross-national histories, by contrast, can tell us about the circulation of objects, peoples, and ideas across national borders; about the history of cultural transfer, and about international phenomena.[9] And, for that matter, a number of comparative histories (maybe the best) are also cross-national histories, such as Charles Maier's *Recasting Bourgeois Europe*.[10]

Given the real differences of aims and outcomes between the two approaches, cross-national history is not (despite what its advocates claim) likely to render comparison obsolete. As Grew reminds us, comparison in history is not a method entailing a single type of inquiry but a set of approaches and "a kind of attitude"; it is, as George Fredrickson terms it, an "imagination."[11] However, Espagne is right to point to the sympathies between cross-national and cultural or intellectual history, whereas comparative history seems to have prospered, if anywhere, in social and political fields, in subjects such as welfare, labor, and most recently, war.[12]

Other chapters in this book challenge the well-worn verities of comparative history. Marta Petrusewicz's essay offers perhaps the most stimulating alternative, elaborating Marcel Detienne's call for "comparing the incomparable," with a method of concept transfer. My own chapter, by contrast, focuses upon lower-risk strategies. I seek to identify hazards and to offer suggestions about minimizing them. It reads as deflationary but is not intended to discourage. I begin with observations about the perils of comparative research, turn next to its pleasures, and conclude with some reflections on the kinds of work most likely to succeed. Because the rewards of comparison have so often been trumpeted, the first section is the longest.

I

Comparative history is a tremendously uncertain business. There are many perils that await the unsuspecting. There is the time needed to master different historiographies. There are archival snafus. What happens, for instance, if the researcher is unable to find comparable sources, given different countries' archival practices? To take just one example of many: whereas hospital records are plentiful and easily accessible in Britain, in German archives they are both rare and governed by privacy restrictions. There is the awkwardness of structuring and writing comparative books. Should the countries be treated separately or interwoven within chapters? How many times can "by contrast" or "unlike in France" appear within one volume without overtaxing a reader's patience? And all of these concerns are overshadowed by the worries of whether anyone will indeed read a comparative study. But let me confine myself only to the conceptual dangers.

Comparative studies can come to grief in a bewildering variety of ways: because the historian cannot substantiate the distinction she is drawing; because comparison does not evoke anything new; because the comparisons that are drawn cannot answer the problems that are posed. As Thomas Welskopp rightly observes, there has been too much work that compares mindlessly, as if comparison were a worthy aim in itself rather than a means to a larger end.[13] Excruciating for the comparativist is the reviewer who states that he has learned little or nothing about the case he knows best, or worse, that the historian has committed fundamental errors. Faulty conceptualization is not a pitfall limited to comparative history, although it is very glaring there: picking up a heavy comparative book requiring languages and historiographies may cause even the well disposed to wonder why the author has gone to so much trouble for so few genuine discoveries. This may explain why comparative studies rely so heavily on the paradox as a point of departure.

Most difficult to pull off are those comparisons that take as their object of study apparently analogous phenomena in disparate settings. Three studies—George Fredrickson's *White Supremacy*, Peter Kolchin's *Unfree Labor*, and Shearer Bowman's *Masters and Lords*—demonstrate the problems that dog such topics.[14] Widely admired by comparativists for their mastery of the form, both Fredrickson and Kolchin have been taken to task by South African and Russian historians for their characterizations of racial distinctions and serfdom, respectively. What appear to the comparativist as neat and revealing juxtapositions seem to the specialist unwarranted liberties with the historical evidence. Similarly, Bowman's comparison of slavery in the American South and serfdom in Prussia in the first half of the nineteenth century suffers from its author's reliance upon an outdated portrait of the *Junker*; German historians seem to have paid little attention to his book.

Studies such as these are plagued by very fundamental questions of "comparability." Are the countries under examination too different to yield meaningful contrasts? Does their juxtaposition for the purpose of comparison eliminate the important distinctiveness of each? It may be that we ask too much of these sorts of efforts when we evaluate them according to the yardstick of each national historiography's own body of knowledge. What studies such as Fredrickson's and Kolchin's do most successfully is to dispute the easy exceptionalist narratives that thrive where there are no competitors; they add, too, to our understanding of the general features of phenomena such as slavery while demurring from grandiose social-scientific abstractions. These are pursuits that seem more palatable to historians in the form of an essay where the intent is manifest: where provocation rather than comprehensive interpretation is the clearly intended goal. Although Kate Brown's comparison of Karaganda, Kazakstan, and Billings, Montana, probably does not persuade many readers that the two cities are (as her title announces) "nearly the same place," the commonalities of their inhabitants' experiences, despite the obvious and acknowledged dissimilarities of context, nonetheless provoke thought.[15] Extended over the course of a book, however, her case would probably become weaker, not stronger, the deft rhetorical touches that frame her argument ever more strained.

An inherently more difficult problem for comparative history is that of local particularities. In focusing on the national unit, and especially upon the state, comparative historians have tended to obscure the distinctive histories of regions, to homogenize differences under the rubric of the nation. There are, of course, notable exceptions, studies such as Detlef Lehnert's *Kommunale Politik,* which compares local governance in the cities of Berlin and Vienna from 1919 to 1932.[16] But at a time when some dispute the very existence of the nation, much comparative history is characterized by what seems an old-fashioned sensibility. In part, this focus upon the nation and the state has been dictated by the topics chosen. When comparison was concerned primarily with institutions, social movements, or periods of transformation, historians sacrificed, perhaps by necessity, rich depictions of the local for the larger prize of national patterns; the state was central. As comparative historians grapple with the history of everyday life (and here Laura Lee Downs' *Manufacturing Inequality* offers an excellent example of a comparative history that is also a social history from below), the heterogeneity contained within nations may enter through the back door.[17]

The thorniest of the problems that comparative history raises is that of causality. The problem becomes especially acute in bipartite or two-country comparisons and most difficult of all in those cases that focus on differences. In attempting to explain why X happened or developed in country A and not in country B, comparative studies tend to place explanatory weight on a few factors. Put differently, a focus on *why* (in a narrow sense) replaces attention to *how*. My own book offers an example.[18] I ask why German veterans, who received comparatively generous pensions and the best social services in Europe, turned against the Weimar Republic that favored them, whereas British veterans, neglected by successive governments, proved loyal subjects. My research led me to the conclusion that the role of the public, and voluntarism, was crucial. Veterans in both countries suffered shabby treatment at the hands of the state; the critical difference was how they felt about their fellow citizens. Although I note other fundamental differences between interwar Britain and Germany (perhaps most importantly, the barriers to extraparliamentary action and the war's resolution), they serve principally as context and not as explanation.

In its search for causes, my book follows in a time-honored, though to me now not entirely satisfactory, vein. Fredrickson has summed up the prevailing tradition: "For most historians and social scientists, comparative history is a way of isolating the critical factors or independent variables that account for national differences."[19] But is it in fact possible to build arguments by isolating critical factors? And how do historians, who are, after all, not white-coated rationalists operating in a laboratory, disentangle one factor from the other? If we demonstrate that Protestantism was not necessary for the development of capitalism in country A, have we necessarily diminished its significance in country B? What is beyond dispute is that Protestantism cannot, as a rule, entirely explain the development of capitalism writ large. Comparison thus makes a large dent in the "generalizing" explanations of the comparative historical sociologist or political scientist. However, within the individual case, the significance of Protestantism cannot be dismissed so easily, nor even can its primacy be cast in doubt.

If similar phenomena have different causes and if different outcomes stem from apparently related factors, how do we isolate the critical variables? Rather than being "a technical instrument…capable of giving positive results," as in Bloch's description, comparison may well lead the researcher into deep and murky waters.[20] Sophisticated causal explanations require more than sifting through independent variables. After all, revolutions Y and Z may share a precipitating event, but that commonality might well mask deeper—and divergent—underlying explanations. At issue is the interplay *between* different factors, left unaccounted for in many comparative arguments. Variable X may function very differently in countries A and B, depending upon the context. In country A, it may be of primary importance, in country B, only of negligible significance.

Every comparativist who seeks explanations for differences eventually confronts the problem of distinguishing the causal from the contextual. The causal is the explanation, whereas the contextual furnishes the background. While national historians' arguments tend towards the multicausal, drawing upon all of the factors that can explain a particular phenomenon, comparativists are often caught in a mono- or bicausal trap. How, after all, can national differences be satisfactorily explained by reference to national differences? Comparative books often begin with a chapter on context before setting out an argument intended to demonstrate that the factors often taken as the self-evident cause of X phenomenon do not suffice to explain what happened, that there was a more powerful force (or forces) at work revealed by attention to similar or different developments in another country. As might be expected, the weight of the explanation falls upon tangibles: movements whose strength can be measured, a class whose predominance is unchallenged, welfare programs whose growth can be charted. Most often, the cultural and ideological context is shorted in favor of such structural elements.

If comparativists still carry the lonely banner of causality, it is, generally speaking, a very particular kind of causal explanation that we offer. Comparison, as Heinz-Gerhard Haupt and Jürgen Kocka point out in the second chapter of this book, necessarily means abstraction. The mere fact of abstraction often requires relegating to the background this or that element in order that a comparison can be undertaken at all. The point here is not that comparativists should abandon the search for causes, but that we should pursue it more alive to the costs. In his illuminating study of universities in the German Democratic Republic, Poland, and the Czech lands, John Connelly explains his solution to the problem: "Political culture is part of the story but also part of the explanation."[21] Connelly's is a frank acknowledgment of the difficulty of distinguishing context from cause: the reader in search of a tidy explanation will not find it. His overriding aim is to demonstrate variation in East Central Europe.

II

So why should we compare? First and foremost, as American exceptionalism and the *Sonderweg* demonstrate, because we do it anyway—and usually badly. There are the normal pleasures of reading widely, of attention to interdisciplinary debates (by no means confined to comparativists), and the genuine discipline that comparison imposes on those who tend towards pointilism. For graduate students, comparison can provide a first line of defense against obscurantism; it forces one, at an early stage, to answer why the project matters and to engage different historiographies.

Let me offer some more basic reasons to compare. First, although not as often as one might wish, comparison provides a counterfactual glimpse that illuminates a path not taken, policies not pursued, which serve to throw a wrench in overdetermined historical narratives. Comparison can return contingency to history. Comparison can lead the historian to ask questions that spark genuinely new interpretations. Bloch's study of enclosure is the most famous (and most oft-cited) example. Peter Baldwin's juxtaposition of the British welfare state and the Scandinavian system (as contrasted with the French and German models) is a marvelous example of revelation-by-association. Susan Pedersen's inquiry into the failure of the British feminists' campaign for family allowances led her to a little-known chapter in the development of the French welfare state: employers' efforts to disaggregate the male wage by offering family allowances to their workers. In my own work, the predominance of voluntarism in Britain caused me to wonder what had happened to the German charities that dominated provision for disabled soldiers in the first years of the Great War. This question, essentially a comparative starting point, pointed the way to a development that had largely gone unnoticed: the regulation of charities by state authorities from the last years of the war through the Weimar Republic.

More often, what comparisons illuminate are not hitherto unknown developments, but the significance of institutions and phenomena that national historians take for granted. Fredrickson's splendid comparison of South Africa and the American South, *White Supremacy*, did not uncover any smoking guns, but served to place the development and the hardening of racial categories in a new and enlightening context. Similarly, Christoph Jahr's study of deserters in the British and German armies during the First and Second World Wars demonstrated, through painstakingly compiled empirical evidence, the strange legacy of a British army that was notably out of step with civilian public opinion.[22] In my own case, the renowned traditions of British voluntarism proved more than simply a national peculiarity; charities served to check veterans' radicalism by brokering a truce between the grateful public and those who had suffered. Comparison can also modify historiographic exaggerations. In Connelly's work, the GDR, when compared with Poland and the Czech case, appears still more authoritarian than the recent literature on resistance in East Germany would allow.

What sorts of comparisons work best? Those historians who have commented on the subject point to "middle-range" comparisons. As Raymond Grew argues: "comparison is most enlightening when...attention is paid to the intricate relationships between the elements compared and the particular societies in which they are located....The search is for patterns of behavior and circumscribed hypotheses, and it is as likely to result in the recognition of unexpected connections between aspects of society previously thought to be unrelated as in general theory."[23] According to both Grew and Baldwin, studies aimed at this middle range avoid the stratospheric heights of social-scientific conclusions.[24] Less clear from their descriptions is what might constitute too limited a topic. What, for instance, might a comparative microhistory reveal? Johannes Dillinger's reflections on the differences between American spiritualism and German sectarianism, as viewed through the cases of the New York Fox sisters and a late eighteenth-century Württemberg ghost sect, indicate the promise of a comparative microhistorical approach that proceeds by juxtaposition rather than abstraction.[25]

Least likely to go wrong are those topics that begin from a point of relation, those that seemed to contemporaries themselves inherently comparative. When you work on these kinds of topics, you uncover a rich international discussion that itself revolves around similarities and differences. This is what Nancy Green calls the "interactive comparative method" in her insightful book about the garment industries in Paris and New York, *Ready-to-Wear and Ready-to-Work*.[26] There are many fine examples of this type of comparison, among them Charlotte Tacke's study of monuments in nineteenth-century France and the German states and, along similar lines, Michael Jeismann's account of French and German images of the enemy.[27] The comparativist, thus, has the opportunity to say something not merely about the national contexts but about a wider phenomenon. Comparison has the potential for demonstrating something that historians do not already know without casting events, classes, or statistics adrift from their social moorings.

Along these same lines, we should not hold doggedly to the nation as the principle unit of comparison. As Heinz-Gerhard Haupt has suggested, we should also seek out other "entities of comparison."[28] The problem of homogenizing the differences within nations is a real one and should be taken seriously. Studies of cities, studies of regions, more local comparisons of institutions, investigations of minority populations within a nation: all of these are potentially lower-risk strategies that preserve particularities.[29] An elegant and short example of this genre is the historical sociologist Howard Kimeldorf's *Reds or Rackets*, a study of why and how longshoremen in New York got tied up with the Mob, whereas their counterparts in San Francisco became communists.[30] Ultimately, of course, all history is—at base—comparative, although often not explicitly so.

Finally, we ought, both as comparativists and as the patient audience that they hector, lower our expectations of what the "method" can achieve. In 1928, Marc Bloch described the comparative method thus: "The historical specialist asks for a method which is a technical instrument, generally used, easily manageable, and capable of giving positive results....The comparative method is precisely such an instrument."[31] This faith in comparison has been shown in the last seventy-odd years to have been misplaced. Rather than chasing the divine revelations that comparisons grant on occasion, we might content ourselves with smart juxtapositions, with parallel histories that shed light upon cross-national phenomena. Comparison was, in Bloch's words, "a powerful magic wand" that allowed historians to see beyond local conditions to develop more comprehensive explanations.[32] Looking back over the literature and my own experiences, we should be on guard lest Bloch's "magic wand" become, like the trick in some modern-day evangelical conjuring act, a poisonous snake.

REFERENCES

This chapter is a revised version of an essay that first appeared in the *Bulletin of the German Historical Institute* 29 (Fall 2001), 23–33. My thanks to Maura O'Connor and the participants in the GHI-Taft workshop, "Europe in Cross-National and Comparative Perspective."

1. Marc Bloch, "Pour une histoire comparée des sociétés européennes," paper delivered at the Sixth International Congress of Historical Sciences held in Oslo in 1928 and printed in *Revue de synthèse historique* 46 (1928): 15–50; Marc Bloch, "Toward a Comparative History of European Societies," in Frederic C. Lane, ed., *Enterprise and Secular Change: Readings in Economic History* (London, 1953), pp. 494–495.

2. Harmut Kaelble, "Vergleichende Sozialgeschichte: Forschungen europäischer Historiker" in Jürgen Kocka and Heinz-Gerhard Haupt, *Geschichte und Vergleich: Ansätze und Ergebnisse international vergleichender Geschichtsschreibung* (Frankfurt a. M., 1996), p. 99; see also Kaelble, *Der historische Vergleich: Eine Einführung zum 19. und 20. Jahrhundert* (Frankfurt, 1999).

3. Charles Tilly, *Big Structures, Large Processes, Huge Comparisons* (New York, 1984).

4. Among others, see Theda Skocpol and Margaret Somers, "The Uses of Comparative History in Macrosocial Inquiry," *Comparative Studies in Society and History* 22 (1980), 174–197; Antoon van den Braembussche, "Historical Explanation and Comparative Method: Towards a Theory of the History of Society," *History and Theory* 28 (1989), 1–24; Charles Ragin, *The Comparative Method* (Berkeley, 1987); Victoria E. Bonnell, "The Uses of Theory, Concepts and Comparison in Historical Sociology," *Comparative Studies in Society and History* 22 (April 1980), 155–173; John Walton, "Standardized Case Comparisons: Observations on Method in Comparative Sociology" in Michael Armer and Allen Grimshaw, eds., *Comparative Social Research* (New York, 1973), pp. 173–191; Morris Zelditch, Jr., "Intelligible Comparisons," in Ivan Vallier, ed., *Comparative Methods in Sociology* (Berkeley, 1971).

5. Raymond Grew, "The Case for Comparing Histories," *American Historical Review* 85: 4 (October 1980), 773.

6. Michel Espagne, "Sur les limites du comparatisme en histoire culturelle," *Genèses* 17 (September 1994), 102–121; Michel Espagne, *Les transferts culturels franco-allemands* (Paris, 1999); see also Wolfgang Schmale, *Historische Komparatistik und Kulturtransfer* (Bochum, 1998); Eric Fassin, "Fearful Symmetry: Culturalism and Cultural Comparison after Tocqueville," *French Historical Studies* 19: 2 (Autumn 1995), 451–460.

7. Ian Tyrrell, "American Exceptionalism in an Age of International History," *American Historical Review* 96 (October 1991), 1033–1038, specifically, 1036.

8. Bénédicte Zimmermann, Claude Didry, and Peter Wagner, *Le travail et la nation: Histoire croisée la France et de l'Allemagne* (Paris, 1999), p. 4; Michael Werner and Bénédicte Zimmermann, "Vergleich, Transfer, Verflechtung. Der Ansatz der Histoire croisée und die Herausforderung des Transnationalen," *Geschichte und Gesellschaft* 28:4 (2002), 607–636; Michael Werner and Bénédicte Zimmermann, "Penser l'histoire croisée: Entre empirie et réflexivité," *Annales HSS* (January–February 2003), 7–36.

9. Daniel T. Rodgers, *Atlantic Crossings: Social Politics in a Progressive Age* (Cambridge, MA, 1998).

10. Charles Maier, *Recasting Bourgeois Europe* (Princeton, NJ, 1975).

11. Grew, "The Case," 776–777; George M. Fredrickson, *The Comparative Imagination: On the History of Racism, Nationalism, and Social Movements* (Berkeley, 1997).

12. Examples include Susan Pedersen, *Family, Dependence, and the Origins of the Welfare State: Britain and France, 1914–1945* (Cambridge, 1993); Peter Baldwin, *The Politics of Social Solidarity: Class Bases of the European Welfare State, 1875–1975* (Cambridge, 1990); Peter Baldwin, *Contagion and the State, 1830-1930* (New York, 1999); Gerhard A. Ritter, *Der Sozialstaat: Entstehung und Entwicklung im internationalen Vergleich* (Munich, 1991); Alisa Klaus, *Every Child a Lion: The Origins of Maternal and Infant Health Policy in the United States and France, 1890–1920* (Ithaca, NY, 1993); Seth Koven and Sonya Michel, "Womanly Duties: Maternalist Politics and the Origins of Welfare States in France, Germany, Great Britain, and the United States, 1880–1920," *American Historical Review* 95 (1990), 1076–1078; Ann Taylor Allen, "Feminism, Social Science, and the Meanings of Modernity: the Debate on the Origin of the Family in Europe and the United States, 1860–1914," *American Historical Review* 104 (1999), 1085–1113; Michael Geyer, "Ein Vorbote des Wohlfahrtsstaates: Die Kriegsopferversorgung in Frankreich, Deutschland und Großbritannien nach dem Ersten Weltkrieg," *Geschichte und Gesellschaft* 9 (1983), 230–277; Michael Prinz, *Brot und Dividende: Konsumvereine*

in Deutschland und England vor 1914 (Göttingen, 1996); Stefan Berger, *The British Labour Party and the German Social Democrats, 1900–1931* (Oxford, 1994); John N. Horne, *Labour at War: France and Britain, 1914–1918* (Oxford, 1991); John Breuilly, *Labour and Liberalism in Nineteenth-Century Europe: Essays in Comparative History* (Manchester, 1992); Christiane Eisenberg, *Deutsche und Englische Gewerkschaften: Entstehung und Entwicklung bis 1878 im Vergleich* (Göttingen, 1986); Jürgen Kocka, *Bürgertum im 19. Jahrhundert*, 3 vols. (Munich, 1988); Susan Grayzel, *Women's Identities at War: Gender, Motherhood and Politics in Britain and France During the First World War* (Chapel Hill, NC, 1999); Jay Winter and Jean-Louis Robert, eds., *Capital Cities at War: Paris, London, Berlin, 1914–1919* (Cambridge, 1997); Laura Lee Downs, *Manufacturing Inequality: Gender Division in the French and British Metalworking Industries, 1914–1939* (Ithaca, NY, 1995). On the need for comparative cultural history of colonialism, see Ann Laura Stoler, "Tense and Tender Ties: The Politics of Comparison in North American History and (Post) Colonial Studies, *Journal of American History* (December 2001), esp. pp. 831, 847–850; 861–4.

13. Thomas Welskopp, "Stolpersteine auf dem Königsweg: Methodenkritische Anmerkungen zum internationalen Vergleich in der Gesellschaftsgeschichte," *Archiv für Sozialgeschichte* 35 (1995), 339–367; Werner Daum, "Fallobst oder Steinschlag: Einleitende Überlegungen zum historischen Vergleich," in Helga Schnabel-Schüle, ed., *Vergleichende Perspektiven—Perspektiven des Vergleichs: Studien zur europäischen Geschichte von der Spätantike bis ins 20. Jahrhundert* (Mainz, 1998), pp. 1–2.

14. Shearer David Bowman, *Masters & Lords: Mid-Nineteenth-Century U.S. Planters and Prussian Junkers* (New York, 1993); George M. Fredrickson, *White Supremacy: A Comparative Study in American and South African History* (New York, 1981); George M. Fredrickson, *Black Liberation: A Comparative History of Black Ideologies in the United States and South Africa* (New York, 1995); Peter Kolchin, *Unfree Labor: American Slavery and Russian Serfdom* (Cambridge, 1987).

15. Kate Brown, "Gridded Lives: Why Kazakhastan and Montana Are Nearly the Same Place," *American Historical Review*, 106 (2001), 17–48.

16. Detlev Lehnert, *Kommunale Politik: Parteiensystem und Interessenkonflikte in Berlin und Wien 1919–1932* (Berlin, 1991).

17. Downs, *Manufacturing Inequality*; see also Jakob Vogel, *Nationen im Gleichschritt: Der Kult der 'Nation in Waffen' in Deutschland und Frankreich, 1871–1914* (Göttingen, 1997); Gunilla-Friederike Budde, *Auf dem Weg ins Bürgerleben: Kindheit und Erziehung in deutschen und englischen Bürgerfamilien, 1840–1914* (Göttingen, 1994).

18. Deborah Cohen, *The War Come Home: Disabled Veterans in Britain and Germany, 1914–1939* (Berkeley, 2001).

19. George M. Fredrickson, "From Exceptionalism to Variability: Recent Developments in Cross-National Comparative History," *Journal of American History* 82: 2 (September 1995), 587.

20. Bloch, 495.

21. John Connelly, *Captive University: The Sovietization of East German, Czech, and Polish Higher Education, 1945–1956* (Chapel Hill, NC, 2000), p. 283.

22. Christoph Jahr, *Gewöhnliche Soldaten: Desertion und Deserteure im deutschen und britischen Heer 1914–1918* (Göttingen, 1998).

23. Grew, "The Case," 773.

24. Baldwin, *Politics of Social Solidarity*, 39.

25. Johannes Dillinger, "American Spiritualism and German Sectarianism: A Comparative Study of the Societal Construction of Ghost Beliefs," *Bulletin of the German Historical Institute* 28 (Spring 2001), 55–73.

26. Nancy Green, *Ready-to-Wear and Ready-to-Work: A Century of Industry and Immigrants in Paris* (Durham, NC, 1997).

27. Charlotte Tacke, *Denkmal im sozialen Raum: Nationale Symbole in Deutschland und Frankreich im 19. Jahrhundert* (Göttingen, 1995); Michael Jeismann, *Das Vaterland der Feinde. Studien zum nationalen Feindbegriff und Selbstverständnis in Deutschland und Frankreich 1792–1918* (Stuttgart, 1992).
28. Heinz-Gerhard Haupt, "Die international vergleichende Geschichtswissenschaft: Ein Relikt der Strukturgeschichte?" unpublished paper, German Historical Institute, 2000.
29. See, for example, Maud Mandel, *In the Aftermath of Genocide: Armenians and Jews in 20th-Century France* (Durham, NC, 2003).
30. Howard Kimeldorf, *Reds or Rackets? The Making of Radical and Conservative Unions on the Waterfront* (Berkeley, 1988).
31. Bloch, "Toward a Comparative History," 495.
32. Ibid., 501.

5

ACROSS BATTLE FRONTS: GENDER AND THE COMPARATIVE CULTURAL HISTORY OF MODERN EUROPEAN WAR

Susan R. Grayzel

> If warfare is as old as history and as universal as mankind, we must now enter the supremely important limitation that it is an entirely masculine activity.
>
> John Keegan, *A History of Warfare*[1]

Military history offers an example of a field in which comparative history has been and is a thriving industry. From Clausewitz to Keegan, all wars are fodder for discussions of war *as such*. Universal declarations about the nature of warfare then are not uncommon. But if military history has been more willing than other fields to embrace the possibility of comparison, it is still structured by the one "natural" border that separates the categories of men and women. In order to refute these still dominant ideas and to reshape the master narratives that condition how we think and teach about modern Europe, we need comparative and cultural history, especially of war.

In the span of time between the French Revolution and Napoleonic Wars, which ushered in the nineteenth century, and the First World War, which set in motion the twentieth, the gap between combatants and civilians grew enormously. Yet, this did not diminish the sense that the modern army relied on the support of, and was tied to, the entire nation. The internal conflicts of revolutions and revolutionary wars were certainly experienced by men and women alike, but over the course of other nineteenth-century conflicts, the codification of new modes of warfare led to a protected "citizenry" of civilians, as seen in the Hague Conventions aimed at "civilizing" war. Therefore, part of the shock of World War One was that these barriers began to unravel and to unravel in almost all sectors of the war.

This chapter takes my own work in the history of gender and the First World War as the starting point for a discussion of the difficulties and rewards of comparative cultural history. In the first part, I trace the path that I followed in writing my first book, considering especially the differences between studies that focus upon states and social policies and those—like mine—that attend to the more intangible realms of culture. The second part explores my new book project on air raids to ask whether causality need necessarily be the highest aim of comparative history. Comparing cultures requires attention, above all, to representations and meanings, subjects that may be obscured by a preoccupation with causal explanation. The chapter concludes with general observations about the promise of comparative cultural history.

THE PROBLEM OF FRONTS

What general histories of women in warfare exist have usually been written by political scientists and sociologists. Those who have followed Jean Elshtain's influential *Women and War* into the field have had to contend with what she identified as fundamental differences between women and men when it came to war: the contrast between the idealized feminine "beautiful soul" and the masculine "just warrior."[2] The universality of Elshtain's categories called for more archivally based research into the pervasiveness of such binary oppositions. And yet, efforts to historicize the experiences of women in war demonstrate that such studies may suffer from their own problems of definition and inclusion. In her survey of women and war "from prehistory to the present," Linda Grant De Pauw defines woman as "any human who self-identifies as female," dividing such beings as they appear "in war" into several broad categories: victims, instigators, camp followers, viragoes, and androgynous warriors.[3] Such totalizing classifications, while implicitly rebuking scholars such as John Keegan by insisting on the significance of women's actions, do not, on the whole, address either the origins, or the fluidity, of their roles.

Here then is the principal utility of detailed comparative history. The virtues of comparison are, of course, evident to us in the classroom. Despite challenges to teleology and totalizing narratives, we teach survey courses, of necessity, in broad comparative frameworks, emphasizing those massive events such as wars that lend themselves to cross-national studies because they are the most vivid reminders that national borders matter. We cannot ignore them (even if we would wish to) because they are usually such traumatic events that their legacies are long, complicated, and entangled for both winners and losers. Modern wars are further fundamentally different because of the existence of the nation-state and its power to call upon *everyone* within the nation.

Although situating women in the total wars of the twentieth century may not disrupt any master narrative, a comparative approach can raise questions about the meanings attached to what happened to women, to civilians, and to the borders between "home front" and "front line." Examining centuries of state-sanctioned conflict in the mold of De Pauw and Keegan was not going to tell me very much about the evolving understandings of modern warfare in light of gender. Yet, any project, comparative or not, begins by wondering about the complexity of all of the individual, let alone national, stories. At the time that I was formulating my ideas and embarking on the research for what would become my first book on the First World War, there was already a well-established literature on women's international opposition to war, especially at the dawn of the twentieth century. However, the full range of women's responses to the war, and their lived experiences, had received relatively little attention from scholars. Moreover, the "new" stories of women's courageous defiance of the war-making apparatuses of their respective nations often fit too neatly into stereotypes. Those celebrating rather than examining the actions of women opposed to war tended to see them as the "natural" counterpart to soldiers: women support peace as men support war. The longer I read and thought about women's feminist pacifism, the more I wondered what enabled these women to defy the prevailing emphasis on support for the war; this question led me to want to investigate not just women pacifists but also patriots.[4] I was curious about the range of responses to the war.

In the course of moving from a proposal to research to the actual writing of a book, several inspiring works of comparative history offered rich examples of the kind of project that I hoped to undertake. These works focused on the two nations, Britain and France, that I had become interested in as the potential focus of my research. Of course, the experience of occupation—which France endured, while Britain remained largely, although not entirely, protected from the "direct" effects of the conflict—enormously influenced these two countries' reactions to the war. And yet, however significant such differences, the two nations' similarities in terms of ideas about gender identity were striking. I learned much from Susan Pedersen's study of the origins of welfare-state policies centered around the family in interwar Britain and France, from John Horne's work on divergent labor policies in these two nations, and Laura Lee Downs' research on the strict differentiation between the work of women and men that prevailed in both countries.

In all of these studies, the recovery of the experiences of individuals in these two states came through an investigation of answers to social policy questions. How could states mobilize men? By promising to care for their families and using incentives that might help to rebuild a diminished population. How could these same states sustain productive labor and realign workplace activity without disturbing gender hierarchy and thus alienating male workers and employers? By redefining categories of "work" and "skill." These are not only vital questions and significant answers but also ones for which there are clear-cut sources with which to engage them. Social policy produces archival evidence in abundance: government records and documents, legislative debates, official statistics, trade union minutes and publications, and newspaper coverage. And in general, such records are theoretically easy to compare: "Country X produced this type of legislation, Country Y another."[5]

Asking something far more intangible—what happened to the understanding and the meaning of gender during the war?—proved more challenging than I had imagined. For instance, the First World War allowed the concept of the "home front" to come into being as a space separate from the "front," yet vitally connected to it.[6] This was one of many innovations that accompanied a newly modern type of warfare, but the categorization of this front as a separate space also made the contributions of those at home appear less significant. Only when you invent the "home front" can you both define and cross the border separating it from some "real" front. By the end of my research, I was ready to argue that when studying wars, we need to interrogate this early twentieth-century idea of the home front and the prevailing vocabulary of front line, where, military historians such as Keegan tell us, the truly significant developments take place. We need to think of modern wars as fought along a continuum starting with the home and ending with the battlefield, arenas that are intimately connected. If we do so, we will not be able to regard any one space or participant as being somehow more authentic and significant than another.

I came to realize, then, that the actions of one country's government and the representations and challenges to official ideas found in its media and artifacts of popular culture could tell me something, yet perhaps not enough to make sense of the bigger picture. Like all historians, I would be telling a particular story with, I hoped, general implications. A comparative look at shared and divergent cultural values could help me attempt to understand something beyond the nation-state. I was searching, therefore, for something that constituted a pertinent and viable comparison, and I found myself sifting through several options. I could have looked at nations on different sides of the war, considering how the construction of enemies, for example, utilized similar ideas about gender. To investigate two allied countries, by contrast, might reveal divergences in a seemingly united effort. Indeed, when I looked at the allied nations Britain and France, I found startlingly different attitudes towards, for instance, prostitution and the spread of venereal disease within the military. In the meantime, new work by Mary Louise Roberts on postwar France and Susan Kent on postwar Britain had been published, and although both scholars offered insights into post-war understandings of gender, neither seemed (perhaps because each dealt with only one nation) to address fundamental questions about the war itself.[7]

Given that our investigations of the history of warfare rely on archives generated for the most part by masculine institutions, such as governments and armies, that have often defined women out of war, finding women beyond the easy images, propaganda, and social policy can be arduous. Looking under the category "women" in the Public Record Office in London or "femmes" in the Archives Nationales in Paris can uncover little beyond the official organizations set to monitor women's work. However, a search for articles by and about women in national and regional media yields ample evidence concerning a large range of behaviors and occupations. Moreover, Britain offers the unparalleled resources of the Imperial War Museum's Women's Work Collection and the National Library of Women (formerly the Fawcett Library), and France has the smaller Bibliothèque Marguerite Durand. Yet even these institutions, which house personal archives, rely upon the choices made by specific individuals as to what was worth saving during the war and what was deemed worthy of collecting in later years.

The French and British archives held differing and sometimes conflicting types of sources. Many British suffragist organizations kept minutes of their meetings during the war and, through them, one gets a sense of their own accounting of their strategies and priorities.[8] In

France, by contrast, I had to rely on the records of feminist meetings produced by informants for the Sûreté and the Parisian Prefect of Police.[9] In both cases, it quickly became obvious that these accounts needed to be balanced by public utterances and, when possible, private correspondence. In an effort to understand the relationship of the war and women's struggles for public, political, and civic rights, I turned to published material, such as feminist newspapers, that lent itself more directly to comparative research.

My interest in the language used by sources further led me to turn to other disciplines, such as cultural and literary studies. Trained in an era when no text was "transparent," I wanted and needed to pay close attention to how the sources defined their terms. Looking at more than policy, without neglecting it, I had to determine what was available in the wider culture that would allow individual women to make sense of their own experiences. So, I investigated the cultural cues about gender propagated by men and women, including those generated by literature and popular fiction. This also led me to models of cultural and literary theory as I tried to remain attuned to the use of certain images and languages, to what could and could not be said.

Working with two countries actively speaking to each other and trying to sustain a joint effort meant that I discovered some wonderful examples of texts published in close succession in Britain and France. Thus I could examine the censorship imposed on, for example, Marguerite Yerta's *Six femmes et l'invasion* in French and the passages left untouched in a hastily translated British edition of *Six Women and the Invasion*. Both versions of this book, which examine the harsh conditions experienced by French women in the invaded and occupied zones of France, appeared in 1917. The French version, like its translation, reminds readers of the terror imposed upon civilians left to fend for themselves under German occupation; some of these threats were explicitly sexual, and the collective circumstances served to unite the French population. Yet the English version contains not merely references to limited instances of French mistreatment of their fellow citizens, but also more explicitly recounts that some French women had sexual relations with German soldiers and were not just victims of rape or abuse. In the French version by contrast, the story is tidied up so that heroic French women always resisted barbaric Germans. Given that Britain was not similarly attacked, such a story was less necessary there. Thus even seemingly simple differences in translation told me something about each country while raising larger questions about how the feminine experience of this war was communicated.[10]

As the example of Marguerite Yerta suggests, I found some women's published memoirs of the war tremendously interesting. On the whole, however, I made little use of them and virtually none of the unpublished memoirs or those published after the war. The few female-authored autobiographies and memoirs that were available raised questions of selection for publication and of the narrowness of much of this material. For one thing, we have few voices of working-class women (just as we have few voices of working-class soldiers). Rather, my strategy was to find widely circulated ideas and images. So much material on women appeared in the news media, for instance, that this could have become not merely one of my main sources, but my only source. Discussions of the treatment of French women under German occupation in the winter and spring of 1915, with related debates about "children of rape" presumably resulting from such circumstances appeared in a broad range of newspapers. The breadth of circulation not only helped suggest their overall importance for shaping an understanding of gender and the war but it also provided some access to a range of voices.

But how to make sense of these voices as a cultural historian? Here, I was influenced by other disciplines' techniques for examining cultural media, turning, for instance, to Mary Poovey's notion of the "ideological work of gender" as a way to make clear how significant the allegedly separate female experiences and women's articulations were for the war effort. Texts like Marguerite Yerta's, I argued, performed an ideological task as significant as official propaganda. And I also borrowed some concepts from disciplines such as sociology that gave me a vocabulary to speak of the "emotional work" done by women who supported men at war. Waiting, encouraging, smiling through tears, and mourning were forms of labor that exacted their own tolls.[11]

Because I wanted to avoid dividing experiences between front line and home front, or attempting to determine the equivalent male and female occupations (fighting versus munitions work or fighting versus nursing), I found myself in search of a way to organize what I was learning about gender, women, and the war. The method that evolved organized material thematically, with a focus on the body and the body politic. I began by investigating the construction of a spatial divide between war and home front for and by women and men. Subsequently, multiple examples led me to investigate the resounding interest in women's maternity, evident in debates in France about the "children of rape," in British concern about "war babies," and in both states' debates over production versus reproduction. Rhetoric on both sides of the Channel reflected a consuming interest in motherhood and in threats to maternity posed by "dangerous" non-reproductive female bodies. In contrast to most military historians, who separate women from war making, I wanted to insist on women's active public, "political" debates, which used motherhood as a basis both to take a stand against the war and war itself and to claim access to civic and national identities as well as associated rights such as voting.

After finishing my first book, I ventured upon a new synthetic project that examined the First World War and women globally, entitled *Women and the First World War*.[12] I subdivided the subject into categories such as propaganda and social policy, waged and unwaged labor, sexuality and morality, pacifism and revolution, and finally, the war's effects, ranging from voting to mourning. Only in one chapter called "In the Line of Fire" did I examine women's participation in the most traditional spheres of warfare, the categories that De Pauw and Keegan restrict themselves to: namely, combatants and "victims." The daunting task of gathering information from Australia to Malawi, from India to Scotland, from Russia to the United States, also strengthened my belief in the value of comparative, synthetic, and analytical work. This expanded international approach to the subject taught me that regardless of geographic location or national identity, states defined women, and most importantly women defined themselves, as having a *distinct* relationship to each of these larger sets of issues and to their wartime states. My current research takes this insight to ask an even broader set of questions about gender's role in defining the nature of war. I am beginning with this one: what does it mean to fight when the home front becomes the front line?

THE CASE OF AIR RAIDS

Comparisons can begin with big questions and the search for alternative narratives; they can be serendipitous or investigate parallel sites: the cathedral city or munitions factory, official government policy concerning public health or reproduction. They can also take an innovation, such as the mass mobilization of women into waged work, however temporarily, during the First World War or the invention of air warfare, that happened in several places simultaneously and figure out its multiple meanings. We can choose comparisons or comparisons will choose us. Some comparisons, it would seem, are more easily made across national borders than others. And yet, even those comparisons that may at first appear relatively straightforward—comparisons of laws, for instance—upon closer reflection present their own difficulties, as laws both reflect and in turn shape cultural understandings. Our understanding of the subjects we take as our own may well depend on our ability to place them in a context larger than the nation-state; this seems particularly true when it comes to "culture."

The invention of the air raid, the subject of my current book project, is an event, a technological novelty, and decisions to use aerial bombardment count as political and even military history, but it is an innovation that is also made "real" by the way it is received and imagined. A cultural understanding of what this shift meant suggests the desirability of looking at its impact in the multiple places in which it was felt. The air raid has mostly been seen as a strategic technique, an obvious part of aviation or military history. However, it really marks a cultural break with the past. The air raid breaks down the borders between battle and home front, men and women, and nation-states, by penetration and not necessarily invasion of national boundaries. Once the air raid can occur, no place is safe, but just as it made everyone a potential victim, so too it made everyone a potential hero.

Starting in 1914, Germany launched zeppelin and airplane raids against its enemies. To some extent, this innovation fit in with other wartime technology that Germany introduced, such as submarines and chemical weapons. Both U-boats and air raids provoked outrage because of their targeting of "innocent" civilians, including women and children. Yet, to attack civilians in a ship at sea meant something different than attacking them quite literally in their homes. This expansion of the battle zones reworked what separated legitimate and illegitimate targets of war. Unfortunately, for civilians of twentieth-century wars, this decision ultimately made cities, towns, and villages far removed from so-called front lines places where war could be and was waged. This expansion ultimately culminated in the Cold War doctrine of Mutual Assured Destruction.

My examination of the reaction to air warfare in the First World War has revealed the significance of gender to the ways in which this new type of war was experienced. From the outset, propaganda highlighted the fact that those killed in air raids included women and children. Not only did something fundamental go awry when those meant to be protected from war fell under direct attack, but such events called upon "men" to be "men" defending "women and children." The targeting of private homes and the destruction of a school in London's East End in the daylight airplane raids of 1917 contributed to feelings ranging from unease to panic to indignation.[13] Public accounts, thus, also high-lighted the bravery of women who acted stoically and endured the raids without succumbing to "air raid shock," the civilian equivalent of shell shock.[14] Newspaper articles emphasized the "calm" bravery after "each of the recent raids" shown "by the inmates of those little cottages which were destroyed or just escaped destruction by a happy chance…in most of these suburban homes there were only women and children."[15] As air raids intensified over the course of the war, and certainly by the time Gothas bombed Paris, it was clear that the raids inspired new kinds of state and individual responses, and were read as something new and worse. At the same time, these new terrors also called into being new civilian bravery. One of the leading feminist newspapers, *La Française,* explicitly reminded its presumably female readers in February 1918 that, with their calm bravery, they emulated "those at the front."[16]

As part of the response to changes such as air and chemical warfare in interwar Europe, an international movement arose to deal with the threat of future wars and all they might entail. Given what had hap-pened in World War One, it is hardly surprising that this effort absorbed the energy of prominent feminists. As members already active in a transnational movement, some of those previously involved in the struggle for women's suffrage turned their attention to demon-strating that they took seriously their newly endowed public voice. Using feminist pacifist arguments developed during and even prior to World War One, many also spoke now of their new understanding of the costs of war, not just for men and for those in the military but also for the entire population. For those women who gathered at the Inter-national Council of Women's meeting at Wembley in May of 1924, the lessons of the war were vividly apparent: women must act in the world to curtail the development of new armaments because they and their children were now directly at risk.[17]

There are, it seems to me, two approaches to the subject outlined above, both valid, both rich, and both viable. One version of this history (the cross-national) would place a nation such as Britain at the center of the story of air raids. The other more daunting, time-consuming, fully comparative task would want to examine what happened in several places. Such a story would need to consider Italy's use of air raids in the Horn of Africa, to look at Spain and the international response to the raids of the Spanish Civil War, and to investigate the impact of air war-fare on Hamburg, Dresden, and Berlin. Fruitful comparative cultural history can thus be broad or narrow, and clearly both synchronic and diachronic. There is, in such a project, too, an implicit comparison of various wars, certainly, of the First and Second World Wars.

However, neither version of this project nor similar comparative investigations need to be framed with causality in mind. Comparative history's purpose has too often been viewed as the discovery of causes. By contrast, my own interest as a cultural historian has been in the *meanings* that events take on in different places, at different times. I ask, for instance, what significance does the air raid gain when it occurs and recurs? Such a comparative approach can offer insights into similarities and differences between regions and nations without resorting to an exclusively causal frame. Although there is obviously nothing wrong with asking why particular events happened, too often an emphasis on causality results in a "Goldilocks approach" to comparative history: when conditions are "just right," you get the anticipated result.

CULTURE AND COMPARISON

The challenge of comparative cultural history starts with figuring out what culture is, itself no small task. Part of this challenge comes from the tendency to view the cultural landscape from the top down, erasing variations within the nation-state and even among nation-states. Yet an investigation of the manifestations of culture in multiple places shows, sometimes more clearly than simply national studies do, contemporary efforts to bridge local (intranational) differences; comparative analysis allows us, too, to explore wider pan-European notions and, sometimes, different chronologies and interpretations as well. Historians of European nations have to account for regional variation, as well as the broader cultural interactions between nations. Britain's history has largely been written as English history, but, in addition to Ireland, Wales, and Scotland, regional differences matter historically, and one can even find many separate cultures within London. Comparative and cross-national cultural history can fruitfully interrogate the myths—the sustained shared beliefs—of the nation.

My own work to date has traced the recurring problem, across place and time, that women posed for wartime states. The repugnance towards women in combat was a broadly held sentiment. So what did states do about women? There was a variety of responses, from making women members of the nationally sanctioned military, often but not always restricted to support roles, to denying them this status entirely. During the First World War, Britain initiated the Women's Army Auxiliary Corps to put women in the military, whereas French women who performed similar tasks remained civilians.[18] Both sets of women did the army's "housework" as the French so eloquently put it, but only one set received official recognition. And only under Russia's Provisional Government in the summer of 1917 did women form combatant battalions. By looking across national boundaries, we stand to learn more about the meaning of women's participation in warfare and about the importance of context and culture for understanding governmental decisions about women in arms. Such an approach also provides the opportunity to challenge easy assumptions about the forces of "progressiveness" or "backwardness" in Europe.

Comparative cultural history sets itself the task of identifying elements of culture that are wider than the national, while paying close attention to specific contexts. In its richest variant, it takes as seriously the varying representations in wartime media of women in uniform as it does the laws governing their rights (or lack thereof) to don the garb. Trying to determine what anything means leads us to culture and, in the context of modern Europe, to culture(s) shaped by forces broader than the national.

To some extent, comparative history fits easily into military history, which has a long tradition of examining broad patterns across national lines and even across centuries. At the same time, however, a multitude of local and individual studies aims to shed light on warfare through the experience of a battalion, regiment, or representative soldier, with, of course, special emphasis on military leaders. What made Pershing or Pétain tick? How do we account for the success of Patton or Rommel? What made "ordinary" soldiers fight or win? Such studies have often meant, until recently, that war making can be placed in a tidy little box of information that stands alone, unconnected on some essential level to the vicissitudes of its cultural context.

As wars involve multiple participants with contradictory loyalties and identities, the history of modern European warfare strikes me as a subject that virtually demands cross-national and even comparative cultural research. There are some obvious obstacles: it understandably takes longer to do the research, and it requires greater flexibility to deal with sometimes conflicting types of sources. I also found that the actual writing of comparative history raises constant questions about how much of the larger national narrative history to tell. For instance, in my first book, I wondered about how much needed to be said about the role of Catholicism in France. How much space should one devote to explaining the longer history of British suffragism or French socialism in order to understand women and World War One? What sorts of knowledge about each nation could I assume the reader possessed?

The benefits of doing comparative history have been clear all along as well. If the research presented challenges, it was also invigorating and exciting to uncover the sometimes unexpected similarities and differences. I might not have paid as much attention to the issue of British "war babies" had I had not been alerted to the issue of soldiers' illegitimate offspring being legitimized by proxy marriages in France. I concluded my first book hoping that, through the comparison, I had been able to provide a more nuanced picture of each national experience and of the overall subject of woman and "the war." The process of researching and writing *Women and the First World War* raised even more complicated questions and opened up new insights. How do we do justice to the experience of colonial women when we know so relatively little about the experience of colonial soldiers? How do we acknowledge the role of women in both war and revolution? And ultimately, what did women's experiences mean to them and to us? One can always confront the argument that wars are decided on battlefields, but in the case of total war on the scale of the First World War, understanding the battles is clearly not enough. However inexact cultural comparisons or comparisons of cultures might be (and they are), they still provide insight into war's immediate impact and longer-term legacies.

Individual works and national case studies can provide crucial groundwork, but the main virtue of the comparative project—as far as the history of warfare goes—is the ability to challenge the traditional reification of the "masculinity" of combat and the feminized task of "keeping the home fires burning." Cross-national history vividly shows not only how ideas such as military valor or self-sacrificing motherhood may be deployed powerfully for different ends, but also how a shared Western gender system works to sustain modern wars. As teachers, as scholars, and as citizens of a world shaped by the wars of the twentieth century, I think we are obligated to understand these events in all their full, messy complexity. To do so requires that we cross, figuratively and otherwise, national borders, disciplinary boundaries, and even battle fronts.

REFERENCES

I would like to thank Deborah Cohen and Maura O'Connor for their comments on earlier drafts of this essay and for organizing the conference that gave rise to it, the conference participants for their stimulating ideas, and Joe Ward for his critiques and support.

1. John Keegan, *A History of Warfare* (Report, 1994, New York, 1993), 75–76.
2. Jean Bethke Elshtain, *Women and War* (New York, 1987).
3. Linda Grant De Pauw, *Battle Cries and Lullabies: Women in War from Prehistory to the Present* (Norman, OK, 1998), pp. 1–25, quote on p. 1.
4. For examples of such work, see Jill Liddington, *The Long Road to Greenham: Feminism & Anti-Militarism in Britain since 1820* (London, 1989); Anne Wiltsher, *Most Dangerous Women: Feminist Peace Campaigners of the Great War* (London, 1985); Danielle Le Bricquir and Odette Thibault, eds., *Féminisme et Pacifisme: Même Combat* (Paris, 1985); and essays in Ruth Roach Pierson, ed., *Women and Peace: Theoretical, Historical and Practical Perspectives* (London, 1987).
5. Laura Lee Downs, *Manufacturing Inequality: Gender Division in the French and British Metalworking Industries, 1914–1939* (Ithaca, NY, 1995); John Horne, *Labour At War: France and Britain 1914-1918* (Oxford, 1991); and Susan Pedersen, *Family, Dependence, and the Origins of the Welfare State: Britain and France 1914–1945* (Cambridge, 1993).
6. See the discussion of this in Susan R. Grayzel, *Women's Identities at War: Gender, Motherhood, and Politics in Britain and France during the First World War* (Chapel Hill, NC, 1999), Ch. 1–2.
7. Mary Louise Roberts, *Civilization without Sexes: Reconstructing Gender In Postwar France, 1917–1927* (Chicago, 1994) and Susan Kent, *Making Peace: The Reconstruction of Gender in Interwar Britain* (Princeton, NJ, 1993).
8. Those of the largest such organization, the National Union of Women Suffrage Societies, are housed in the Fawcett Library, London.
9. Christine Bard, *Les filles de Marianne: Histoire des féminismes 1914–1940* (Paris, 1995).
10. Marguerite Yerta, *Les six femmes et l'Invasion* (Paris, 1917); the English version lists two authors: Gabrielle and Marguerite Yerta, *Six Women and the Invasion* (London, 1917). These books are discussed more fully in Grayzel, *Women's Identities*, pp. 39–42.
11. See Grayzel, *Women's Identities*, Ch. 1–2; Mary Poovey, *Uneven Developments: The Ideological Work of Gender in Mid-Victorian England* (Chicago, 1988), and Arlie Russell Hochschild, *The Managed Heart: Commercialization of Human Feeling* (Berkeley and Los Angeles, 1983).
12. Susan R. Grayzel, *Women and the First World War* (London, 2002).
13. See Susan Grayzel, "Towards a Prehistory of the Blitz: Air Raids, Memory, and the Meaning of Warfare in Britain, 1914–1939," Paper delivered to the British Study Group, Minda de Gunzburg Center for European Studies, Harvard University, Cambridge, MA, April 2001.
14. Ibid.
15. Marion Ryan, "The Women's Splendid Courage in the Raided Areas. How They Met Frightfulness from the Sky Alone and Unprotected," *Weekly Dispatch*, October 1, 1916. See also "Women Raid Helpers," *Leeds Mercury*, December 15, 1917 on iniatives to train women to safeguard women and children seeking refuge during aerial attacks, and the *South London Press*, December 21, 1917, which records women's bravery as well as the deaths and injuries of women and children resulting from the bombing.
16. Alice Berthet, "La Réponse des Parisiennes au raid des Gothas sur Paris," *La Française*, February 9, 1918.
17. Ibid. 5.
18. See a fuller discussion of this in Grayzel, *Women and the First World War*.

6

COMPARATIVE HISTORY AND WOMEN'S HISTORY: EXPLAINING CONVERGENCE AND DIVERGENCE

Susan Pedersen

I

Is there a particular affinity between the comparative method and the field of women's history? I believe that there is and that this engagement has its own history. Feminists of the 1830s and 1840s, Bonnie Anderson tells us, saw the subjection of women as global and universal: instances of oppression in other lands provided analogies to their own situation; achievements of women anywhere were occasions for celebration and hope. They compared, in other words, in order to connect: examples from abroad were used to establish the commonality of women's subordination and to strengthen cross-cultural sisterly ties.[1] True, the rise of mass nationalism and imperialist rivalries blunted this early optimistic internationalism. By the late nineteenth century, Western feminists were as likely to compare in order to differentiate and rank-order, dwelling on the oppression of women abroad in order to demonstrate their own cultural superiority.[2] But that international orientation, that tendency to look across the border in sympathy and hope, was never entirely lost. "As a woman, I have no country," Virginia Woolf insisted in 1938, and although her countrywoman Eleanor Rathbone, with her eye on Hitler's Germany, begged to differ, she too admitted that she had trouble as a feminist "remembering or bothering about national distinctions."[3]

When Western feminist movements reemerged in the 1970s, they began by reasserting these global claims, but in a somewhat different fashion. Whereas early feminists had drawn on, and sometimes reacted against, their experiences with abolitionism and early socialism, "second-wave" feminism drew intellectual inspiration, and sometimes political outrage, from the strategies and analyses of the social movements of the Sixties. A productive contentious engagement with Marx (and, to a lesser extent, Freud) spurred a first generation of samizdat, and then suddenly popular, theoretical writings aimed at claiming for women the position of a subjected class,[4] and by the mid-seventies there were the beginnings of a more properly academic literature as well. These were the days of "dual systems theory," of arguments over the analytical usefulness of "patriarchy," of Heidi Hartmann's brilliant dissection of the "unhappy marriage" of Marxism and feminism, and of efforts to forge a more "progressive union."[5] True, like their "first-wave" foremothers before them,[6] some "second-wave" feminists delved into Engels, anthropology, and various idealized versions of pre-history in search of a world before male domination, but for the most part, academic feminists took as their analytical subject "women's oppression today,"[7] turning to history, sociology, and economics to explore its character and causes.

Once again, the comparative imagination asserted itself. Feminist scholars easily jumped across national lines, their forays into foreign lands often driven transparently by a search for models or "lessons" to bring back to the struggle at home. "Does socialism liberate women?" asked Hilda Scott in her 1974 book of that title (concluding it did not);[8] Judith Stacey, by contrast, insisted in 1975 that Western feminists could learn "positive political lessons" from the Chinese revolution's family reforms.[9] Economic inequality, feminists knew, was only one aspect of women's oppression, but economics nevertheless occupied the analytical pride of place: it was the drive to explain stratified labor markets and unequal pay that spurred investigation into the economics of the family, and not vice versa.[10] And although that scholarship grew in sophistication, it retained its international orientation, its flagship journals (*Feminist Studies, Signs*) resolutely transnational in coverage (and, to a degree, control), and its analytical terms ("patriarchy," "separate spheres") tested and applied across national lines.

It is hard for me to write dispassionately about this early "second-wave" scholarship, for it was the enabling foundation of my own intellectual formation. Decanted into graduate school in 1982 with an education in the classics of European social theory, I was in those days only by formal enrollment an historian. True, I had learned a thing or two about nineteenth- and twentieth-century England; I had spent some months as an undergraduate trawling through archival sources. But my goals were political and sociological: I was after nothing less than patriarchy's smoking gun, the root cause of women's oppression. Thus, when my undergraduate investigations into labor relations and economic structures revealed only that women's economic marginality could persist even during conditions (dire labor shortage, rapid training in new skills) likely to break it down,[11] I, like generations of feminists before me, suddenly realized that I needed to broaden, and perhaps even to reverse, the optic. Perhaps women's labor market inequality was as much the consequence as the cause of their domestic powerlessness; perhaps one needed to conceptualize the connection between the relations of production and reproduction, between men's domestic power and their economic power, differently.

One place to begin this project was with that unrealized but durable ideal, the male family wage. From the late 1970s (and, although at first they didn't realize it, long before), feminist economists and historians had identified the "family wage" as a crucial nexus of women's oppression, as the means by which claims to economic privilege based on family needs and male domestic dominance became mutually reinforcing.[12] But how historically specific, and how variable, was this wage form? And, more pointedly, how crucial was this particular gendered organization of economic life to women's subjection? By the spring of my first year in graduate school, I had begun working on this question. This time, however, I decided to work comparatively, juxtaposing my narrative of the emergence of a male-breadwinner norm in Britain (and of feminist assaults upon it) with a study of the development, in France, of different understandings of appropriate family structure and different models of economic support.

What led me to make this "comparative turn"? Ambition and emulation certainly played their part. I was studying with Charles Maier and, having admired his work, wanted to try my hand at something equally, or nearly as, ambitious in significance and scope.[13] But my sociological training had persuaded me that general questions, like the origins of women's subordination, would be better understood after consideration of more than a single case, and I was still enough of a "social scientist" (and not enough of an historian) to be undaunted by the scope of the project I was undertaking. Admittedly, but probably fairly typically, my turn to France was somewhat accidental: I was in the market for a second "case." Since my German was simply not good enough at that stage for me to attempt serious research with German sources, and I had some background in French history, I decided to make an initial foray into French materials. But, as I quickly discovered, the choice of France proved fortuitous. I found that I had stumbled across one of the great untold stories of twentieth-century economic history: the story of French industrialists' determined efforts to combat the ideal of a male family wage and their inadvertent creation of an unusually successful and unusually structured welfare state. Unlike in Britain, where feminists struggled with limited success against a male breadwinner ideal supported by male trade unionists and government officials alike, in France, a peculiar alliance of industrialists and prona-talists collaborated to construct a wage system that, in essence, seques-tered a portion of aggregate wages for the support of dependent women and children alone. Indeed, in light of the French story, the widespread British deference towards male-breadwinner ideals began to look somewhat peculiar.

The dissertation, and ultimately the book, that resulted from this investigation thus moved away from questions of women's subordina-tion to seek to understand the evolution of different normative models of family life and different welfare states, and to specify what made those different outcomes possible. Although a number of factors were discussed, including different long-standing attitudes towards married women's wage-earning, different patterns of industrialization, different women's movements, and very different foreign-policy concerns (and hence different attitudes towards population growth), the structure of industrial relations in the two countries moved to the center of the story. The determination of French industrialists and the relative weak-ness of French unions, in contrast with accepted patterns of collective bargaining in Britain and a wide public agreement that welfare mea-sures were the business of the state, made possible a degree of wage dis-aggregation in France that had as its result one of the most comprehensive sets of policies to prevent family and child poverty any-where in the world.[14]

But what did this mean for my initial question about the subjection of women? Here, comparison proved illuminating but also sobering. As I delved into my case, it became clear that the French system assur-edly was not born out of feminist demands, nor even out of some greater cultural valorization of the work of motherhood. If anything, this system was made possible by the weakness of the French feminist movement and the propensity of all groups to subordinate questions of women's individual rights, whether as mothers or citizens, to arguments about the need to support "families" more generally. Although mothers certainly benefited from family allowances and maternity support, it would be hard to argue that the French system made women "more emancipated," for familial entitlements were bought at the cost of a corporatist rhetoric that denigrated the importance of women's suffrage and other *individualist* rights and sought to bolster the authority of the male *chef de famille*.

What, then, had comparison contributed to my work? It had, I felt, had very considerable payoffs. First, it made clear the historical specificity and particularity of British economic and political patterns (the male-breadwinner wage norm, the insured-breadwinner-based welfare state) that had been, especially in the Anglo-American historiography, too often seen as normative for industrial societies in general. Second, it allowed me to specify more clearly both the character and the causes of the different wage and welfare systems by which different societies came to support families, and to show the ways in which those very different distributive "logics" (which I termed in my book a "male-breadwinner logic" or a "parental logic") contributed to or strengthened particular patterns of gender relations and social power. What comparison did not do was to answer my (now seemingly rather naive) question about the causes of, and hence the possible solutions to, women's subordination. To paraphrase Tolstoy, what comparison revealed was that every society subordinates women, but it does so in its own way.

II

Now, my excuse for telling this story isn't simply that it has given me the chance to reflect on—and hence to make sense of—a personal intellectual trajectory that I experienced at the time as a good deal less coherent and logical. Instead, the interest of the story arises, I think, from the extent to which it captures some wider trends within the writing of women's history. For what I see now as my deeply structuralist bias, my tendency to ask sociological rather than historical questions,[15] and my turn to comparison as a means better to understand historical specificity and commonality, were shared by other scholars searching for an adequate approach to the study of women's subordination. The conferences, journals, and networks of interdisciplinary social sciences welcomed and sustained that turn: the annual conferences of the Council of Europeanists and the Social Science History Association,

Comparative Studies in Society and History, and the Social Science Research Council, scholarly centers and communities at Michigan, Columbia, Harvard, and elsewhere, incorporated questions of gender relations and structure into their programs, funding plans, and pages. We see the fruits of this confluence of academic feminism and comparative social science in a whole series of conference papers and dissertations of the 1980s, which became the edited volumes and books of the 1990s. Jane Jenson, Ann Orloff, and Theda Skocpol's work on comparative social policy, Laura Downs' study of gender relations in the metalworking industries in Britain and France, Alisa Klaus's work on French and American child protection, Mary Ruggie's account of employment policies for women in Britain and Sweden, and the volumes that grew out of conferences on the gendered structures of welfare states or the experiences of women in times of war all addressed, explicitly, the question of comparison, seeking to specify the economic, social, political, and cultural forces that resulted in such variable patterns of gender relations and gender power.[16] Out of this as well came a set of early comparative theoretical essays aimed at establishing gendered typologies for states, societies, and movements.[17]

By the time my book was published in 1993, what I was doing seemed academically respectable and, if not exactly normal, not unusual either. If relatively few women's historians wrote fully comparative books, there were plenty of gestures towards comparison and certainly a general perception that scholars working within particular national historiographies had much to gain from "thinking comparatively." That comparative turn spilled over into (and sometimes grew out of) our teaching: routinely, women's history courses would juxtapose works on the French and American revolutions, women and industrialization in Germany and Britain, women's experiences with German and Italian fascism, and the experience of women in the Bolshevik and Chinese revolutions. Implicit in such comparisons was the effort to discover the national particularities and broader commonalities of women's experiences and the reasons why different societies come to pose, and to answer, their "woman question" in different ways. The books, mine among them, that addressed such questions through fully articulated comparison were simply the expression of what I think were broadly accepted assumptions about the centrality of comparison to any intellectually satisfying and theoretically informed history of women. I would single out three assumptions in particular: that women's history should be attuned to both commonalities and differences in the situation of women in different cultures, that it should seek to explain the causes both of particular national patterns and of variation, and that it should accept that the unit of comparison for women's—as for other—history was, in effect, the nation-state.

But do these assumptions still hold? Do women's historians continue to exhibit these preferences for delineating national patterns, undertaking comparative study, and attempting to specify causes? I would argue that we do not and that although we may continue to be engaged in an historical enterprise that seeks to move beyond the purely national case, this attempt at broader discussion no longer takes place largely under the sign of "comparison." Let me now offer some thoughts on the causes of comparative history's relative demise and some speculations about the forms in which supranational women's history might continue to survive.

III

Why, then, has the history of women moved away from comparison? To begin with, it is worth mentioning that comparative women's history operates under the same disadvantage as does all comparative history: the disadvantage that it is quite hard to do. Comparative history, like socialism, takes too many evenings. The good comparativist tends to hold herself to the standard of the best work in any particular national field, and this can mean, frankly, a lot more work. Writing comparative history means mastering many historiographies rather than just one and often many languages as well. It tends to mean more extensive travel to a wider range of archives, and hence more of all those other things we do to support research: more grant-writing, more negotiating for leave, more efforts to work out time in foreign institutes. Of course, these are some of the pleasures of comparative history as well, but they do have costs. Cutting corners begins to seem appealing, but the risks are high: every comparativist lives in fear of the review that waxes appreciative of the wider comparative project but asserts that in the particular national field in which the reviewer is expert, the author has gotten absolutely everything wrong.

So, it doesn't surprise me that, for many historians, comparative history seems a difficult art to sustain. I've been struck by the number of historians who, having written a comparative first book, find themselves redefining themselves as national historians for their second project. Deborah Cohen wrote a comparison of the treatment of disabled veterans in Britain and Germany for her first book;[18] her second will be on Britain alone. Susan Grayzel wrote an account of women's wartime experiences in Britain and France for her first book;[19] her new study of air warfare focuses on Britain alone. Laura Downs turned from a fully comparative account of women's industrial work in interwar Britain and France to work on France alone;[20] I myself am following up a comparative account of welfare-state formation in France and Britain with a biography. Comparison, oddly enough, sometimes seems less the mark of the mature scholar than a luxury we can afford only in graduate school. It isn't just that we become (as we leave graduate school for professorial careers) less likely to have the time for research that good comparative projects require (and that this time-pressure may be felt particularly sharply by women, who may be having children just as they begin to work out the scope of that second major book); nor is it only that we may tire of the multiple conferences and many-fronts publishing required of those who would wish to maintain their scholarly standing in more than one national field. Nor is it just that the historians' job market, with its national subfields, has a knack for sending us down particular national tracks: comparativists, in job interviews, routinely find themselves protesting that they are "really" French or German historians, and then, once in that job, becoming that very thing.

True, all these external pressures exist, but historians turn away from comparison for reasons of intellectual choice and affinity as well. The effort to understand a particular culture well tends to breed attachment, and that attachment, once felt, can be lasting. Certainly, this is what happened to me. I dove into archives in Britain and France to answer my particular questions, but, over time, I became interested in Britain for its own sake: it was, in other words, my growing knowledge of the culture and the place that began to dictate my questions, and not vice versa. I like to think that this was a sign that I was becoming, finally, a historian, that I was "getting the references" culturally just as I had understood the theoretical references so many years before. But there is no doubt that that attachment lessened my drive towards comparative history: the better I came to understand the British case, the more I doubted that I would ever be able to comprehend a second culture that deeply. Those of us who write two-country comparisons are thus particularly likely, eventually, to come down on one or the other "side". I've always found it telling that Peter Baldwin, one of the few younger historians I know who has been able to sustain a commitment to fully comparative work through the second book, has consistently opted to examine fairly universal problems (social security, the management of disease) through multicountry, rather than simply two-country, comparisons and ended up in a history department so large (UCLA) as to be able to support appointments not tied to the teaching of a particular national field.[21]

The demands of the field, the structure of our profession, and the seductive qualities of historical research thus all militate against a lasting commitment to the practice of comparative history. But what I believe to be a turn away from comparison within the historical profession more generally, also has some more immediate causes. First, if comparative history was born of the engagement of historians with social theory and social science, so too its fortunes have waned as the allure of social science for historians has faded. No trend has been more marked in the past few years than the shift by historians away from a concern to specify causes towards a concern to elucidate cultural meanings. Anthropologists and literary scholars, rather than sociologists and political scientists, have been the favored fellow-travelers on this road. Of course, cultural historians may also wish to compare the motifs and meanings of, say, religious belief or aesthetic styles or child-rearing practices in one culture with those of another, but the hermeneutic, "thick descriptive" methods of cultural history discourage such comparison. Inasmuch as the aim of the exercise is often to illuminate the content of, say, Englishness or Frenchness, or to explore cultural patterns not necessarily limited by national or political boundaries at all, cultural historians are more likely to transgress disciplinary boundaries and research conventions than national fields. Showing that themes present in business prospectuses or political economy tracts also show up in serial novels or artistic works seems a more convincing demonstration of their significance than some analysis of either similar or different cultural preoccupations in other lands.

And if the "cultural turn" has made comparative history less pressing, a second challenge can be discerned in the growing interest among historians in locating their inquiries within boundaries other than those of the nation-state. Unsurprisingly, in an era of globalization, the local and the transnational have become common frameworks of analysis. At first glance, this disillusionment with the nation-state might seem favorable to comparative history, for comparative projects need not be state-centered. Cities, regions, or indeed empires can be and have to a degree become productive units of demarcation for comparative study. Yet such approaches remain marginal: for the most part, comparative historians continue to use the nation-state as their primary unit of analysis, whereas those interested in other geographical units only rarely cast their inquiries in a comparative frame. The current vogue for transnational history and, similarly, the powerful turn towards imperial and post-colonial history are not signs of the health of comparative history but of its diminishing attractiveness and, seemingly, relevance. Historians, too, are creatures of their age: small wonder, then, that the effort to provide a genealogy for the world of unfettered trade, supranational sovereignty, and worsening global inequality in which we find ourselves has taken precedence over the task of specifying particular national patterns.

IV

These trends have thrown comparative history on the defensive, and, for complex reasons, women's history has been affected particularly acutely. Its very "newness," its self-conscious openness to innovation and experimentation, makes women's history especially sensitive to methodological and theoretical shifts. No group of historians felt the influence of Foucault more powerfully, none engaged with the "linguistic turn" more seriously, than historians of women, or, as they were now becoming, historians of gender. No doubt the fragmentation and frustrations of feminist political practice contributed to this engagement. When sexual inequality proved resistant to legal and institutional remedy and actual women resistant to feminist organizing, analyses attentive to the complex cultural and psychological aspects of gender identity and inequality understandably gained in appeal. Of course, even in the early 1970s, a few scholars had looked to psychology to explain the resilient flexibility of male domination,[22] but only when some of the field's founding mothers converted to various forms of post-structuralism, and volume one of Foucault's *History of Sexuality* came to replace Marx and Engels as the basic text for feminist reading groups and women's studies courses, did the core preoccupations of the field shift.[23] This shift was not, and still less was it experienced as, a retreat from a concern with women's subjection or with power; indeed, a determination to demonstrate power's multivalent, complex, and even participatory character haunted this new scholarship. Yet insofar as women's historians began to locate inequality as much in cultural norms and practices as in institutions and laws, and dissertations on, say, shopping or seances began to displace those on, say, suffrage or social policy, the allure of comparison began to fade.[24] With power reconceived, the task of describing "how" took precedence over the task of explaining "why," and the former question proved much less easily illuminated by comparison. Power remained in the picture, but since it coursed through the capillaries of "culture," it proved difficult to extract analytically and to hold up to comparative view.

But the challenge posed by post-structuralism had its moral side as well, and this proved especially difficult for a field founded upon, and hence sensitive to, ethically grounded critiques. Women's history was born of the urge both to understand women's subjection and to recover a history of resistance: comparison, then, was resorted to in order to specify the places and strategies by which such subjection might be lessened. But the turn to culture has cast that enterprise and, by association, comparison itself into disrepute: if cultural history—and, still more, post-colonial criticism—has accomplished anything, it has been to call into question the assumption that one can evaluate gender relations in different societies by a single standard and in isolation from the cultural context in which they are embedded.[25] Aware of European women's historic engagement in imperialism and of the ways in which humanitarian rhetoric could be used to justify political subordination, women's historians have become chary of approaches that would use suffrage, involvement in wage labor, or indeed any other abstract measure as a reliable index of women's social standing.

For all of these reasons, then, the "turn towards comparison" in women's history may be on the wane. In saying that, however, I do not mean to suggest that women's historians are retreating to their national bunkers. Far from it. Instead, precisely because new fields tend to experience methodological and theoretical shift particularly acutely, women's historians have been prominent among those seeking to map out new models for what we might call "supranational history." Let me cite a few recent examples.

First, we have seen some creative use of multicountry analysis by women's historians attempting to write gendered histories of global conflicts. Take, for example, Susan Grayzel's prize-winning book on the impact of the First World War on gender identities. Grayzel examines both French and British experiences in this study, but the aim isn't quite to tease out the specificities of the two national cases as it would have been in more traditionally conceived comparative history. Not that she ignores national variations, but these fade into relative insignificance when compared with the powerful and relatively parallel impact that total war had on gender relations in these two belligerent countries. Comparison gives way to a kind of broader transnational history, to an argument about the extent to which, in situations of extreme peril, national particularities fall away. If an implicit comparison exists, it is temporal rather than territorial, a comparison between the range of identities possible for women in times of peace and times of war. Yes, there are two cases here: but the reason for the two-country study is less to isolate the particularities of the two countries' responses than to say something broader about the relationship between gender orders and total war.[26]

In Grayzel's work, we see the traditional aims of comparison subordinated to a (successful) effort to explore supranational trends. In a second recent spate of books, country-based analysis gives way to an international focus. In Leila Rupp's book on international women's organizations in the late nineteenth and twentieth centuries, and in Bonnie Anderson's study of the transnational feminist network of the early nineteenth century, feminism is shown to have been, from its inception, a deeply international movement; although national parties and politicians routinely tried to coopt or contain the movement, those international ties were never entirely severed.[27] For Rupp and Anderson, demonstrating the international character of this movement is itself the story, but other historians have also used a transnational, but not comparative, approach to examine how policy changes usually explored within domestic frameworks alone could be shaped by international and not simply comparable national political movements.[28] We have lost something, these histories imply, by using the nation-state as the "default setting" when framing our analyses.

A third group of historians would agree and offer, moreover, something beyond a topic-driven "history of connections" to put in its place. Spurred by the imperatives of multiculturalism within the academy and taking to heart the powerful intellectual critique offered by African-American and post-colonial theorists, women's historians have been among those most committed to recovering the ways in which imperialism and racial domination marked virtually all aspects of Western life. Initially at least, much of that history continued to be written in a "national" frame: while it sought to demonstrate the ways in which various Western women's identities and movements had been shaped by their engagement with racial and colonial "Others," the nationally defined group or movement remained the focus of study. Indeed, in their tendency, following Said, to focus on imaginative constructions of "the Other" to the exclusion of actual cross-cultural contacts and relations, these works could inadvertently reinforce the propensity to see national cultures as distinct, uncomprehending, and hermetically sealed. Yet some influential voices were always (or became) alive to this danger.[29] Thus Mrinalini Sinha, drawing as much on the world-systems theory of Immanuel Wallerstein as on neo-Foucauldian discourse analysis, placed

British and Indian developments (the construction of imperial and colonial masculinities in Bengal in the 1880s, the shaping of British and Indian feminisms in the 1920s and 1930s) in a single analytical frame in order to reveal the lineaments and webs of power structuring this "imperial social formation" more broadly.[30] For comparativists, such work poses an implicit question. If we accept that gender inequalities, identities, and movements are indeed hybrid in origin and content, should we jettison the practice of "comparing" national cases and instead take as our subject the global patterns of interaction within which they emerge and function?

V

Thus stated, this question seems almost irresistible, and yet the answer, I am convinced, cannot be an unqualified "yes." Or rather, although all of us should learn from and take to heart these new supranational histories, women's history should also continue to exploit the possibilities offered by structured comparison, especially of national cases. The practice of history is not a zero-sum game, and although particular methods may be poorly equipped to answer some historical questions, they may be adept at answering others. The turn towards transnational and imperial history has given us much, bringing into focus connections and global ties that comparativists—with their preference for seemingly hermetically sealed national units—have too often missed. Yet comparative history, I would argue, had its years of glory because it genuinely did, and does, have something distinctive to offer, something that women's historians cannot easily do without. It has, I think, several unique strengths.

First, as comparativists, following Mill, have always argued, well-structured comparison throws into relief the particularities and commonalities of national experiences. For women's historians, this is significant not only because we can then go on to specify patterns and identify and order possible causes, but also because the simple act of juxtaposition often performs a crucial "de-normalizing" function. Certainly this was one of the main benefits of comparison for my own work: only the comparison with France, a society both like and unlike Britain, forced me to recognize the particularity of British domestic ideals and policy choices, and to see them not as given but as something to be explained. In this sense, comparison is the analogue of post-structuralism, which has so productively insisted upon the constructed and historical nature of gender and subjectivity itself. Gender identities and relations are, as we know, particularly prone to "normalization"; when approaching such subjects, then, comparison can be an unsettling and useful tool. Women's history has always insisted that women's subordination is historical, variable, and not natural: surely, then, it must retain analytical approaches that give force to that basic point.

Yet although comparison historicizes national particularities, it does so, critics charge, by reifying the nation-state, thus ignoring the many ways in which cross-cultural interactions and global movements themselves shaped specific national patterns. This is certainly true, for although comparisons of "national cultures" certainly exist (witness Richard Biernacki's study of factory cultures in Britain and Germany or Ida Blom's work on gendered nationalisms[31]) comparativists do tend to have a statist and structuralist bias and to see the nation-state through Max Weber's (and not Benedict Anderson's) eyes.[32] But is this necessarily a weakness, or can one see such "bias" as a useful check in an age of globalization? "The history of modern women is best told as parts of the histories of separate nations," Donald Meyer argued in his four-country comparative history of the rise of feminism, for even such global or international forces as modernization and capitalism, patriarchy and socialism, have been adapted and shaped by state power.[33] Migrations and diasporas, movements of goods and of capital certainly also determine women's "life chances," but even in this "post-territorial" age (and certainly before) states retain formidable powers over the disposition and well-being of their citizenry. In a world where women still find their civil and familial rights, their control over their bodies, and (often) their access to economic goods constrained by "reasons of state," it behooves us to hold on to modes of analysis adept at specifying some (not all) of the roots and relative impact of those societal patterns.

Finally, comparison remains important precisely for the reason it fell into disfavor: because it provides a foundation for relative judgment, for modifying claims to significance with the crucial adjectives "more" or "less." This is, of course, also the point at which comparison gets tricky, for one scarcely wishes to jettison either the more holistic approaches of anthropology or cultural history, or the moral critique offered by post-colonial studies, and to return to the world of feminist paeans either to bourgeois individualism or socialist egalitarianism. Yet the "relativizing" aspect of comparison need not function in this way, for constructing some league table of modernization or emancipation is no longer (if it ever was) the comparativist's main scholarly goal. Rather, historians tend to use comparison in order to identify and determine the salience ("more" or "less") of a variety of different factors, and to show how such factors combine to produce often unexpected and singular results. They, too, wish to describe whole societies, albeit with more analytical precision; if they venture into the realm of causation, they do so hoping to offer meaningful explanations for particular outcomes, not to formulate general laws. Thus, as Elizabeth Heinemann has brilliantly shown, the comparative historian responds to the rival claims of national feminist movements (in this case, West and East German) to superior achievements and emancipation not by declaring one side the winner, but rather by uncovering the assumptions and interests that might lead different groups of women to define "emancipation" in such different ways.[34] National particularities are acknowledged, but they are also explained, an approach than enables "women" to retain at least some shred of the common identity, some glimmer of the collective purpose, that feminists began to claim for them two centuries ago.

What, then, would I conclude from this brief and highly personal survey of historiographical trends? We are not, I hope I've made clear, at a moment of isolationism. Women's historians, like other historians, are building bridges and crossing borders, trying out new approaches, and rejecting old statist paradigms. But although this has given us important new histories—transnational and post-colonial histories, histories of how global forces reworked gender across national lines—I do worry that it may have also led us to overlook the extent to which the state has structured and still structures the "life chances" of women and men. Out of the (possibly temporary) convergence of women's history and comparative history came an appreciation for the ways in which national economic and political institutions and movements shaped women's possibilities and lives. Our interest in those findings has waned, but they've not become any less important.

REFERENCES

This paper was first presented at a workshop on "How to Write a Comparative History of Women" held at the Open University in Lisbon, Portugal, in May 2001; I thank my fellow presenters Bonnie Anderson, Ann Taylor Allen, and Karen Offen for their comments, and (especially) Anne Cova for inviting and advising me. Thomas Ertman, Charles Maier, Deborah Cohen, and Maura O'Connor offered useful suggestions for revision, as did David Blackbourn and the participants of the European History Graduate Workshop at the Center for European Studies.

1. Bonnie S. Anderson, *Joyous Greetings: The First International Women's Movement, 1830-1860* (New York: Oxford University Press, 2000), esp. pp. 140–141.
2. A pattern brought to light in Antoinette Burton, *Burdens of History: British Feminism, Indian Women and Imperial Culture, 1865–1915* (Chapel Hill, NC: University of North Carolina Press, 1994), and now much elaborated upon.

3. Virginia Woolf, *Three Guineas* (New York: Harcourt, Brace, Jovanovich, 1938), pp. 108-109; the quote from Rathbone is from a letter to Rajkumari Amrit Kaur, February 29, 1934, Rathbone Papers on India, Fawcett Library, 93/12, London.

4. Notably, Shulamith Firestone, *The Dialectic of Sex: The Case For Feminist Revolution* (New York, Morrow, 1970); Kate Millett, *Sexual Politics* (New York: Doubleday, 1970); *Feminist Revolution* (New York: Redstockings, 1975).

5. The outpouring of feminist writings on such questions defies easy summary, but for me the landmark essay remains Heidi Hartmann, "The Unhappy Marriage of Marxism and Feminism: Towards a More Progressive Union," *Capital and Class* 8 (Summer 1979), 1–41.

6. Especially, Olive Schreiner, *Women and Labour* (1911; report. London: Virago, 1978).

7. This is the title of Michele Barrett's impressive theoretical synthesis (London: New Left Books, 1980).

8. Hilda Scott, *Does Socialism Liberate Women? Experiences from Eastern Europe* (Boston: Beacon, 1974).

9. Judith Stacey, "When Patriarchy Kowtows: The Significance of the Chinese Family Revolution for Feminist Theory" (1975), rpt. in Zillah R. Eisenstein, ed., *Capitalist Patriarchy and the Case for Socialist Feminism* (New York: Monthly Review, 1979), pp. 299–348.

10. Once again, the gold standard is the work of Heidi Hartmann, "Capitalism, Patriarchy, and Job Segregation by Sex," in Eisenstein, *Capitalist Patriarchy*, op. cit., pp. 206–247.

11. Susan Pedersen, "Explaining the Persistence of Gender Hierarchy at Work: The Dilution of Labour in British Munitions Industries, 1914–1918," B.A. thesis, Harvard-Radcliffe, 1982.

12. Most notably by Mary McIntosh, "The Welfare State and the Needs of the Dependent Family," in Sandra Burman, ed., *Fit Work for Women* (London: Croom Helm, 1979), pp. 153–172; and Hilary Land, "The Family Wage," *Feminist Review*, 8 (1980), 55–78. These writers, along with Heidi Hartmann, also rediscovered Eleanor Rathbone's brilliant work on this subject; especially Eleanor F. Rathbone, *The Disinherited Family: A Plea for Direct Provision for the Costs of Child Maintenance through Family Allowances* (1924; report. 3rd ed., London: George Allen & Unwin, 1927)

13. Charles Maier, *Recasting Bourgeois Europe: Stabilization in France, Germany and Italy in the Decade after World War I* (Princeton, NJ: Princeton University Press, 1975).

14. Susan Pedersen, "Social Policy and the Reconstruction of the Family in Britain and France, 1900–1945," Ph.D. Dissertation, Harvard University, 1989; Susan Pedersen, *Family, Dependence, and the Origins of the Welfare State: Britain and France, 1914–1945* (Cambridge, UK: Cambridge University Press, 1993).

15. Certainly, at least at the outset, I approached history as a morass of fact from which one could elicit data relevant to questions arrived at through a review of theoretical and secondary works (a classically sociological approach), rather than as a research enterprise through which one would arrive at the questions themselves.

16. Ann S. Orloff and Theda Skocpol, "Why Not Equal Protection? Explaining the Politics of Public Social Spending in Britain, 1900–1911, and the United States, 1880s–1920s," *American Sociological Review*, 49: 6 (December 1984), 726–750; Jane Jenson, "Gender and Reproduction: Or, Babies and the State," *Studies in Political Economy*, 20 (Summer 1986), 9–46; Laura Lee Downs, *Manufacturing Inequality: Gender Division in the French and British Metalworking Industries, 1914–1939* (Ithaca, NY: Cornell University Press, 1995); Alisa C. Klaus, *Every Child a Lion: The Origins of Maternal and Infant Health Policy in the United States and France, 1890–1920* (Ithaca, NY: Cornell University Press, 1993); Mary Ruggie, *The State and Working Women: A Comparative*

Study of Britain and Sweden (Princeton, NJ: Princeton University Press, 1984); Seth Koven and Sonya Michel, eds., *Mothers of a New World: Maternalist Politics and the Origins of Welfare States* (New York: Routledge, 1993); Gisela Bock and Pat Thane, eds., *Maternity and Gender Policies: Women and the Rise of the European Welfare States, 1880s-1950s* (London: Routledge, 1991); Margaret R. Higonnet et al., eds., *Behind the Lines: Gender and the Two World Wars* (New Haven, CT: Yale University Press, 1987).

17. This literature developed in part through engagement with Gøsta Esping-Andersen's influential *The Three Worlds of Welfare Capitalism* (Princeton, NJ: Princeton University Press, 1990); for feminist responses and alternative typologies, see especially, Mary Langan and Ilona Ostner, "Gender and Welfare," in Graham Room, ed., *Towards a European Welfare State?* (Bristol: School for Advanced Urban Studies, 1991), 127–50; Ann Shola Orloff, "Gender and the Social Rights of Citizenship: The Comparative Analysis of Gender Relations and Welfare States," *American Sociological Review*, 58 (1993), 303–328; also Seth Koven and Sonya Michel, "Womanly Duties: Maternalist Politics and the Origins of Welfare States in France, Germany, Great Britain and the United States, 1880–1920," *American Historical Review*, 95:4 (October 1990), 1076–1108.

18. Deborah Anne Cohen, *The War Come Home: Disabled Veterans in Britain and Germany, 1914–1939* (Berkeley: University of California Press, 2001).

19. Susan Grayzel, *Women's Identities at War: Gender, Motherhood and Politics in Britain and France during the First World War* (Chapel Hill, NC: University of North Carolina Press, 1999).

20. Laura Lee Downs, *Manufacturing Inequality: Gender Division in the French and British Metalworking Industries, 1914–1939* (Ithaca, NY: Cornell University Press, 1995).

21. Peter Baldwin, *The Politics of Social Solidarity: Class Bases of the European Welfare State, 1875–1975* (Cambridge, UK: Cambridge University Press, 1990); Peter Baldwin, *Contagion and the State in Europe, 1830–1930* (Cambridge, UK: Cambridge University Press, 1999).

22. Juliet Mitchell, *Psychoanalysis and Feminism* (London: Allen Lane, 1974); Nancy Chodorow, *The Reproduction of Mothering: Psychoanalysis and the Sociology of Gender* (Berkeley: University of California Press, 1978).

23. I am thinking, here, of such profound shifts in approach as that found between, e.g., the Joan Scott (with Louise A. Tilly) of *Women, Work and Family* (New York: Holt, Rinehart and Winston, 1978) and the Joan Scott of *Gender and the Politics of History* (New York: Columbia University Press, 1988); between the Michele Barrett of *Women's Oppression Today: Problems in Marxist Feminist Analysis* (London: New Left, 1980) and the Michele Barrett of *The Politics of Truth: From Marx to Foucault* (Cambridge, UK: Polity, 1991); between the Judith Walkowitz of *Prostitution and Victorian Society: Sex, Class and the State* (Cambridge, UK: Cambridge University Press, 1980) and the Judith Walkowitz of *City of Dreadful Delight: Narratives of Sexual Danger in Late-Victorian London* (Chicago: University of Chicago Press, 1992). It would be easy to multiply such examples.

24. I am aware that no cultural historian would accept the distinction I am making here.

25. One particularly influential statement being Chandra Mohanty, "Under Western Eyes: Feminist Scholarship and Colonial Discourses," *Feminist Review*, 30 (1988), 60–88.

26. Grayzel, *Women's Identities at War*.

27. Leila J. Rupp, *Worlds of Women: The Making of an International Women's Movement* (Princeton, NJ: Princeton University Press, 1997); Bonnie S. Anderson, *Joyous Greetings*.

28. See, e.g., Ian R. Tyrrell, *Woman's World/Woman's Empire: The Woman's Christian Temperance Union in International Perspective, 1880-1930* (Chapel Hill, NC: University of

North Carolina Press, 1991); Daniel T. Rodgers, *Atlantic Crossings: Social Politics in a Progressive Age* (Cambridge, MA: Harvard University Press, 1998).

29. Antoinette Burton's influential work instructively demonstrates this shift. *Burdens of History* sought to establish the imperial location and imperialist assumptions shaping British feminism. However, her more recent essays have questioned this "national" focus to concentrate instead on the ways in which global and imperial power relations produced and structured movements and identities across national lines. See Burton, *Burdens of History; At the Heart of the Empire: Indians and the Colonial Encounter in Late-Victorian Britain* (Berkeley: University of California Press, 1998); and, most interestingly, her review essay "Some Trajectories of 'Feminism' and 'Imperialism,'" in Mrinalini Sinha, Donna Guy, and Angela Woollacott, eds., *Feminisms and Internationalism* (Oxford: Blackwell, 1999), pp. 214–224.

30. Mrinalini Sinha, *Colonial Masculinity: The "Manly Englishman" and the "Effeminate Bengali" in the Late Nineteenth Century* (Manchester: Manchester University Press, 1995); and Mrinalini Sinha, "Suffragism and Internationalism: The Enfranchisement of British and Indian Women under an Imperial State," *The Indian Economic and Social History Review*, 36: 4 (1999), 461–484.

31. Richard Biernacki, *The Fabrication of Labor: Germany and Britain, 1640–1914* (Berkeley: University of California Press, 1995); Ida Blom, "Gender and Nation in International Comparison," in Ida Blom, Karen Hagemann, and Catherine Hall, eds., *Gendered Nations: Nationalisms and Gender Order in the Long Nineteenth Century* (New York: Berg, 2000), pp. 3–26.

32. This is not to say that Weber is less attuned than Anderson to the power of ideas and ideal interests in shaping political and cultural affiliations, but rather to point out that he has an adequate theory of the state, as well as an appreciation of the nation.

33. Donald Meyer, *Sex and Power: The Rise of Women in America, Russia, Sweden, and Italy* (Middletown, CT: Wesleyan University Press, 1987), p. 629. Richard Evans would agree. Although his landmark study is now twenty–five years old and some of the literature on which it was based has been superseded, it remains valuable and unusual in its effort to provide both a comprehensive typology of, and an explanation for the variations between, nationally specific Western feminist movements. Richard Evans, *The Feminists: Women's Emancipation Movements in Europe, America and Australasia, 1840–1920* (London: Croom Helm, 1977).

34. Elizabeth D. Heinemann, *What Difference Does a Husband Make? Women and Marital Status in Nazi and Postwar Germany* (Berkeley: University of California Press, 1999), esp. epilogue, pp. 239–246.

7

THE NATION AND THE COMPARATIVE IMAGINATION

Glenda Sluga

The idea that the nation is the appropriate unit of analysis for the past has been a firmly entrenched aspect of the development of history as a discipline. In the late nineteenth century, the professionalization of history coincided with the general scientific view that nations were natural, inevitable, and highly evolved units of social organization, sociability, and individual subjectivity. History also helped sustain that view. We need only think of the ongoing predominance of nations in the organization of the discipline and in the writing of history, or the ways in which historians have made a practice of commonly evoking national collectivities (the Americans agreed, the English disagreed, for example), and conflating differences that are not regarded as national or "racial." The eminent historian of race, George Fredrickson, has even stated that there is no getting around the nation.[1] Indeed in *The Comparative Imagination*, Fredrickson claims that the nation and national history are fundamental to comparative history.

This chapter looks at *how* the nation has been pivotal to comparative history and the "comparative imagination". Recently, historians have begun to turn to comparative history as a means of escaping the exceptionalist and parochial state of many national histories, arguing that comparison enables a more nuanced understanding of individual nations.[2] However, as I argue in the first part of this chapter, conventional characterizations of the nature of nations are themselves the ideological products of the processes of comparison. The processes of "othering" that historians and social scientists regard as critical to the formation of national identities and the imagining of national communities are framed by the same ways of seeing the world that structure comparative histories.[3] To the extent that nations are imagined communities, they are imagined also through comparisons.

Comparative histories that disregard the ideological function of comparisons in the constitution of national differences are liable to take as self-evident what has been constructed and further entrench those differences rather than analyzing them. In this context, the current historiographical challenge to the nation as a paradigm for historical research and writing has a great deal of relevance for the idea and practice of comparative history. That challenge simultaneously addresses the constructed nature of nations and the forms of power exercised by nations as states.[4] In particular, some historians have suggested that the historical emphasis on nations as an important locus of power actually contributes to the power that nations can exercise or, at least, that can be exercised in their name. They argue that in order to escape this bind it is necessary to seek out and recover the spaces of the past that transcend national frameworks.[5] The second part of this chapter takes as its focus the current interest in transnational history and its impact on both the reconceptualization of the sites of comparative historical analysis and the historical uses of the comparative imagination.

THE COMPARATIVE IMAGINATION

Historians of Britain have emphasized the significance to the formation of a British identity of comparisons with a French "other," while historians of France have noted comparisons and contrasts with Germany in the articulation of a modern French identity.[6] More broadly, Larry Wolff has detailed the conceptions of East European difference which, since the eighteenth century, have contributed to the formation of a European (understood as Western) identity. Wolff has shown that the discursive invention of Eastern Europe was a process "whereby Western Europe also identified itself and affirmed its own precedence."[7] Similarly, Maria Todorova has surveyed the literary construction of the Orientalist subcategory of "the Balkans" by Western intellectuals at the turn of the twentieth century.[8] These studies reveal what Wolff refers to as the "perceived pattern of similarities and differences" that achieved widespread political and cultural authority in Western Europe since the

Enlightenment, and have framed the cultural and political status of specific European nations.[9]

My argument here is that antithetical comparisons have not only shaped ways of seeing (or "imagining") nations and national differences, they have also structured historical analyses of European places and their inhabitants. According to the comparative imaginary outlined by Wolff and Todorova, those nations and nationalities that are defined as Eastern are also rendered backward in comparison with Western states. They are constructed by historians as places where the liberalism that defines Western Europe is not indigenous and where nationalism has consistently produced a "seething cauldron of ethnic and national conflict."[10] We need only consider the example of Trieste, a port city on the Adriatic that until the First World War had been part of the Habsburg empire and that has straddled the cultural and political division of Western and Eastern/Balkan Europe. In academic and populist histories, Trieste is proffered as the point at which European nationalisms have bifurcated: west of Trieste nationalism was benign, but east of Trieste "it was likely to be horrible."[11]

At various moments during the twentieth century, Trieste was claimed by both Italy and Yugoslavia, and at the end of the Second World War it was administered for nearly ten years by a British-American Allied Military Government before it was handed over to Italian authorities in 1954. Historians have commonly attributed Trieste's turbulent political past to the problem of nationalism; that is, how to draw a border separating the two key national groups in the region, Italians and Slavs. Yet, a historical analysis can show that a perceived pattern of similarities and differences such as that outlined by Wolff and Todorova had a strikingly persistent influence on representations of national identities in the region and on interpretations of the political significance of diversity there. Intellectual and political representatives of the states, Britain and the United States, who played key roles in the post-Second World War period in deciding the nationalist political fate of the region reduced complex forms of political and cultural affiliations to the opposition between Italians and Slavs, and to the forms of comparisons between East and West, and the Balkans and Europe, in which they rested. They also represented diversity in Trieste as a problem essentially different from the acceptable manifestations of diversity in their own, British and American, societies. Their representations resonated powerfully with widespread images of the endemic barbarism of the East or "Balkans" in comparison with the civilization of the West, overwhelming any attempts at the local level to counter the forces of exclusivist nationalism or to create the basis for the kind of tolerance of difference that was regarded as fundamental to the functioning of British and American societies. During the Cold War, the British and American authorities who governed Trieste also associated communism with the East and Slavs, and portrayed Trieste itself as Western, Italian, and thus anticommunist, despite the strength of local communist organizations and of communist attempts to cultivate a nonnationalist basis for citizenship.[12]

How such reductive comparisons have influenced politics and come to structure accounts of the past of European peoples and places has its own history. What is striking in that history is the key role of progressive anglophone intellectuals and their emphases on the nation as the most important political form for social progress.[13] For example, in early twentieth-century England, historians such as Arnold Toynbee, Ramsay Muir, Robert Seton-Watson, and Lewis Namier made comparisons between Eastern and Western European states, and, especially between the British and Habsburg empires, central to their theories of nationhood as well as to the writing of national histories.[14] Seton-Watson, founder of the School of Slavonic Studies at the University of London, was a key British advocate of aligning political borders with Europe's natural ethnographic map in Eastern Europe – a process which he summed up as the principle of nationality. Before the First World War, he viewed the "Dual Monarchy" (the Habsburg empire, also known by this time as Austria-Hungary) as the representative of European culture in southeast Europe. It was to be an empire in the image of Britain – with different ethnic and racial groups, united in the figure of the monarch Franz Joseph and the practices of parliamentary institutions.[15] Seton-Watson proposed that "racial" diversity could be held together by a single monarch's exercise of will and by the state's encouragement of rational patriotism—in the image of the British model of statehood.

However, with the outbreak of war, Seton-Watson began to revise his views of the Habsburg Empire, interpreting its diversity as a political problem.[16] The Habsburg empire's failure was now presented as the product of a quasi-natural law of nations, of the need for correspondence between state forms and racial or national identities in what was, by definition, Eastern Europe. These denunciations of the Habsburg empire were heavily implicated in the validation of the existence of diversity within Britain. The Habsburg empire's status as an "Eastern sultanate," and its imperial ambitions were compared and contrasted with the cultural/racial heterogeneity of the British Empire, and the latter was represented as an idealized commonwealth ruled according to the precepts of nationality, autonomy, cooperation, and liberty.[17] "Our [British] belief in racial freedom," Seton-Watson argued, "whether in a liberal confederation of self-governing peoples or in the absolute independence of each, is no fetish. It is an historic truth driven home to our minds by the experience of the British Commonwealth."[18]

Why weren't the national independence movements of Ireland, India, Egypt, or South Africa relevant to Seton-Watson's view of Britain in the same way that nationalist groups within the Habsburg empire were used to redefine the latter's relevance and functionality? The point is that only some comparisons were regarded as legitimate or significant. Intellectuals from Britain, along with France, and the United States—together the three states that took the major responsibility in 1919 for formulating a new national world order—denied the relevance of the principle of nationality for democratic change in their own states despite the demands of the Irish, Catalans, African-Americans, and others. They justified this inconsistency by reference to a comparative understanding of the different proclivities of nations nestled in comparatively different regions of Europe. During the First World War, the plausibility of these inconsistencies (at the time referred to by the American philosopher John Dewey as a "curious anomaly")[19] relied not only on comparisons with the Habsburg empire, where the coexistence of different national/racial groups was presented as unnatural, or places such as Trieste, where the claims of nationalist lobbies were even then regarded as inevitable and unavoidable, but with Germany, where the alleged predominant (Teutonic) disposition licensed a deterministically racial view of the nation and the state. Such conceptions of the different significance of diversity in Eastern and Western Europe have persisted, on the one hand, in historicizations of the racial dimensions of a German *Sonderweg* and the inevitable demise of a "racially" diverse Habsburg empire and, on the other hand, the relative lack of interest in the political implications of racialism and nationalism in states such as Britain.[20]

Written as "cross-national history," comparative history, Fredrickson claims, takes "two stories in two different contexts that are presumptively true by the normal standards of historical evaluation and juxtaposes them in the hope of finding a deeper meaning for each narrative and beyond that, if possible, a larger meaning that applies to both."[21] However, in the examples above—British and American perceptions of the Trieste problem and the history of early twentieth-century ideas of nation—I have taken a slightly different perspective. At one level, these cross-national comparative studies suggest that stories about national differences are intrinsically comparative; on another level, they can be vested with a larger meaning, namely, that *trans*national discourses have shaped and legitimated nations, and established their supposed differences. The history of ideas is particularly conducive to thinking beyond the spatial framework of the nation; in the cases of the historicization of Trieste and of the Habsburg empire, it provides a useful basis for highlighting the importance of the transnational to comparative history in general.

COMPARISON AND TRANSNATIONALISM

A comparative historical perspective can cast into relief complicating evidence of both sameness and difference in the face of neat theoretical patternings of national ideas and identities. Comparing early twentieth-century attitudes towards diversity that emerged in Britain, the United States, and the Habsburg empire can show us that despite the differences and the socially specific resonances of those attitudes in each of these places, there was a similar faith in the possibility and practice of diversity. Comparative history can show us that national histories are deeply interrelated and what is taken as true about them are products of the construction of histories as "national." Thus British intellectuals in particular used the Habsburg empire as a foil for smoothing over the ambivalences and ambiguities in the conceptualization and management of diversity within the British Empire. Comparative histories of nations and of national identities also invite reassessments of the units out of which they are constituted—that is, the nations/states that are the subjects of comparison. Two recently revived trends in historiography are most pertinent to any such possible reassessments: *histoire croisée* and transnational history.[22] Both invoke the notion of intersecting histories rather than pasts neatly bounded in national spaces, even though a comparative account of their development could reveal the respective national origins of their current manifestations: *histoire croisée* as specific to French and German historiography and transnational history to the United States. Here I limit myself to a discussion of transnationalism, if only to emphasize its applicability to a European context.

In 1991, the *American Historical Review* published a forum on transnational history that raised fundamental questions about the place of the nation in the writing of history. The historian Ian Tyrrell critiqued the historiography of the United States for its unreflective investment in the idea of American exceptionalism. Tyrrell argued that historical interest in nations has not simply reflected an objective reality: historians and history continue to be complicit in the making of national identities.[23]

On this basis, he proposed the importance of a comparative approach to national history. Like Fredrickson, Tyrrell claimed that parochialism could only be avoided through comparative studies. Tyrrell has gone on to become a vocal advocate of placing comparative histories in a transnational framework. "Comparison of parts of nations, and of particular movements and issues," he argues, "is absolutely essential to an internationalizing project. Comparative history must be set within broader themes of transnational history, so as to demonstrate the contingent and ever-changing character of the nation."[24]

The term "transnational" evokes the possibility of transcending as much as traversing national spaces. It has emerged in historiography as a means of conceptualizing an alternative spatial framework to the nation, and of offering a critique of the nation itself. In this sense, transnational histories can take many forms. Histories that focus on border regions, historical studies of travel and empire, or of international movements, are all potentially transnational. Indeed, some historians are increasingly hypothesizing and discovering the significance of transnational "imagined communities" such as the Atlantic (or transatlantic) world. Others, such as Tyrrell, argue that even the Atlantic transnational model is too narrow, encouraging as it does (in Tyrrell's words) a Euro-American-centrism. Tyrrell offers instead thematically oriented units of comparison such as "settler societies." This particular comparative focus would bring together the study—if we consider only English-speaking options—of the United States, Canada, Australia, and New Zealand, with the emphasis on their becoming rather than being national.[25]

Transnational histories have in common with comparative history a multinational base. If we were to seek other similarities, we could argue that both place in tension the forms of sameness and difference that shape modes of identification and experience. However, transnational and comparative histories tend to differ in their objectives. Obviously, comparative history usually aims to compare histories of nations, whereas transnational history aims to find links between nations.[26] In the case of Trieste, a comparative study of British and American foreign policy reveals the existence of mutually reinforcing narratives of national difference, particularly the alleged differences between Italians and Slavs. At the end of the Second World War, these narratives bolstered the realism of an Iron Curtain drawn across Europe inevitably separating antagonistic political cultures (Eastern/Slav and Western/Italian) and gave a cultural depth to the conceptualization of the Cold War in the Trieste region. Consequently, a transnational analysis reveals the existence of a narrative of national differences, available and utilized across the Atlantic and sharing hierarchical typologies of nations. Indeed, the authority of this narrative lay in its transnational referentiality. My conclusions are not unlike those reached by Prasenjit Duara, a historian of China, who, by focusing on the shifting borders of the politics of literature, has shown that "the construction of national authenticity in East Asia draws on circulating cultural resources within this transnational region, or at the very least, the region filters global processes."[27]

Given then that all national histories, like national identities, are intrinsically comparative, the question that I have been faced with in each of my historical projects is whether histories that involve more than one nation should explicitly compare nations. If I discover links across and between nationally bounded experiences and ideas that enhance my understanding of their similarities and differences, to what extent is it important to use that understanding to recast our knowledge of individual national histories? By referring transnational histories back to the nation, am I not reinforcing the forms of historical and cultural imagining that reify national communities? Can I avoid reinforcing the borders of the nation? Should we feel the compunction to refer transnational analyses back to national models when the power exercised by the nation-state, or its representatives is not the specific focus of analysis? What about when it is?

In answer to some of these questions, Tyrrell argues for a comparative history sensitive to transnational forms of power that can shift our perspective of, in the case he offers, the national history of the United States.

> What is needed is the linking of comparative analysis of settler societies with transnational contexts of imperial power and the expansion of global markets under capitalism. With this modification, settler society models can be useful for enriching American historiography. The result would not be to provide ready-made reinterpretation of American historiography but, rather, to open up new questions and challenge unthinking assumptions concerning unilinear and homogenous national patterns. American history from this perspective looks different than it does from within, and from that of a purely European or Atlantic re-take on American events.[28]

In a similar fashion, Fredrickson enjoins the comparative historian to be wary of national exceptionalism by beginning with the assumption "that each of her cases may be equally distinctive, equally likely to embody a transnational pattern or to depart from it."[29] In both of these examples, the nation functions as a critical framework because here nations as states exercise direct forms of power. But although understanding national differences *per se* is a key objective of modern historiography, its virtues are limited, particularly because the practice of history is itself so profoundly complicit in the comparative imagining that gives shape to those differences.

There are, as Tyrrell suggests, contiguities between the comparative and transnational approaches to history that are relevant to the problem of national history. Comparative historians such as Fredrickson propose that in order to write good comparative history it is necessary to master the history of one nation, learn the history of more than one nation, and gain proficiency in a number of languages. Multilingualism, which might mean a sensitivity to dialect as much as national language, is also a prerequisite of many forms of transnational history, although not all. But, importantly, transnational history encourages making nations the subject of interrogation and rethinking the units out of which histories are made.

At its most challenging, a transnational approach usually draws upon the kind of multidisciplinarity that has nurtured post-colonial studies, in particular, knowledge of social and literary theory, in order to critique the forms of comparative imagination that merely accept or assume the nation and, further, to cultivate a comparative imagination that imagines beyond the nation. As a result, transnational history also potentially undermines the possibility of a comparative history grounded in nations. What is there to be compared *between* nations if one is working at uncovering processes that occur *across* or *in spite of* them? Although states exist as nations, the historian does have to go on working with the nation at the same time as she recalls that the conventional forms of comparison which inform the writing of history need to be illuminated before alternative kinds of comparison can be "imagined." Any comparative history, even if its subjects are cities or empires, has to begin with a deconstruction of the history of representations of nations; as Duara has argued: "it is necessary not merely to overlook different boundaries but also to see how modern territorial boundaries are illusory means of keeping histories apart."[30]

My brief historical examples of the construction of national identities and differences in Europe in the first section of this essay should alert us to the ways in which comparative histories built out of assumed differences between nations replicate conventions that have their own history. In the cases of Trieste and the Habsburg empire, those histories involve the conventional ways of seeing specific national differences that were articulated and reified in the early twentieth century. There is no ground zero for comparative history, no untainted past that we can pare back to in order to arrive at an originary point from which new narratives completely disentangled from value judgments about differences and the reasons for them might be constructed. If we can contemplate a dictum for the writing of comparative history, it might be to consider the framework of transnationalism. When that history involves ideas specifically, it should also consider the extent to which the movement of ideas across and between national borders constitutes and has constituted a primary site of political and cultural "power," be it in regard to the creation of nonnational identities or the dissemination of ideas about nations and national differences themselves.

***

In a survey of historical writing on nationalism, Anthony Smith has argued that historians have a tendency to extreme skepticism towards the idea of the nation and national identity.[31] However, putting the counterargument—that this historical tendency has been accompanied by a fascination with the functionality and inevitability of nations and their borders even in the writing of comparative and transnational histories—would hardly arouse controversy among historians. This is evident in the current debate among historians about transnational history and its value, as well as the more general anxiety that any threat to a national framework of historical study tends to arouse. There are many examples of the resilience of the national frameworks that organize the discipline and which historians themselves police.[32] Even in the excavation of representations of difference and identity that structure comparisons, in the interrogation of implicit and explicit comparisons that inform historical assumptions concerning a particular place, it is no easy task to write, let alone think, outside the nation. Yet those who evoke transnational history aspire to re-evaluate the place of the nation in history. A history engaged with the (transnational) movement of ideas across nations might still use a comparative basis to question the constructions of national difference that lie at the heart of comparative history. It might then simultaneously ask not only the question of how different are nations, but what can I learn about the thing I am comparing, about its identity as a thing in itself, through the process of comparison. In this context, what is required is not less skepticism or fewer comparisons, but more historical emphasis on "curious anomalies," on the recovery of the complexity and ambivalence of past narratives of nations, sameness and difference, with the emphasis on the changing political significance of difference itself.

REFERENCES

1. George Fredrickson, *The Comparative Imagination: On the History of Racism, Nationalism, and Social Movements* (Berkeley: University of California Press, 2000).
2. Susan Pedersen, 'What is political history now?' in *What is History Now,* D. Cannadine, ed. (Palgrave, 2002) p. 48.
3. This is not a new perspective. Since the late nineteenth century, historians and social scientists have been pointing this out, if within different theoretical frameworks.
4. Fredrickson argues that we cannot abandon the nation as the unit of comparative study because of the power exercised by nations as states. Yet he also states that nations are the key unit of a specific form of comparative history known as "cross-national history," and that the comparative history of nations is important if we are to remove parochialism from the study of individual nations.
5. See J. M. Hansen, *The Lost Promise of Patriotism: Debating American Identity, 1890–1920* (Chicago, 2003), and Prasenjit Duara, "Transnationalism and National Histories," in Thomas Bender, ed., *Rethinking American History in a Global Age* (Berkeley, 2002)
6. See, for example, the work of Linda Colley and Pierre Nora.
7. Larry Wolff, *Inventing Eastern Europe: The Map of Civilization on the Mind of the Enlightenment* (Stanford, CA, 1994), p. 360.
8. Maria Todorova, *Imagining the Balkans* (New York, 1997).
9. Wolff, p. 371.
10. Roger Brubaker, "Myths and Misconceptions in the Study of Nationalism", in J.A. Hall, ed., *The State of the Nation: Ernest Gellner and the Theory of Nationalism* (Cambridge, 1998), pp. 273–274.
11. Ernest Gellner, *Nationalism* (London, 1998), p. 56.
12. For the contradictions in the communist position see G. Sluga, *The Problem of Trieste and the Italo-Yugoslav Border: Difference, Identity and Sovereignty in Twentieth Century Europe* (Stony Brook, NY: State University of New York, 2001), Ch. 3–6.
13. G. Sluga, *What is a Nation? A History of Ideas of Nation and Nationality in Britain, France and the United States, 1871–1921* (forthcoming).
14. However, in each case the representations of national difference and identity that accompanied/informed the comparisons both fit and did not fit the enveloping narratives of regional (i.e., Western or Eastern) identities.
15. R. Seton-Watson, *The Southern Slav Question and the Habsburg Monarchy* (London, 1911), p. 341.
16. R. Seton-Watson, *The War and Democracy* (London, 1914), p. 256.
17. In some cases too, Austria-Hungary was the antithesis of the United States, whose "Anglo-Saxon" core defined the centrifugal tendencies of national combination; see, e.g., C. Pergler, *The Heart of Europe* (address in Washington DC, December 11, 1916, Conference of Oppressed or Dependent Nationalities (Bohemian [Czech] National Alliance, Chicago, 1917), p. 16.
18. R. Seton-Watson, "The Passing of the Status Quo," *New Europe* 64 (January 3, 1918).
19. John Dewey, "The Principle of Nationality," *Menorah's Journal* 3 (1917), 203–208, republished in Dewey, *The Middle Works 1899–1924, vol 10: 1916–1917,* ed., Jo An Boydston (Carbondale, IL, 1980), pp. 286–287.

20. Even the notion that such comparative characterizations might reflect some obvious or common sense kernel of truth about national differences is more distracting than helpful historically. At specific historical moments the political significance of the diversity of the Austria-Hungarian empire could be construed in radically divergent ways, or England's Englishness could be both German and anti-German.

21. Fredrickson, *The Comparative Imagination*, p. 14.

22. I argue that they have been revived on the basis that *histoire croisée* has been borrowed from Marc Bloch, and transnational history is the latest manifestation of attempts since the nineteenth century to cast history in an international context.

23. Ian Tyrrell, "American Exceptionalism in an Age of International History," *American Historical Review* 96: 4 (1991), 1031–1055.

24. Ian Tyrrell, "Beyond the View from Euro-America: Environment, Settler Societies, and the Internationalization of American History," in T. Bender, ed., *Rethinking American History in a Global Age*, p. 176.

25. Most of the essays in this volume support the same impetus that lies behind the attempt to revisit comparative history, that is, an interest in the transnational as a unit of experience and analysis.

26. See G. Sluga, *The Problem of Trieste and the Italo-Yugoslav Border: Difference, Identity and Sovereignty in Twentieth Century Europe* (Stony Brook, NY: State University of New York, 2001).

27. P. Duara, "Transnationalism and National Histories," in T. Bender, ed., *Rethinking American History in a Global Age*, p. 34.

28. Tyrrell, "Beyond the View from Euro-America: Environment, Settler Societies, and the Internationalization of American History," p. 171.

29. Fredrickson, *The Comparative Imagination*, p. 52.

30. Duara, "Transnationalism and National Histories," p. 43. Duara also argues that deconstruction is an unavoidable task for the historian, p. 38

31. A. Smith, "Nationalism and the historians," in G. Balakrishnan, ed., *Mapping the Nation* (London, 1996), p. 182.

32. This is evident from the first essay in the collection *Rethinking American History in a Global Age* and authored by Duara, who states that the objective of transnational histories should be to make the nation the subject of interrogation. By contrast, the book's editor, Thomas Bender, has disassociated the imperative of rethinking the transnational context of United States' history from any fundamental critique of national history. From his standpoint, transnational history exists to enhance the national history of the United States.

8

COMPARATIVE AND CROSS-NATIONAL HISTORY: APPROACHES, DIFFERENCES, PROBLEMS

Michael Miller

This chapter makes a simple argument. Cross-national history may become comparative history, but the two approaches are different kinds of historiographical animals with different objectives and differing benefits. There are, of course, those who would disagree and who would argue that all history that crosses boundary lines, particularly those of countries in a period dominated by the nation-state, is, by definition, comparative. I advocate a more limited framework that aligns with what comparativists have always argued: that comparative history explains in ways noncomparative history cannot. Comparative history, I would suggest, comprises primarily, but not exclusively, several pursuits: (1) searching for explanations through the comparison of similar historical phenomena with varying outcomes; (2) scrutinizing actors and factors by looking in one subject area for what has been found elsewhere; and (3) testing theory by subjecting it to the messiness of history.

In all these cases, the emphasis is on causality or the opening up of vistas heretofore obscured by a lack of alternatives. To a very large extent I am conflating comparative history with a history of contrasts, where differences, rather than similarities, drive explanation. But I also include under the comparative rubric the weighing of similarities against previously presumed differences, or the identification of common patterns that have tied particular national experiences together. In both cases the accent remains on specific (often national) cases and common lines of development that can be traced in each. What ties all of comparative history together, as I understand it, is the deployment of a comparative methodology to say something meaningful about similarities or differences.

By cross-national history I imply the pursuit of a historical story across several national experiences without the impulse to make comparative evaluations. What had been done (or might have been done) within national history is here done through multinational histories. Ineluctably, cross-national history will take on comparative dimensions. Yet this need not be its defining feature. In fact, as I discuss below, eliding cross-national history into comparative history can have a crimping effect and, in any event, will alter the agenda, and consequently the shape and direction, that cross-national history might otherwise assume.

My present project—Europe and the maritime world in the twentieth century—is one I would define as more cross-national than comparative, although the two methods intertwine throughout the study. The dominance of one approach despite the persistent, if limited, intrusion of the other has challenged me, however, to investigate their divergences. I have especially been drawn to examining what barriers in comparative history have blocked a more comprehensive commitment to that perspective in my own multinational research. I have considered, too, the greater rewards to be culled from doing cross-national history. It is this questioning that informs the following essay.

In my study of the maritime world over the past century, I have spread my research over five countries—Belgium, Britain, France, Germany, and the Netherlands—and I have utilized secondary sources to be still more geographically expansive. By maritime world I meant the seaborne movements of peoples and goods. To study these movements I have cast the topic broadly to include nearly all business sectors from shipping companies to ports, intermediaries such as ship agents and freight forwarders, stevedore and terminal operators, trading companies, plantations, markets, and riverboat feeder companies. I have concentrated on European-based networks of operations and flows, but the very nature of the topic rendered my coverage global.

My motivations for undertaking this project have been several. For many years I have taught mostly European-wide history courses, so it made sense to journey beyond national history (modern French history in my case) for a new project at this stage in my career. If learning a new language (Dutch) was the price that would have to be paid, the opportunity to live and conduct research in cities I scarcely knew was a sufficient inducement. In addition, I sought a subject that would allow me to stitch together the two halves of twentieth-century history and to place modern European history within its proper global setting. A study of the maritime world fit both particulars. Most of all, since my first book on the Bon Marché Department Store[1], I have been drawn to the business enterprise as an organizer of the processes of modern life. What interests me are the exchanges between business and its wider context over the past century.

My intent, therefore, is to reconstruct how this maritime world worked and, in particular, the networks through which it worked. Then comes the question of exchange: how European and global history shaped the workings and culture of the maritime business community and how that community's operations have in turn affected the world in which we live. Several themes run through the account I am writing. One is an examination of maritime business culture, its complex dichotomies, and the fundamental changes introduced into that culture by the container revolution. A second theme focuses on the linkages between maritime history and the history of imperialism, including the retreat from empire following the Second World War. Encompassing these two themes is a third, the shift from an earlier globally focused system to the globalized world of today.

The comparative method has been built into this design, as one example, the comparative history of European twentieth-century ports, demonstrates. The flows of peoples and goods into and out of Northwestern Europe, the most heavily developed and industrialized quadrant of the continent, pass through many harbors, but over the past hundred years they have mostly converged on seven great ports. Five of these—London, Liverpool, Hamburg, Rotterdam, and Antwerp—have traditionally led, followed by two others, Bremen and Le Havre. Yet the fortunes of all these ports have varied over time. Of the big five, the three continental ports have continued to flourish. In the 1960s, Rotterdam overtook New York as the largest port in the world. Antwerp's vast installations are among the most impressive in the world. Hamburg has had its ups and downs since the Second World War, but it is still one of the continent's largest container ports.

Fate has been less kind to London and Liverpool. Throughout the first two thirds of the century, London was probably the greatest

European port. When the PLA (Port of London Authority) was formed in 1908 to run the great docks of the Thames, there were another three hundred private wharves with fifteen miles of quays extending up and down the river. Within this extraordinary entrepôt, over a half million tons of goods at a time were stored in PLA warehouses. On the eve of the Second World War, London led Europe in the arrival of ships (by net registered tons), and its seaborne traffic in metric tons was second only to Rotterdam, where bulk cargo dominated.[2] By the 1970s, however, nearly all the private wharves had shut down as had the great docks, save Tilbury far downriver: London had fallen off the international charts. Liverpool's fate was even sadder. Once home to some of the most renowned shipping lines and Britain's principal port for exports, Liverpool has become a second-tier port. Today it is one of Europe's poorest big cities, its still striking mercantile architecture testifying only to past glories and vanished wealth. As for Bremen and Le Havre, they remain major European ports but play a smaller role in world trade than in the past. Bremen has been overshadowed by Hamburg. Le Havre, a port of considerable potential in the nineteenth century, lost ground in the twentieth to the great North Sea ports: Hamburg, Rotterdam, and Antwerp.

To explain these successes and declines invites a comparative perspective. To point to London or Liverpool's fall without simultaneously accounting for Rotterdam or Antwerp's continued prosperity would only account for half the story. What must be explained is what one did right that the other did wrong, or what one could do that the other could not, or what befell one that did not befall another. No single answer will do, but a series of comparisons can suggest useful explanations.

One approach is to compare these cities spatially. Liverpool was never a one-product harbor, but its proximity to Lancashire and Manchester turned it into Britain's premier cotton importing and textile exporting port. The port of London had the greatest consumer concentration in Europe as its hinterland, shared the same space as the world's financial and trading center, and, with Liverpool, operated as the nodal point of the world's largest empire. On the continent, Rotterdam and Antwerp rose to preeminence with the unification and industrialization of Germany. Waterways from Rotterdam extended deep into the Ruhr and along the Rhine watershed. No North Sea port city was better positioned than Antwerp for rail connections to southern Germany, north and northeastern France, Switzerland, and northern Italy and the Danube, as well as to the heavily industrialized Belgium–Luxembourg zone. Space, in the form of hinterlands and trading networks, determined what ports could become.

Alterations of space also had their negative effects. After Germany seized Alsace-Lorraine in 1871, the railroad and business connections that were then constructed shifted Alsatian, Swiss, and northern Italian trade from Le Havre to Antwerp.[3] The separation of eastern and western Europe after World War Two seriously disrupted Hamburg's Elbe-based hinterland and consequently its former competitive position. Most of all, spatial alterations slashed London's and Liverpool's competitive advantages by the second half of the century. Decolonization meant the end of trade patterns centered on the two great imperial ports. Australian trade with Japan, for example, surpassed Australian trade with Britain after the war. British trade focused increasingly on Europe. Liverpool was poorly positioned for this transition, however, and Channel ports other than London offered superior locations, especially with the coming of roll-on/roll-off shipping. Containerization, which revolutionized shipping in the 1960s and 1970s, put paid, spatially, to the two ports. Liverpool was on the wrong side of the country for anything other than transatlantic traffic. Traffic to Europe divided between main ports and feeder ports, with London consigned to the latter. Containerization demanded easy road access in and out of harbor terminals, and older big-city ports like London had trouble meeting these requirements. Britain would command a large container trade, but, in humiliating fashion, its largest container port became Felixstowe, a location off the map to all but the initiated.

Meanwhile post-war spatial arrangements continued to favor Rotterdam and Antwerp. The pre-war success of both cities had been linked to Germany's driving role in the European economy. Both benefited from the post-war economic revival of Western Europe and the West German "economic miracle." The director of the port of Rotterdam explained the port's advantages comparatively in the late 1960s. Within a distance of five hundred kilometers of Rotterdam could be found practically all the important industrial and demographic centers of Europe, with a total population of 160,000,000 inhabitants, whereas 50,000,000 people lived within the same radius of New York. The Rhine was the busiest river in the world, the North Sea "the heaviest navigated sea," and Rotterdam lay at the intersection of both.[4]

Varying degrees of state intercession offer another explanation. All states intervened in one way or another to promote their seaborne economies. But some states intervened more effectively or with greater resources. Asking why again requires comparative analysis. For instance, a number of states granted preferential rail rates to deflect rail traffic from one port to another. Germany did this to advantage Hamburg and Bremen, whereas geographical and business imperatives should have directed that traffic to Rotterdam or Antwerp. France likewise sought to channel Antwerp traffic to Dunkirk, but its policy was less systematic in part because French industrialists in the east preferred to ship via Antwerp, where they could get the best rates, the best connections, and the best conditions. In statist France, practically all networks ran through Paris, where ministerial decision making had to balance the conflicting interests of shippers and ports. Nor was this balancing inward surprising since the reigning mentality in Paris has always been more continental than maritime. Consequently, when the Common Market was first created it was the Dutch and Belgians who maneuvered for water and roadway advantages for their harbors; French priorities lay elsewhere. The British state, for its part, let matters run their course while containerization gutted old port facilities. A traditional commitment to market forces might have had some bearing here, but it is difficult to argue only that case as Labour was in power for a good part of this period. Government reports and direct intervention—particularly into the organization of dock labor—testify to state activism. More likely, the critical reason for state neglect was once again spatial. Unlike the competition among continental ports, the competition in Britain was simply between one British port and another. The traffic was going to come and go, whether through London, Liverpool, Dover, or Felixstowe.[5]

Port fortunes also rose or fell as a consequence of the role of business communities and networks. Hamburg and Bremen port communities soldered civic identities to merchant commerce and international trade. Alongside powerful port networks, there were international networks built through trading companies, ship agencies, forwarders, and some of the world's largest shipping companies. Thus when two world wars wiped out infrastructures, the identities, pride, networks, and contacts remained, constituting a reservoir of knowledge and skill that could be used in rebuilding. Rotterdam, too, developed powerful overseas networks, although they required substantial adjustments in a post-colonial world. To attract shipping and trade, the city built the New Waterway in the latter part of the nineteenth century, allowing for easy passage up the Maas without bridges or locks. Working together, port authorities and terminal operators provided superior facilities for the bulk cargo traffic in which the port dominated. Large integrated operators offered services and rates to attract inland business. In the

1960s, the port and business community aggressively proceeded to deepen the channel, encourage business investment, and, most critically, to obtain the first transatlantic containerized routings. Antwerp businessmen just as aggressively developed networks and practices to attract and hold traffic. They established quick dispatch as an Antwerp specialty, promoted extensive liner service, lobbied for government investment, and jointly resolved areas of conflict: harbor interests were held paramount. In Le Havre, on the other hand, earlier business energies flagged, while power fell to Paris-based business groups whose interests did not always coincide with those of the port.

Liverpool's business networks in many ways approximated those of Hamburg. This was a city of international merchants and major shipping companies. The latter joined together in a powerful lobby, the Liverpool Steamship Owners Association, to represent interests often intertwined with those of Merseyside. The Liverpool Cotton Exchange further fixed business through the port. Abroad, port representatives worked closely with Liverpool shipping men to promote shipping through Liverpool. But whereas Hamburg's trading and maritime networks remained a source of strength, Liverpool's slowly unravelled. Increasingly, shipping or trading headquarters shifted from Liverpool to London. The city's proudest shipping companies entered London-based groups or retreated before the tide of containerization, and the Cotton Exchange declined after the Second World War. London's networks also faltered. There, too, markets and home-based companies withered. The post-war city, as David Kynaston writes, became far more financial than commercial. In a larger sense, London's networks flowed through the city, which remained one of the great capital and service hubs of the world. However, city merchants and financiers, especially in the new maritime business culture of the late twentieth century that did not require one ever to set foot on a quay, felt no personal commitment to making their money through the port of London. Whereas business networks formed the backbone of certain ports, elsewhere they failed to perform that function, or simply lacked the wherewithal to do so.[6]

So far so good. Yet, if comparative history excels in depicting broader patterns of similarities and differences,[7] and in exhuming the causes for each, it nonetheless also possesses its pitfalls, blind spots, black holes, and dead ends, as I discovered at an early stage in this project when I contemplated what it would take to write a comparative history of port cities. Initially, my plan was to do simply that, with the presumption that in port cities the port played the defining role in city

life, politics, and identities. A quick review of the most basic of municipal documents, city council minutes, and discussions for Liverpool or
Rotterdam revealed, however, that city attentions were focused occasionally on port matters, but far more often on topics such as schools,
churches, roads, gas lines, transportation, and the like, in effect the
same preoccupations of any sizable urban agglomeration in modern
times. Obviously there would be more to the story than just the affairs
of city council meetings, but immediately the issue arose of to what
degree had the presence of the port been *the* defining feature of the history of these cities.[8] By the logical implications of comparative methodology, to elucidate whether port cities had a specific history and to
distinguish just what that had been, I would, it seemed, be required to
extend the comparison to include one or several non-port cities as well.

That could be done, but at the price of forgoing a deep knowledge of
all these cities and their people. How, for instance, could power relations be delineated without knowing how power worked, the family,
business, or personal networks through which power operated, the
sources of counterpower that could be brought to bear, and thus who
or which groups truly possessed power at specific moments in a city's
history? And without such knowledge for a port city, how would it be
possible to comprehend the degree to which port business or port
affairs determined city affairs? Something similar could be said for city
identities and mentalities. To scratch beneath the surface to determine,
for instance, just how cosmopolitan in outlook or personal relations
port-city people were would require a deep familiarity with the city
and its inhabitants. All this knowledge could be obtained, but it would
be difficult to do for more than two cities, and even then, knowing each
city as well as the other would be an exceptional accomplishment.

In the end, I chose to pursue a more comprehensive study of the
modern maritime world because this corresponded to my larger interests concerning business and society, Europe and the world, and global
flows. Yet the initial experience was instructive, because it pointed to
the unresolved flaw in comparative history: what is gained in scope is
most likely surrendered in depth. That is a trade-off that can be accepted but not ignored, and certainly not dismissed. Writing good
national history remains a daunting task because no one can be com-
petent in all dimensions of one country's past. Still, we strive to make
our focused histories meaningful to national specialists who may care
precious little about our particular topic but who want to know how it
might make them rethink the larger national context and the arguments that have structured the historiography. We do this by training

as French or German or British historians and by supposedly "mastering" the historiography of our chosen fields. We, of course, rarely master anything outside our focused research, but "comparatively" we attain a feel for our national history fields that is difficult to replicate across the continent or even across one frontier for the simple reason that these national histories remain the starting point and their historiographies are immense and growing.

As a consequence, most comparative history that has been undertaken has been limited to two, perhaps three countries. In one exceptional example from the past decade, Susan Pedersen's work on the origins of differing welfare systems in Britain and France,[9] the author succeeds because of her sophisticated conceptual apparatus but no less because of her deep research in both British and French archives and printed materials. Yet how many other historians will be prepared to dig as deeply as Pedersen has into two national histories? How more exceptional still an effort would it have been had Pedersen extended her analysis (with equal quality) to a third or fourth European country? Reading a few secondary works on another nation or region does not make one a comparative historian. Even extended study of a second national history does not necessarily qualify one as a true comparativist. It is one thing to have a familiarity with the secondary literature of other countries and something else again to be able to subject the arguments of these works to the same rigorous evaluation one brings to texts in one's principal geographical focus of study.

Like most modern Europeanists, my training was divided between concentration on modern European history and a specific national field, in my case France. For over twenty years, I have mostly taught courses that are European-wide, including the survey course in modern European history every spring semester at Syracuse University. Throughout my current research, however, I have never felt that I could bring to my examination of documents in Hamburg or Rotterdam, or London and Liverpool the same authoritative perspective that I could for research on France. When examining French documents, I see where they may fit with current interpretations or where they may not. I determine their meaning, moreover, based on my own evaluation of the persuasiveness of the professional literature. But it has not been possible to research, write, teach, serve on committees, and simultaneously to obtain, let alone sustain, a comparable knowledge of the vast secondary literature on Britain or Germany. Here again is where depth does matter. The wider the scope, the thinner is the command. Comparative history has the power to raise questions about similarities and differences, and in the process to provoke new ways of thinking about old verities. It is less well endowed to challenge those verities because it depends upon them as a platform from which to embark. As a result, the comparativist is more likely to affirm orthodox interpretations than to marshall evidence that forces us to rethink a field, as monographs in national history do at their best. In vaunting the strengths of comparative methodology it is also necessary to recognize its greatest shortcomings: claiming knowledge yet depending on received wisdom; circular argumentation that proves the explanatory framework with which one began; and, as a parody of the comparative promise, reducing one nation's history to a foil for another's. It would be wise to recall, also, that the best comparative history to come will ineluctably rely upon the best scholarship in national history.

There are other difficulties to doing comparative history well or at all; some of these I confronted almost daily in my research. One was the incomparable character of source materials. A good example is shipping company archives. These tend to be enormous, sometimes filling entire warehouse bays or the equivalent of several football fields in linear shelf space. But their contents vary from one company to another. Whereas Dutch shipping company archives have preserved extraordinary runs of correspondence, the Hapag correspondence records in Hamburg are far spottier, and the Compagnie Générale Transatlantique in Le Havre appears to have lost nearly all its correspondence files. Certain company records such as the Hapag files are strongest on the first sixty years of the century. The Compagnie Maritime Belge archives in Antwerp have primarily preserved materials since the Second World War. Some records provide superb glimpses into the early days of containerization. Others do not. Some records reveal top-level decision making. Others are stronger on day-to-day operations. None of these variations has created insurmountable difficulties. With the aid of secondary works or research in other kinds of collections, it is often possible to fill in the gaps. But how actually does one *compare* under these circumstances? Clearly certain similar features crop up from one archive to the next, but not all. Absences are one way that comparativists can proceed, but not very well if the absence is determined by source problems rather than by contemporaries' choices. At very low levels of interpretation, the problem can be most apparent. For instance, Holland-America Line correspondence was so voluminous that I was obliged to select certain years for a close examination of company practice and policy. The results, however, could not be compared with other companies where I had to settle for what correspondence was available. At more general levels of network formation or ship agency relations, the depth of information again varied from one collection to another—an indication of remnants, but not necessarily of past realities. For trading companies with sparser records and histories, the comparative limitations could be still sharper.

Paradoxically, comparative history can also suffer from similarities rather than differences. Again shipping company records are instructive. What struck me was how much one collection read like another, despite gaps. The firms ran their operations the same way. Their business trips reported on the same matters and pursued the same agendas. Their departments carried out the same functions in much the same manner. Their agency relations were frequently identical. The problems of one firm are reminiscent of the problems of the others.

Common attributes need not be an obstacle to comparative insight, of course. In her work on gender in metalworking industries in the era of the First World War, Laura Lee Downs remarks that she adopted a comparative perspective "in order to suggest how national culture and differences in state structures defined distinctive routes to what were, in many important respects, rather similar outcomes."[10] For shipping, a parallel approach might be rewarding, but what if there were not distinctive routes or if looking for these only repeats what we already know of different national contexts with shipping stirred in? Then we would have advanced a little, but not very far, and in the process the very pursuit would obscure the more central story of a common European business history better served through a cross-national approach where different questions drive narrative and analysis.

Finally, comparative history for modern times implies comparison across frontiers or oceans, whereas the most fertile territory for certain comparative topics may remain within national boundaries. Let me return to the history of ports. I have shown how comparative history can chart the relative fortunes or misfortunes of ports in five countries, yet it would be just as correct to cast the comparison as one of intrastate rivalries, which occurred in nearly all maritime nations: Hamburg versus Bremen; Amsterdam versus Rotterdam; Le Havre versus Dunkirk and Rouen; Bordeaux versus Marseilles; London versus Liverpool. It would be interesting, of course, to compare two or three of these competitive sets. Still, a study of, say, Hamburg and Bremen would in the end dig deeper into the history of these two maritime communities than would an interstate comparison. It would identify different questions, and it would tease out issues in German national history that an international comparison would be less likely to produce.

All of these limitations have bearing on writing a multinational history of trade flows, geographical shifts, business, and business culture in the twentieth century. Where national differences clearly did matter, for example, regarding the fate of ports (despite the final caveat above), then comparative methodology determined design. But what of the larger outlines of the history? For instance, to reconstruct how the maritime world worked and the networks through which it worked, I have looked at company histories, how networks were built and sustained, the problems of running a shipping company or a port or a ship agency or a trading company, and how all these components interacted to provide the basic transportation infrastructure a global economy requires. I have scrutinized scheduling and routing questions. I have observed the business side of moving people as tourists, administrators, pilgrims, or plantation coolies. I have examined war experiences and training experiences. I have examined business cultures that are at once national and cosmopolitan, clubby yet tough-minded, and I have traced the development of a new shipping culture that reflects the revolutionary changes that have come with containerization as well as more general business changes. At the most basic level, I have wished to know what shipping companies, trading companies, agents, forwarders, terminal operators, and port authorities did on a day-to-day basis, because this is the material from which an understanding of the system and its workings must be built. None of these concerns is especially advanced through comparative history, and the very effort of delineating a system runs counter to national differences or even national "routings." Many of the preceding subjects would fit poorly into a purely comparative study. To attempt to do so would leave too much historical footage on the cutting-room floor and force the argument. Moreover, where sources are uneven, a strictly comparative framework would itself run into difficulty. If comparative history had definite advantages, nonetheless the better fit was a cross-national study that pursued a historical story across several national experiences and where the accent was on the larger maritime history rather than on the national crucibles through which it emerged.

At their best, cross-national and comparative histories are complementary rather than competing methods of writing multinational history, and it is difficult to write one without incorporating the other, as I have attempted to demonstrate in my discussion on ports. But their agendas, or the questions they ask, are not the same. Whereas comparative history's strength is its ability to explain varying patterns, cross-national history's advantage is its ability to reach beyond what could be accomplished through comparative history alone. To illustrate this point, it is only necessary to examine the interweaving of maritime history with the history of colonization and then retreat from empire following the Second World War.

International shipping and trading before 1945 was global, yet to a strikingly large degree imperially focused. Britain's largest shipping company, the P&O, and the greatest of Liverpool-based firms, Alfred Holt & Company (also known as Blue Funnel or Ocean Steamship Company), centered their lines on imperial ports to the East. Two of the most prominent Dutch companies, the Rotterdamsche Lloyd and the SMN (Stoomvaart Maatschappij "Nederland") ran their principal lines to and from the Dutch East Indies. The French Messageries Maritimes focused on the East, particularly ports such as Saigon and Shanghai. The Compagnie Générale Transatlantique ran primarily on the North Atlantic route, but it also built a sizable business to French North Africa and the Antilles. Belgium's largest shipping company, the Compagnie Maritime Belge, evolved out of shipping to the Congo. Of the five countries I have concentrated on only Germany, with no empire after the First World War, broke the pattern. Still, all the great German companies, in one way or another, operated in conjunction with the colonial systems.

Many enterprises worked with or through trading houses that were themselves often nexuses of their own imperial trading, shipping, plantation, and manufacturing networks. Managing P&O's agency network in the East was Mackinnon Mackenzie, a powerful company on the Asian subcontinent that controlled or managed tea properties, cotton mills, and shipping and riverboat lines. Lord Inchcape (James Lyle Mackay) who turned the P&O group into the largest shipping company in the world after the First World War, was a Mackinnon Mackenzie man. He and his successors were to build their own Inchcape Group into a vast shipping, trading, and managing empire extending from India to Southeast Asia, East Asia, the Persian Gulf, and East Africa. The Dutch Rotterdamsche Lloyd operated through Internatio (N.V. Internationale Crediet–en Handelsvereeniging "Rotterdam"), a large Rotterdam trading and plantation company based in the Dutch East Indies with over thirteen hundred office personnel in the East in 1939.[11] A list of other significant Dutch Trading Companies in the East Indies would include Borsumij (Borneo Sumatra Handel Maatschaapij), Geo Wehry, Hagemeyer, and Tels and Company, and a British list for only the East would need to mention James Finlay & Co., Ralli Brothers, Harrisons & Crosfield, W. Mansfield & Co. (Holt's Singapore agent), Butterfield and

Swire (Holt's agents in China), Jardine Matheson, and the Borneo Company simply for a start. Another list could be compiled of West African companies such as the huge United Africa Company that was part of the Unilever network, or the French CFAO (Compagnie Française de l'Afrique Centrale).

The Second World War, and particularly Japanese conquests in East and Southeast Asia, set in motion the end of this system. After 1945, many of the trading companies showed considerable energy and inge-nuity in starting up again. But they found burned plantations, plun-dered supplies, colleagues who had wasted in internment camps, and, most notably, a new political environment of contestation and disorder that made returning to pre-war conditions impossible. Retreat from empire, communist victory in China, and new nationally oriented regimes in India and Indonesia forced shipping and trading companies to seek new markets, networks, and territories.

A natural response was to pursue alternative tropical activities else-where in Asia or in Africa, although often the result was simply delayed repetition of what had been experienced on imperial home ground. Some firms found more success pioneering new markets or routings to the Dominions, especially Australia. Some companies, such as Swires, which had been forced off the Chinese mainland, used their assets and knowledge to diversify and thereby continued to prosper. A far more common response, however, was a thorough revision in company iden-tity and location, frequently with a new focus on North America or Europe rather than the post-colonial world.

The experience of decolonization, despite territorial variations, thus launched a new stage in European maritime history. Yet the story of change was also a far more complicated one. Three other fac-tors—technological, managerial, and geopolitical—were no less influ-ential than retreat from empire in altering the late twentieth-century shipping and trading world. First, there was the demise of seaborne passenger traffic aside from ferries or cruises. In 1958, Pan American initiated jet travel across the Atlantic. By the early 1960s, trans-Atlantic crossings by ship fell from fifty percent of the market to less than one quarter. In 1973, 12,000,000 passengers flew across the Atlantic, whereas about 130,000 sailed. At roughly the same time, the P&O ran its last passenger ship to India.[12]

Second, containerization revolutionized nearly every aspect of mari-time business. The turn to containerized traffic was immensely complex, requiring new terminal, logistical, documentary, design, transport, and business strategies. It nonetheless offered the compelling opportunity to cut turnaround time in ports from days to hours, to lower labor costs, and to pare back theft. By the late 1960s, containerization on major routes was well underway, and by the 1970s it had spread to cover vast portions of general cargo. Its consequence was a rewriting of the hierarchies of companies and ports, the end to much shipping as it had been known, the demise of many companies, and the formation of interfirm alliances or consortia unlike anything in the past. By lowering freight costs and opening the way for more efficient, rapid, and cheap flows, it also provided a basis for today's globalized economy. Third, geopolitical and geoeconomic shifts, especially the rise of powerful Asian economies, rewrote maritime history after the Second World War.

The intertwining of European maritime history and decolonization was thus merely one aspect of a larger European experience that, in its multiple effects, has produced the current stage of globalization. Europe, once the organizer of economic flows, has come to function, with North America and East/Southeast Asia, as one of three interlocked great trading blocs. Whereas routings in the past proceeded between two fixed geographical points, for instance between imperial territories and home nations, or between Europe and one of the Americas, they now moved round the world. Maritime company operations, even company bases, have become globally focused and interdependent. Business cultures and identities have altered accordingly.

It would be possible to approach this evolution through comparative history. There are, however, two problems in trying to do so. First, it would sometimes be most appropriate to compare the experiences of nations and sometimes the experiences of firms. Locations, commodities, and routings could also be compared. Just to take one set of examples, it would be no less valuable to compare and contrast the experiences of Holt with P&O, the Holland America Line with the companies that formed Nedlloyd, Hapag with NDL or the two with Hamburg Süd, the Compagnie Générale Transatlantique with the Messageries Maritimes and the Chargeurs Réunis as it would to compare and contrast British, Dutch, German, and French experiences with decolonization and containerization. How to set up such a comparative framework would pose serious organizational challenges, and one would have to be careful to avoid the familiar apples-and-oranges syndrome.

Second, what stands out most throughout the historical evolution I have described is a common European experience that would fit ungracefully into a purely comparative structure of description and analysis. Such a structure, moreover, would force a line of argument that would be instructive in certain ways yet limited in others. Here

the cross-national approach seems more appropriate. Where comparative history tends toward the exclusive, cross-national history wel-
comes the inclusive.

The history of imperial focus and decolonization, joined to technological, managerial, and geopolitical change, would need to address
how colonial business was organized and worked, how men (and some
women) were recruited, their work and leisure experiences, and the
company culture that informed these, and the history of commodities
and consumer or industrial demand that forced new routings, cultiva-
tions, and trading patterns, for a start. It would have to include no less
than the business of moving varieties of peoples, from administrators
and businessmen, to settlers, pilgrims, and plantation workers. It
would have to proceed to the varied experiences of the Second World
War, then the efforts to penetrate liberated areas, what businessmen
found when they returned, how they started over again, what they
could accomplish, and what had changed forever. Then one would
need to follow alternative strategies of adjustment and redesign, where
these succeeded and where they failed. The history of passenger travel
and its collapse in the three decades following the war would require its
own narrative. The history of containerization would begin with needs
and advantages and proceed to revolutionary changes and their
consequences for firms and their cultures. In between, the story of
investigating, organizing, strategizing (firm alliances and competitive
postures), and executing would require many pages. Correspondence,
internal memos, firm restructurings, the shift in hierarchies by ports,
companies, or sectors would need to be told. The history of globalization would be contained within all of these stories, but a closer look at
markets and flows, as well as at the promotion of consumer cultures in
nonwestern lands would also be necessary. In particular, globalization
would in this case make Europe—or a European-wide dimension
rather than individual nation–states—the vanishing point of the perspective. I know how to write this story as cross-national history, but
I can imagine only the problems of writing it as comparative history. In
the latter I would have to leave out, or marginalize, far too much in
order to give the comparison sharpness and coherence.

In the end, the choice between cross-national and comparative history
will reflect personal inclination or predisposition. Each accomplishes
one way of writing multinational history while sacrificing another. My
own preference has been for the former, in part because I find it easier to
incorporate comparative methods into cross-national ones than vice
versa. Yet I have also found that the larger questions about European

experiences that have motivated my study can be better served within a cross-national framework. As my own work has led more in one direction than another, I have been forced in turn to reflect on what there is in the stricter comparative approach that I have found wanting. In the hands of superior practitioners like André Vigarié, Charles Maier, or, more recently, Susan Pedersen and Dominic Lieven, comparative history remains breathtaking in its accomplishment.[13] Still, as the bandwagon for comparative history gathers speed in our supposed era of transnational institutions, it is wise to reflect on its limitations as well as its strengths, or on Alan Milward's reminder that it has been the enduring interests of nation-states that have shaped the European Union.[14] Comparative history should be done more, but not necessarily by everyone. It is not a panacea and scarcely "the best way." Moreover, as this essay has contended, it is only one way of writing history across boundaries and regions.

REFERENCES

I would like to thank the Deutscher Akademischer Austauschdienst, the National Endowment for the Humanities, and the John Simon Guggenheim Memorial Foundation for supporting the research that went into this article.

1. Michael B. Miller, *The Bon Marché: Bourgeois Culture and the Department Store, 1869–1920* (Princeton, NJ: Princeton University Press, 1981).

2. R. Douglas Brown, *The Port of London* (Lavenham: Terence Dalton, 1978), pp. 88–90, 94; J. Schraver, ed., *Rotterdam the Gateway to Europe: History of the Port and Trade of Rotterdam* (Rotterdam: A.D. Donker, 1948), pp. 111, 113.

3. André Vigarié, *Les Grands ports de commerce de la Seine au Rhin, leur évolution devant l'industrialisation des arrière-pays* (Paris: S.A.B.R.I., 1964), pp. 265–266, 287–288, 322.

4. F. Posthuma, "Het Havenbedrijf der Gemeente Rotterdam, 1945–1965," in *Rotterdam Europoort 1945-1970*, ed. G.E. Van Walsum (Rotterdam: A.D. Donker, 1972), p. 75.

5. Antwerp, Stadsarchief, MA 36 Havenbedrijf 24272; Vigarié, *Grands ports*, pp. 485–503, 613–616, 619–627. Ministry of Transport, *Report of the Committee of Inquiry into the Major Ports of Great Britain* (London:HMSO. 1962); Ministry of Labour, *Final Report of the Committee of Inquiry under the Rt. Hon. Lord Devlin into Certain Matters Concerning the Port Transport Industry* (London: HMSO, 1965); Brown, *Port*; Geoffrey Ennals, Port of London Authority, interview with author, London, June 2, 1998.

6. Susanne Wilborg and Dr. Klaus Wilborg, *1847-1947. Unser Feld ist die Welt. 150 Jahre Hapag-Lloyd* (Hamburg: Hapag-Lloyd AG, 1997); Herbert Wendt, *Kurs Südamerika. Brücke zwischen zwei Kontinenten* (Bielefeld: Ceres, 1958); Siegfried Zimmermann, *Theodor Wille, 1844–1969* (Hamburg: Hanseatischer Merkur, 1969); Werner Klugmann and Walter Seeler, *Hafen Hamburg 1945–1965. Zwanzig Jahre Aufbau und Entwicklung* (Hamburg: Okis, 1965). H.(Hugo) van Driel, *Samenwerking in haven en vervoer in het containertijdperk* (Delft: Eburon 1990); Schraver, *Rotterdam*. Antwerp, Stadsarchief, MA 36 series, Contact Commissie files; Fernand Suykens et al. *Antwerp: A Port for All Seasons*, 2nd ed. (Antwerp: MIM, 1986); Interview with Jacques Damster (Managing Director/ Compagnie Générale Maritime Benelux n.v.), Antwerp,

January 13, 1998; Vigarié, *Grands Ports.* Francis E. Hyde, *Liverpool and the Mersey: An Economic History of a Port 1700–1970* (Newton Abbot: David & Charles, 1971), pp. 209–210; Malcolm Falkus, *The Blue Funnel Legend: A History of the Ocean Steam Ship Company, 1865-1973* (London: Macmillan, 1990); Geoffrey Jones, *Merchants to Multinationals: British Trading Companies in the Nineteenth and Twentieth Centuries* (Oxford: Oxford University Press, 2000); Liverpool, Merseyside Maritime Museum, MDHB/Management Files/Australian Trade, April 2, 1948, January–September 1948 ("Visit to Australia and South Africa"); David Kynaston, *The City of London*, vol. 4, *A Club No More, 1945–2000* (London: Chatto & Windus, 2001), 4. Interview, Ennals.

7. The above three comparisons do not exhaust the possible perspectives for investigating port histories. Comparative studies of labor militancy, managerial competence, and port costs would be no less revealing.

8. For an excellent discussion of this problem, see Frank Broeze, "Port Cities: The Search for an Identity," *Journal of Urban History* 11 (February 1985), 209–225.

9. Susan Pedersen, *Family Dependence and the Origins of the Welfare State: Britain and France 1914–1945* (New York: Cambridge University Press, 1993).

10. Laura Lee Downs, *Manufacturing Inequality: Gender Division in the French and British Metalworking Industries, 1914-1939* (Ithaca, NY: Cornell University Press, 1995), p. 12.

11. Rotterdam, Archieven van de Internationale Crediet—en Handelsvereeniging "Rotterdam," 168, June 1944.

12. Antoine Frémont, *La French Line face à la mondialisation de l'espace maritime* (Paris: Anthropos, 1998), pp. 17–19, 85; David Howarth and Stephen Howarth, *The Story of P&O*, rev. ed. (London: Weidenfeld and Nicolson, 1994), pp. 176–177.

13. Vigarié, *Grands ports*; Charles Maier, *Recasting Bourgeois Europe: Stabilization in France, Germany, and Italy in the Decade After World War I* (Princeton, NJ: Princeton University Press, 1975); Pedersen, *Family Dependence*; Dominic Lieven, *Empire: The Russian Empire and Its Rivals* (New Haven, CT: Yale University Press, 2000).

14. Alan S. Milward, *The European Rescue of the Nation-State,* 2nd ed. (London: Routledge 2000).

9

CROSS-NATIONAL TRAVELERS: RETHINKING COMPARISONS AND REPRESENTATIONS

Maura O'Connor

Comparative history and cultural history have not been the best of friends. But this need not be the case unless one is primarily concerned with pointing the way towards causal explanations. If comparative history's focus on separating the important from the incidental acts as its guiding principle, then cultural history's relationship to the comparative will remain only casual. Instead, I want to encourage a more intimate relationship between the two by taking a slightly different strategy. I propose that we consider the tensions between the comparative and cross-national alongside those between the structural and the post-structural. I do not want to argue that one approach is right and the other wrong, but to use the tensions between them as a creative way of understanding cultural transfer and influences, differences, and similarities. Given the skepticism that has arisen between proponents of these different approaches, my strategy here might require a leap of faith. But it is one worth taking because it will, I hope, encourage invention and flexibility, analytical rigor and imagination. Perhaps more important, it will encourage an exchange between historical inquiries that share a great deal in common.

I offer this essay not only to invite revision, but to use my own shortsightedness to consider anew the relationship between representations and comparisons, between cultural history's emphasis on interpretation and meaning, and comparative history's focus on similarities and differences. In this chapter I examine the tensions between the admittedly eclectic cross-national approach that I used in my own study about nineteenth-century English travelers to Italy and a comparative approach. Because my aim was to analyze the meanings of political, cultural, and diplomatic exchanges across borders, *crossing* became the central theoretical focus—at times a metaphor, at times a trope—for understanding and rethinking the role imagination played in the creation of nations and national identities. Comparing the ways that English middle-class travelers represented an Italian nation with what Italians themselves said was of considerably less importance. Yet had I been more interested in explicitly comparing, my arguments about the significance of crossings and exchanges to the cultural construction of the nineteenth-century nation might have been more persuasive. Giving my cross-national approach a comparative emphasis would have forced me to examine the role of representation from both sides of the border. Instead, the Italian nation that I was at pains to take seriously was often undermined by representation and metaphor, much to my analytical chagrin. Thus, this essay is an attempt to use comparative history's attention to difference and similarity as a way to push representation further, to rethink cultural approaches of exchange and crossings.

I

Although I was trained to think as a comparativist about modern European history, and although I teach as one, I had a proclivity towards the cross-national before I ever used these words to describe what I wanted to do. I had difficulty settling on a national focus. I wavered between British and French history and contemplated pursuing a comparative dissertation study. I even had what I considered a wonderful topic. Based on an undergraduate research paper called "Soap in the City," I planned to investigate the social world of laundresses and public bathhouses; to undertake a comparative cultural study of water and its availability in nineteenth-century London and Paris; to examine the many ways in which soap became "an actual yardstick of civilization" in the nineteenth century, an idea that I borrowed from Sigmund Freud in his book *Civilization and Its Discontents*.[1] I was quietly discouraged, however, from undertaking a comparative research project because of the practical difficulties involved. The first had to do with securing access to research funding for two countries; but the second, and more serious difficulty from the perspective of my advisors, was the inevitability of falling through the cracks in a bleak job market that still defined the modern European period around national fields. I saw no need at the time to challenge the advice of my mentors and discovered another subject that literally and figuratively kept me moving across national boundaries: exploring the political consequences of foreign travel and examining the cross-cultural relationships between nineteenth-century English men and women and their Italian counterparts.[2]

What I learned along the way was that although travel writings were themselves highly impressionistic sources, they could reveal something important about the role of both the writer's and reader's imaginations in framing and interpreting experiences abroad and informing political opinions. In this regard, they shared a great deal in common with nineteenth-century diplomatic records. I argued that English travel writers, much like British diplomatic representatives abroad, created an Italian nation of their own discursive making as they moved from region to region and city to city.[3] This was easy to do in part because the history of the Italian peninsula, with which many were familiar, provided them with a rich blueprint from which to borrow. Despite the obvious historical distances between the ancient, medieval, and modern political geography of Italy, English travelers, in the wake of the Napoleonic Wars, saw these Italian pasts as connected. Indeed, Italian nationalists in Britain would emphasize some of these same connections by the 1840s and 1850s.[4]

Moreover, many British diplomats and Foreign Office representatives also viewed the politics of national unification through an idealized representation of history and a romanticized vision of nationalism. Gendered images of the Italian peninsula became some of the most compelling and sympathetic representations to emerge from diplomatic records and travel texts alike.[5] Images of Italy's beauty, despair, hope, and readiness for nationhood, and particularly representations of Italian cities as queens, wives, mothers, whores, and maidens emerged as a language of signification that many understood. Despite the assumptions of some nineteenth-century diplomatic history that correspondence from the Foreign Office reveals a truth unmediated by cultural values, my reading of diplomacy encouraged a different interpretation. An analysis of diplomatic records, I insisted, should pay attention not only to what is said but how it is said and the connections between the two.[6] Thus, I began to read diplomatic correspondence as a form of travel writing. To be sure, travel narratives and diplomatic records served different purposes, but they also shared important similarities, including the gendered rhetorical strategies both deployed to sell the idea of Italy as a nation.[7]

When my interest shifted from the comparative social history of cities to the history of nationalisms, I realized that theories about the growth of state power, economic change, and even the role of revolution in the nineteenth century could not explain why or how the nation became an almost inevitable category of social, political, and cultural belonging. The cultural Marxism that had earlier attracted me to the study of European history and literature[8] could not adequately account for nationalism's overwhelming popularity. Far from being the natural outcome of political and economic modernization, the attraction to nationalism proved both obvious and subtle. Gramsci understood something that Marx did not about the utterly seductive power of the nation-state as an ideal worth fighting for, even when the benefits of belonging were unevenly distributed. I began to pay more attention to how nineteenth-century men and women described this process; how, far from being simply imposed from above, the nineteenth-century phenomenon of nation-building started from the ground up. The building proved to be far more elaborate, complicated, and contradictory than Marx, or even Gramsci, could have imagined.

That process of building the nineteenth-century nation, and especially imagining it as a political community, often took place outside its geographical borders. Giuseppe Mazzini wrote all of his major works about Italian nationalism in London. Yet Italian historiography, although sometimes acknowledging this fact, seldom takes it into consideration.[9] Some recent works that have been influenced by cultural studies and post-colonial interpretations of nationalism, however, have begun to look outside Italy for clues.[10] Still the historiography fails, by and large, to emphasize how the Italian question traversed boundaries and crossed borders.[11] In my book, I argued that nineteenth-century nationalism, especially before 1870, was a cosmopolitan and increasingly liberal preoccupation that saw the English, and not necessarily the French, as its great diplomats. Many among the urban English middle classes became the greatest champions of Italian nation making. English and British preoccupation with European nationalisms was also intimately connected to Britain's growing imperial power. There were important, and often overlooked, intersections between Britain's European diplomacy and imperial expansion that became one important story I hoped readers would take away from my study.

At the same time, however, I underestimated the ways in which a comparative approach might have been useful in complementing my cross-national agenda in this project. By definition, I thought, a study of travelers had to be about crossings and not about comparisons. Part of what guided my hesitancy to compare was comparative history's structural preconditions, a bit of a straitjacket for someone who prided herself on thinking post-structurally. At the same time, there was virtually no comparative work done on Britain and Italy, unlike other European countries such as France and Germany. I hesitate to criticize Italian historians for not looking beyond Italy, since European historians seldom give the country more than a passing glance. It never occurred to me to compare British ideas about Italian nation-making with Italian ideas, other than Mazzini's and Garibaldi's heroic examples, because England and Italy seemed so incomparable.

But what if instead of following Marc Bloch's "predilection" to compare only the comparable, we did just the opposite?[12] An invitation to compare what is so seemingly different might also help to unsettle certain fictions, inherited from the nineteenth century, about which states were ready to be nations and which were still immature or undeveloped.[13] On the outside, the Italian peninsula's claim to be a nation was no more natural or necessary than the act of Parliament in 1707 that created the United Kingdom of Great Britain. In many ways, comparisons between Great Britain and Italy or between regions of Britain and Italy might be a welcome addition to a European historiographical tradition that has produced many more comparative studies on Britain and France, Britain and Germany, and more recently, Germany and France. I cannot help but think that the persistent contemporary representation of Italy as a nation and a state that is politically dysfunctional owes something to the longevity of nineteenth-century tropes about its beauty and treachery, romance, and ungovernability. Italian historiography has also grappled for generations with the idea that there were/ are two Italies, again, a representation popularized by nationalists (in Italy, Britain, and France) during the nineteenth century.[14]

The cultural or linguistic turn that I, like so many others in graduate school with me in the 1980s, took, was facilitated by first embracing cultural Marxism, discovering Gramsci's ideas about cultural hegemony, and being attracted to the new cultural history influenced by the disciplines of literature and cultural anthropology.[15] I think that those of us who came to post-structuralism via cultural Marxism were often too quick to put structuralism aside without considering its consequences or the ways in which it profoundly shaped post-structuralist thought and practices and even ideas about culture itself. For example, because I was so persuaded by Benedict Anderson's ideas about how the nation functioned as an "imagined community"[16] and, at the same time, excited about literary and cultural theories that emphasized the contingency, constructedness, and representational nature of nation making,[17] I thought too little about comparisons that English travelers drew between themselves and Italians, between English cities and Italian cities, and even between Protestantism and Catholicism. In trying to de-emphasize these comparisons and, indeed, purposely setting aside the structural differences between England and Italy—the political, economic, and religious differences that marked the infrastructures of these regions as they developed historically into states and then nations—I largely ignored major differences. As a result, I obscured the ways in which these structural differences played such important roles in creating English representations and visions of an Italian nation. English travel accounts commented on structural differences all the time. Yet, my analysis focused more on *how* the English imagined Italy as a nation and not necessarily on *why* they imagined Italy in these ways. Their impatience, for example, with Catholicism was not only theological in origin, but also cultural and economic. English travelers objected to the opulence and gold in Catholic churches because it sat idle. It was not invested to make more capital, nor was it used to ease the poverty and desperation of poor Italians.

Indeed, I downplayed religious and social differences most of all, and in retrospect, this was a mistake. It mattered enormously to English middle-class Protestants, many of whom were Nonconformists, that Italy be rescued from what they perceived to be the superstitious clutches of the papacy and the corruption of the Catholic Church. I did not ignore this factor entirely, but I minimized its importance considerably because I thought that the historiography had exaggerated religious intolerance for Catholics and made anti-Catholicism the central motive behind and explanation for British support for Italian nationalism.[18] To explore instead the allure of an imaginary Italy that had the capacity to appeal to a larger audience of English armchair travelers who never ventured to the Italy, I focused my analysis on English representations of the different cities and regions on the Italian peninsula. But I hesitated, at least initially, to compare how English travelers viewed Italy vis-à-vis England. Perhaps equally important, in my determination to emphasize the political role played by the imagination in creating sympathetic public opinion in England, I did not include in my story those English and Irish Catholics whose views of Italian nationalism differed from their Protestant counterparts. In wanting to argue for consensus, for a certain unified English vision of an Italian nation, I missed an opportunity to refine my argument further by including a comparative analysis of religious differences within Britain.

Let me continue by introducing into this discussion Elizabeth Barrett Browning's long poem, *Casa Guidi Windows* (1851). In her famous nationalist text that galvanized so much British support for the Italian cause among the Victorian middle classes, Barrett Browning vehemently rejected the figure of *la bell' Italia*, as literary scholar Esther Schor has persuasively argued.[19] Her rejection has much to teach us about the assumptions too often embedded in representations and the limits of the imagination to create political agency. Barrett Browning did not want to reduce Italy to the sum of its parts nor did she hope to inspire sentimental reforms. Instead, as Schor has shown, Barrett Browning believed that Italy's ability to become a nation rested on the Italian people's abilities to act on their political aspirations, to exercise, we might say, their political agency by first recognizing that their own historical consciousness had been piqued.

Elizabeth Barrett Browning, I suspect, would not have enjoyed my book, for in it Italy was often cast as a competing representation of its many historical selves. That was never my intention; nevertheless, my cross-national approach focused on representations of Italians rather than Italians themselves and thereby obscured their political agency. Those representations were undoubtedly significant—they contained English imaginings about Italy and served to inspire political support and diplomatic cover over time—but they did not encompass or account for Italians' own voices or representations of their national liberation. In taking my cue not only from Edward Said's now classic study, *Orientalism*, but other cultural studies of colonialism and travel,[20] I was seduced by a binary analysis that argued for dialogue and a dialectical understanding of identity, but fell short of achieving this understanding partly because the voices in my study were so overwhelmingly English. I did not spend enough time or devote enough space to examining how the Italians might have responded to English arguments or how Italian representations of nation making compared to English representations. Comparing how the English and Italians imagined the nation could better demonstrate the similarities and differences between competing representations of an Italian nation. Clearly, opening up comparative history to more cultural approaches is equally important. The desire to be a nation, and all that such a desire entails culturally, cannot be easily separated, nor should it be, from the practical strategies involved in making the nation a political and diplomatic reality. The cultural work is always an intimate part of the political strategies and vice versa. What the history of cultural transfer and a cross-national approach can potentially teach us is how to connect the similarities and differences so that interpretations and meanings can be read, analyzed, argued about, and pondered.

Although I argued that imagining an Italian nation was a cultural and political process that occurred both inside and outside the borders of the Italian peninsula, I actually showed very little of the inside process. I showed how English travelers and diplomats could be politically persuasive in galvanizing favorable public opinion on behalf of the Italian national cause. But I did not compare English arguments to arguments and visions espoused by Italian nationalists, intellectuals, and diplomats alike. These Italian voices were silenced except when I retold the romantic tale of the unification battles themselves. In my insistence that the liberal vision win out, I left liberalism's challengers, both in England and Italy, mute.

Had I consistently compared British diplomatic accounts and travel writings with Italian accounts, my cross-national approach might have been still more convincing because Italian diplomats very self-consciously used British diplomatic sympathy for their own nationalist ends. Furthermore, Italian nationalists created certain gendered images of Italy, popular among English sympathizers, for their own political purposes, especially in the south. Italian scholars have recently shown how much these, too, depended on a variety of travel writings.[21] Thus, analyzing and interpreting these gendered representations of Italy and Italian nationalism that frequently made their way into British diplomatic records demonstrated how tropes took on a life of their own. I argued that such tropes mattered a great deal for English political support. Still, interpreting meaning from a comparative perspective, showing how these tropes also mattered to Italians, would have provided more persuasive evidence about the benefits of a cross-national approach.

For Italy to emerge only as the symbolic and representational construction of the English middle-class imagination certainly negated the agency of Italian nationalists and their followers. But it also usurped, unintentionally, contemporary Italian historiography by emphasizing time and again the English telling of this nationalist story. What complicated matters further was my keen interest in showing how integral to Englishness was this continual erasure of Italians from the history of their own making; as an imperial nation Britain too easily claimed nation making as part of its own peculiar understanding of its roles in Europe and the world in the nineteenth century. What got lost along the way, as a result, was the fact that there were Victorian English men and women, such as Barrett Browning and others less famous, who saw things differently. In highlighting consensus and arguing for the importance of certain representations, my analysis overemphasized one vision at the expense of others. A better cross-national approach would have included an analysis of the Italians answering back. It also would have differentiated somewhat between English supporters in England and English supporters residing on the Italian peninsula by comparing both of their responses to the Italian national question. I assumed that their responses were similar, but I took too much for granted without providing enough evidence or analysis.

Part of the problem was that I did not want to argue that English cultural affinities towards Italy necessarily translated into political support for Italian nationalism. Instead, I wanted to emphasize how a certain narrative and representation of an idealized and romanticized Italy inspired English sympathy and considerable political support. But the difference between cultural affinities and representations was not very clearly developed in my study. The contrast could have been redrawn to make the difference more apparent had I shown how, in the post-unification period, English sympathy and support continued to rely on romanticized fictions of what they hoped Italy could be, and not on the practical realities of what Italy was. Using Italian historiography to refine my approach would have been very helpful here. My study showed that there were important political and even diplomatic implications to this cultural work of imagining an Italian nation. But I had tried to avoid the causal argument by circumventing it, and yet I had failed to make the dialectical argument work. As long as my primary focus was Englishness, I was at a disadvantage. In sum, the cross-national approach that I used privileged one nation over the other. Had I engaged more thoroughly with the tensions between the cross-national and the comparative, I would have produced a book that might have shown more convincingly, I now think, the dialectical nature of nineteenth-century nationalism at work in both England and Italy.

The methodological shortcomings of my own study, however, are part of a more general problem with cross-national and transfer history. Using a cross-national approach is no less taxing or historiographically challenging than using a comparative approach. Comparative and cross-national approaches should not be engaged in isolation or as methods in and of themselves. Rather, as the example of my own work indicates, these approaches should be rigorously employed with other theoretical tools and questions. Instead of considering the nation itself as the subject of comparative or cross-national approaches, we should think more about the themes, topics, and questions that we bring to our study of any nation or nations, regions, cities, ideas, or events. The insights gleaned from cultural history can be more compatible with comparative history than at first glance meets the eye. Comparative historians have traditionally set their sights on the institutions of the modernizing state, on questions of labor, war, welfare, women, slavery, and revolution. The new cultural historians were (and are) no less interested in the state and the nation; we just looked for evidence of its cultural power and hegemony in different kinds of places.

Above all, this chapter is a plea to heed George Frederickson's advice that "to treat international and cross-national history as mutually exclusive would be a mistake."[22] Comparativists have much to teach us about how to write cross-national history, and those who write cross-national history have learned lessons that comparativists should take into consideration. A comparative focus demands rigorous analysis and pays more attention to the objects being compared whether they are nations, regions, cities, or states. Likewise, the cultural inventiveness of cross-national approaches, their interest in crossing disciplines as well as borders, could encourage historians to be more creative in our work. The pitfall of the cross-national is writing about one crossing more than the other, focusing on one national story to the neglect of the other, being burdened by the daunting task of mastering several historiographies. These are similar to the pitfalls experienced in doing comparative history as well. Yet, thinking more analytically about interactions between societies and cultures helps us to understand where infrastructures differ and why they are the same by showing the connections between them. Comparisons and representations might then be released from their structural and post-structural moorings and in the process, teach us something important about comparing national perspectives and crossing borders.

REFERENCES

1. Sigmund Freud, *Civilization and its Discontents*, translated and edited by James Strachey (New York and London, 1961), see p. 44 in particular.
2. See O'Connor, *The Romance of Italy and the English Political Imagination* (New York, 1998).
3. O'Connor, *The Romance of Italy*, see Ch. 2, pp. 13–55.
4. Here I am thinking about the work of Mazzini and his English friends and followers in London and provincial capitals who would make up the Friends of Italy; see O'Connor, *The Romance of Italy*, pp. 57–92; see also Margot C. Finn, *After Chartism: Class and Nation in English Radical Politics, 1848-1874* (Cambridge, 1993), pp. 142–188 and

Denis Mack Smith, *Mazzini* (New Haven and London, 1994).

5. O'Connor, *The Romance of Italy*, pp. 117–147.

6. For studies that were of interest to me in emphasizing connections between foreign and domestic policies, see John Clarke, *British Diplomacy and Foreign Policy, 1782–1865: The National Interest* (London, 1989) and J.E. Cookson, *The Friends of Peace: Anti-War Liberalism in England, 1793– 815* (Cambridge, 1982).

7. O'Connor, *The Romance of Italy*, p. 121.

8. As an undergraduate, I was influenced by the ideas and political writings of Karl Marx, Antonio Gramsci, Raymond Williams, and E.P. Thompson and early on in graduate school by the work of Edward Said, Stuart Hall, and feminist historians of western Europe, most notably Judith Walkowitz, Susanna Barrows, Lynn Hunt, Catherine Hall, Leonore Davidoff, Joan Scott, and Victoria de Grazia.

9. An exception would be Mack Smith, *Mazzini*, where he emphasizes Mazzini's important connections and networks in London. See in particular, pp. 20–48 and 77–105.

10. See Albert Ascoli and Krystyna von Henneberg, eds., *Making and Remaking Italy: The Cultivation of National Identity around the Risorgimento* (Oxford and New York, 2001).

11. A few important exceptions from cultural and literary studies are Nelson Moe, *The View from Vesuvius: Italian Culture and the Southern Question* (Berkeley and London, 2002); Susanna Ferlito, *Topographies of Desire: Manzoni, Cultural Practices and Colonial Scars* (New York, 2000); and Beverly Allen and Mary Russo, eds., *Revisioning Italy: National Identity and Global Culture* (Minneapolis and London, 1997); also see Krystyna von Henneberg, "Tripoli: Piazza Castello and the Making of a Fascist Colonial Capital," in Zeynep Celik, Diane Favro, and Richard Ingersoll, eds., *Streets: Critical Perspectives on Public Space* (Berkeley and London, 1994), pp. 135–150.

12. See Marta Petrusewicz's essay in this volume as well as Marcel Detienne, *Comparer L'Incomparable* (Paris, 2000).

13. See Glenda Sluga's essay in this volume.

14. See Jane Schneider, ed., *Italy's Southern Question: Orientalism in One Country* (Oxford and New York, 1998); Pasquale Verdicchio, "The Preclusion of Postcolonial Discourse in Southern Italy," in Allen and Russo, eds., *Revisioning Italy*, pp. 191-212; Moe, *The View from Vesuvius*; and John Dickie, *Darkest Italy: The Nation and Stereotypes of the Mezzogiorno, 1860–1900* (New York, 1999).

15. See, Lynn Hunt, ed., *The New Cultural History* (Berkeley and London, 1989), especially the introduction, pp. 1–22.

16. Benedict Anderson, *Imagined Communities: Reflections on the Origin and Spread of Nationalism* (London, 1983).

17. For example, I found the following very helpful: Homi K. Bhabha, ed., *Nation and Narration* (London, 1991); Sudipta Kaviraj, "The Imaginary Institution of India," in Partha Chatterjee and Gyanendra Pandey, eds., *Subaltern Studies VII: Writings on South Asian History and Society* (Delhi, Oxford, and New York, 1992), pp. 1–39; Prasenjit Duara, *Rescuing History from the Nation: Questioning Narratives about Modern China* (Chicago and London, 1995), especially his introduction, pp. 3–16; Larry Wolff, *Inventing Eastern Europe: The Map of Civilization on the Mind of the Enlightenment* (Stanford, CA, 1994); John R. Gillis, ed., *Commemorations: The Politics of National Identity* (Princeton, NJ, 1994); *Gender & History* 5:2 (Summer 1993), Special Issue on Gender, Nationalisms, and National Identities; Geoff Eley and Ronald Grigor Suny, eds., *Becoming National: A Reader* (Oxford and New York, 1996), especially the introduction, pp. 3–37; Silvana Patriarca, *Numbers and Nationhood: Writing Statistics in Nineteenth Century Italy* (Cambridge, 1996); Beverly Allen and Mary Russo, eds., *Revisioning Italy: National Identity and Global Culture* (Minneapolis and London,

1997); and Schneider, ed., *Italy's "Southern Question": Orientalism in One Country*, although this book was not available before mine went to press.

18. See, e.g., C.T. McIntire, *England Against the Papacy, 1858–61: Tories, Liberals, and the Overthrow of Papal Temporal Power During the Italian Risorgimento* (Cambridge, 1983).

19. Esther Schor, "The Poetics of Politics: Barrett Browning's *Casa Guidi Windows*," *Tulsa Studies in Women's Literature* 17:2 (Winter 1998), 305–324.

20. In particular, Wolff, *Inventing Eastern Europe*, Dennis Porter, *Haunted Journeys: Desire and Transgression in European Travel Writing* (Princeton, NJ, 1991); Margaret Hunt, "Racism, Imperialism, and the Traveler's Gaze in Eighteenth-Century England," *Journal of British Studies* 32:4 (October 1993), 333–357; Mary Louise Pratt, *Imperial Eyes: Travel Writing and Transculturation* (New York and London, 1992).

21. In general, see Moe, *The View from Vesuvius*; John Agnew, "The Myth of Backward Italy in Modern Europe," in Allen and Russo, eds., *Revisioning Italy*, pp. 23–42; and Marta Petrusewicz, "Before the Southern Question: "Native" Ideas on Backwardness and Remedies in the Kingdom of the Two Sicilies, 1815–1849," in Jane Schneider, ed., *Italy's Southern Question*, pp. 27–49.

22. George Fredrickson, *The Comparative Imagination: On the History of Racism, Nationalism, and Social Movements* (Berkeley and London, 1997), p. 51.

10

THE MODERNIZATION OF THE EUROPEAN PERIPHERY; IRELAND, POLAND, AND THE TWO SICILIES, 1820–1870: PARALLEL AND CONNECTED, DISTINCT AND COMPARABLE

Marta Petrusewicz

This research project did not begin as comparative history. My aim was to bring to light a body of progress-oriented ideas and practices that were diffused in the European periphery during the first half of the nineteenth century by an elite of modernizing landowners. I was assuming the "objective" existence of a periphery, traditional in a generally understood sense, that is, predominantly agrarian, producing foodstuffs and raw materials for the international market, composed mainly of two classes, landowners and peasants, in which cultural hegemony was uncontestedly retained by traditional elites. In the context of the post-Vienna restoration, I claimed, these elites undertook a serious and long-lasting attempt to reform and modernize their countries; in that, they followed an implicit vision of a "harmonious" development, or a gradual and well-ordered modernization. In order to preserve the leading role in such a process, traditional elites had to "self-modernize" as well, to legitimize their privileged role in the society, by developing a modern capacity for leadership.

My argument draws from three case studies: Ireland, the Kingdom of the Two Sicilies, and the Kingdom of Poland, in the period that runs approximately from 1820 to 1870. Several criteria determined this choice, but each of these countries is representative of the "objective" peripheral condition. In the usual research interaction between the hypotheses and the sources, I selected aspects on which to focus and proceeded to collect examples drawn from each country. I exulted when I found symmetry in behaviors, models, proposals, and organizations, and I was upset by a failure to discover resemblances or/and analogies. It was, I believe, my unsuccessful attempt to find in the Two Sicilies an alternative to the absent "normative novel," so widespread in Poland and Ireland, that made me realize that I was dealing with three specific countries/cultures/histories as well as with an "objective" periphery. Like Monsieur Jourdain, I discovered that I was speaking comparative history.

I

i

Marc Bloch's complaint that researchers only too rarely "take the trouble to record their tentative efforts" emboldens me to share my tentative reflections on what I have learned from my research about the ways of "doing" comparative history.[1] "Tentative," because there is very little in the methodological sense by which comparative historians can go. Comparative history, more than once proclaimed to be the "royal road" and one of the targets of renewal, continues to remain, in Hans Ulrich Wehler's words, "an underdeveloped region."[2] Many speak of comparison, but very few practice it; even its great advocates of decades ago, Henri Pirenne and Marc Bloch, hardly practiced it at all.[3] We are not even sure what comparative history means: an approach? a method? a tool?[4] As an approach, it presupposes a certain distance and an outside knowledge: Marc Bloch tells us that he noticed the existence of enclosures in France because he had read about the English ones.[5] Rudyard Kipling's words, "what should they know of England who only England know," can rightly be assumed as a motto of this approach.[6] As a method, it may very well be, in Bloch's words "the most effective of all magician's wands," but it is one without a methodology. And it certainly is an excellent and exciting tool, although it may be not as easy to manipulate as Bloch suggests.[7] Or it may be a combination of many things, approach, method, and tool. It is interesting to note that among the few European languages that have specific terms for it, the German *Komparatistik* denotes the discipline, whereas the French *comparatisme* refers to the activity (the method) of comparing.

Comparative history has no prophets. The founding text remains Plutarch's *Parallel Lives*, a comparative narrative of the merits of the great ancient protagonists, who were not contemporary with each other. But, due to its exemplary purpose, this is not easily imitable. Equally impractical (and unpracticed) today are huge diachronic comparative studies and universal histories like Toynbee's and Spengler's (or even Sombart's) that sought essential similarities between distant civilizations, also because their very extension excessively impoverished the "real." Similar in scope, but not in method or in purpose, are comparative studies of certain phenomena present in different societies very far removed from each other in space and time, and of institutions specifically different but generically alike. Marc Bloch saw an admirable example of such comparison in James Frazer's *The Golden Bough*, although, in general, he considered such huge comparisons to be too imprecise to be of much use "from the scientific point of view."[8] Comparison *à la grande manière* has been successfully applied by Carlo Ginzburg in *Night Battles*, a study of millenarian myths associated with the witches' Sabbath, and even more recently invoked by Marcel Detienne in a book that compares assembly practices in Ethiopia, ancient Greek cities, and among the fifteenth-century Cossacks.[9] But let's face the truth: most historians fear such comparisons.

Bloch himself, although attracted and fascinated by these broad comparisons, favored a second approach, a parallel study of societies "*à la fois voisines et contemporaines*," societies that exercise a constant mutual influence, that are subject to the same causal mechanisms, and that owe their existence, at least in part, to a common origin. His famous 1928 call was in fact a relatively restrained one for "a comparative history of European societies" in the Middle Ages.

Unfortunately, Bloch's predilection has become a sort of a dogma. The commandment, "do not compare but the comparable," has mostly been interpreted in a narrow sense of comparing similar phenomena, analogous institutions, and contemporary societies, all within a close geographical range. This caused the comparison to lose its most important function: to provoke the "mental shock" that a "sense of difference" brings. But "the comparable" is in no way limited to the temporal or spatial proximity or distance, it is a product of our understanding of what is comparable; moving the object of comparison beyond the similar and parallel towards the different and the divergent can get us out of the predictability of the dogmatic application. This, I believe, is the meaning of Detienne's invitation to "*comparer l'incomparable*" by building comparisons around common questions tested on diverse—temporally and spatially—cultural situations.

ii

Komparatistik, of course, belongs more "naturally" to linguistics and social sciences *stricto sensu* than to history. What Durkheim said about sociology, that *la méthode comparative* was not a particular branch of sociology, but was "sociology itself,"[10] could have never been claimed by an historian. Most modern historians do not compare at all.[11] European historians study mostly their own countries, and the non-European historians of Europe are often interested in a pan-European dimension: I am thinking, for example, of the exemplary works of Arno Mayer or Charles Maier.[12] Thus, when historians do compare, they often borrow from social sciences, both the problematic and the methods. They compare what is "comparable" and what is easily comparable, such as quantitative historical indicators derived from sociology, economy and population studies: price series, population, fertility cycles, consumption, and literacy.[13] Other easily comparable categories are political evolution, bureaucratization, national patterns of modernization, family structures, large enterprises and estates, standards of living, institutions (also such as American slavery and Russian serfdom), classes, movements, political parties, and social groups (recently, there has been a resurgence of comparative studies of elites).[14] European comparisons have been mostly done within the West, in the geographical and conceptual sense, or between a Western and an Eastern situation (or sometimes a Northern and a Southern), and most comparativists deal with periods after about 1850.

This kind of comparative history soon found itself at odds with cultural history, which was focused on the micro-level. Local studies, Bloch believed, could only come to fruition with the help of the comparative method; but it is a precept difficult to practice. Comparisons should be based on facts derived from archival research, but how many historians have the erudition of Carlo Ginzburg? How many have the linguistic ability to master different primary sources? How many feel at ease in tilling more than one field? Certainly, comparative efforts were helped by the structural anthropology of Lévi-Strauss and even more by the cultural anthropology of Clifford Geertz. The recent interest in "border" thinking and the growth of post-colonial studies both lead to comparisons, as they attempt to detect cross-pollination and to be local and global at the same time.[15] I believe that another influence can prove exceptionally fertile on comparative historical studies, namely, literary criticism. As George Steiner said, literary studies and interpretation have always been comparative.[16] Literary *comparatisme* assumes, as a constitutive part of the discipline, the existence of national literatures, which are distinct in their essence but cannot be defined without reference to foreign literatures. Literatures are always in contact one with another, and are part of a vast exchange system, in space and in time. This vast transnational exchange or—in terms of intertextuality—the literary filiation, serves also to transfer information. But, then, transfer brings us back into the local study, within which we can understand the context of reception.[17]

The "why" of a comparison changes when regimes of historicity change. Generally speaking, however, we compare because comparison is useful. Aside from grandiose visions of a Toynbee or a Spengler, for whom comparative history was the first stage of global or universal history, comparison serves many not less important goals. It is an instrument, of an unequaled heuristic value, to elaborate concepts. It helps us detect long-lasting and coherent patterns of historical development. It serves to detect facts: some things are very clearly perceivable in one society, and much less so, for a variety of reasons, in another. It may help explain the difference and the peculiarity (such as many studies of the German *Sonderweg* or the Italian "anomalies") and trace their origins and causes. For Otto Hintze, historical comparison allows us to seize and to bring in evidence of fundamental individual distinctiveness; Michel de Certeau sees it as a way of catching "*les écarts, les résistances, les différences.*"[18] Michel Trebitsch, in his comparative history of intellectuals, praises a "purifying virtue" of the comparative approach, which frees history from ideological sedimentations.[19]

II

i

The simplest and most immediately gratifying application of the comparative method is the parallel observation of two or more societies. We detect similarities among the facts observed and enough of the difference in the environment to make the likeness meaningful and exciting, and the comparison worthwhile. Here is, therefore, my parallel narrative of the three cases, Ireland, Poland, and the Two Sicilies.[20]

The first remarkable resemblance is in the historical journeys of the three countries, from the late eighteenth until the mid-nineteenth century. All three experienced, in the late-eighteenth century, a wave of reformism undertaken by their monarchs with an enthusiastic concordance of a part of the landed property class. Programs of reforms touched on economy, land ownership, education, relations with the Catholic Church, and class and state power structures.

In the newly independent Kingdom of the Two Sicilies, the Bourbons attempted to restrict feudal privilege, reform finances and taxation, and reduce the Church's wealth and power. They negotiated a Concordat, expelled the Jesuits, and, with the *Cassa Sacra* in 1783, experimented with a radical land reform that involved expropriation and redistribution of the Church's land and curtailment of baronial privileges. They also promoted and encouraged innovation and industrialization.

In Ireland, a partial constitutional independence was achieved in the 1780s with the creation of the office of resident Viceroy and the (exclusively Protestant) Irish Parliament. Catholics gradually gained property rights and were enfranchised in 1793. Economic conditions improved "miraculously": the government promoted industrialization, mining, and road and canal building. Popular education was growing, in the context of a relative freedom of the press and increasing responsiveness of Parliament to public opinion.

In Poland, Stanisław August Poniatowski, who was to be its last king, appointed the Ministry of Education and, in 1788, called in the Parliament (which would sit for four years) to deliberate on institutional reforms. A very modern liberal constitution, promulgated on May 3, 1791, introduced constitutional monarchy and large representation, civil rights and religious toleration, strong state institutions, and a (rather vague) emancipation of peasants.

These programs, successfully enacted, soon succumbed to the traumas of the revolutionary 1790s: revolts and defeats, bloodshed, repression, conquest, and revenge. In 1799, a revolution in Naples brought in the Partenopean Republic, which abolished feudalism, confiscated Church lands, proclaimed liberty and fraternity, and after a few months was smashed and drowned in blood. The restored Bourbon monarchy was eager to take revenge.

In Poland, a formidable "national" (and peasant) uprising was led by Tadeusz Kościuszko in 1794 in the last attempt to preserve the existence of the country. The military defeat of the insurrection was followed in 1795 by the final partition of Poland among its powerful neighbors, Austria, Prussia, and Russia.

In Ireland, a French-backed republican revolution broke out in May 1798, led by Theobald Wolfe Tone, that mobilized substantial numbers of Protestants and Catholics alike. The British emerged triumphant and retaliated with savage reprisals, culminating two years later in the Act of Union, a final annexation of Ireland.

After the Congress of Vienna, the restored powers sought some modernization of the state and the society, and created a similar space for positive action in the three countries. In the Two Sicilies, the Bourbons did not restore feudalism, which had been abolished in 1806, and maintained most of the Napoleonic administrative and institutional structure and appointments. After 1830, Ferdinand II granted amnesty, brought the exiles back, carried out an intelligent reform of the administration, initiated railroad construction, and encouraged the development of industry and banking.

In Ireland and in Poland, despite their loss of independence, the occupiers sought forms of limited autonomy and opened up economic possibilities. Czar Alexander granted the Kingdom of Poland a liberal constitution, with the Parliament elected by all estates, including even a handful of peasants, and its own army. Universities were opened in Vilna and Warsaw, and the economic program of Prince Drucki-Lubecki, the prime minister, made the mutilated kingdom into a gem in the Russian crown: the lumber, textile, and weapons industries flourished; immigrants with specialized skills flocked in from Silesia, Saxony, and Austria; the Bank of Poland opened in 1828; and the fiscal system was entirely reformed.

In Ireland, organized Catholic politics under the dynamic leadership of Daniel O'Connell achieved a series of victories, climaxing with the Catholic Emancipation Act of 1829 and the Irish Reform Act, which reduced the influence of the aristocracy in the borough constituencies. Innovations were introduced in public administration and the police. A national primary education system was set up under state auspices, and the creation of a Catholic university was considered. The economy flourished with a cotton and linen industry, steam power, and the mechanization of spinning. The Bank of Ireland, in existence since 1783, was joined by the new joint-stock banks.

The landowning classes were the only "indigenous" partner drawn into this reform action. Even without political power, they retained full cultural hegemony, since the urban bourgeoisie was weak and busy making money, and industries and enterprises were often owned by foreigners or people of a different religion. Landed elites were enthusiastically promoting "modernization," a term they often used. The peculiar way in which they understood and practiced "modernization" is strikingly similar in the three cases, cultural products of similar circumstances. Modernization meant "England," as an explicit and implicit standard, and "not England," in that they rejected the "industrial civilization" of monstrous Manchesters, class conflict, popular misery, and unrestrained greed and materialism. Not opposed to industry in itself, they favored gradual industrialization that corresponded to "local vocation" and to raw materials locally available: wool, linen, and cotton textiles in Ireland; lumber, weapons, and linen textiles in Poland; sulfur and silk in the Two Sicilies; and the processing industry for agricultural products in all three. Industry was to be small to medium in size, located in the countryside and organized around a well-managed agriculture. They were in favor of markets—local, regional, national, international—and free trade, and against protective tariffs. But trade was to grow slowly and gradually around agriculture and manufacturing.

It was an agrarian ideology that held agriculture central to modernization: a true wisdom, a combination of art and science, a natural basis for social harmony, and a depository of moral values. Peasantry was seen as part of agriculture: good agriculture required a happy and productive peasantry, which would be made so by agrarian legislation, an improvement in tenancies (rather than property), and education.

Only some countries were "created for agriculture" in the eyes of these modernizers, but Poland, the Two Sicilies, and Ireland were among them; the modernizers' task was to make agriculture productive and profitable. Theirs was not a purely conservative approach; they promoted plenty of innovations in methods and applied sciences. Poets and scientists alike discussed crops, rotations, and manure. The privileged vehicles of the modernizing discourse were journals, schools, and associations, especially the economic and agrarian societies. These associations were numerous and membership was socially desirable. One must remember that, although all the European landed elites were struggling to produce an alternative model of development, only in the periphery did they lead and dominate the civil society. They published copiously on different levels and also sponsored agricultural education on all levels.

ii

The parallel narratives could stop here, and the questions asked as to what these historical resemblances imply, and what the next step is in the analysis. One possibility is to derive from these narratives a single "objective" pattern of the peripheral alternative modernization. Let me exemplify this intent by briefly analyzing a model for such a construction: Theda Skocpol's rightly acclaimed *States and Social Revolutions*.[21] This is a "comparative analysis" of the three great revolutions of modern times, in France, Russia, and China. The three historical cases are studied in their function of leading towards state building and "modernization" of state structure. The construction is teleological and aprioristic;

the cases are chosen because they fit an established model (which follows that of Skocpol's mentor, Barrington Moore); and from each case only that information is chosen which serves the model. Skocpol uses no primary sources, and no secondary sources in Russian or Chinese. Comparative history is for her simply a tool "to work out an explanation of the causes and outcomes" of the three revolutions; that is, the concrete historical cases are "treated as three comparable instances of a single, coherent social-revolutionary pattern."[22]

Such a use of comparative analysis would allow for a neat construction of a "peripheral" model of progress, where the historical cases of Ireland, Poland, and the Two Sicilies would be seen as three instances of the single pattern of peripheral modernization. The price for this neatness, however, is to ignore and discard all that is not symmetrical, all the distinctiveness of the concrete narratives, all the difference. For an historian, this price is too high, it risks reducing the historical comparison, in Bloch's words, to "no more than a sorry caricature."[23]

Another way of organizing the three countries' narratives could lead to painting a large picture of the periphery, where each single narrative has its own place. An exemplary application of such a procedure can be found in another classic: Jerome Blum's *The End of the Old Order in Europe*.[24] Unlike Skocpol, Blum offers detailed narratives of the histories of the servile lands of Europe, and the changes that occurred therein between the second half of the eighteenth and the second half of the nineteenth centuries. Blum's "servile lands" extend from Russia to Eastern France and from Lombardy to Denmark, comprising almost the whole of Europe. The book is divided in three chronological parts, and each of those is in turn subdivided thematically. Each subchapter lists all the relevant developments in each country, described one after another, with a great wealth of detail drawn from a great variety of primary and local sources. The same questions are asked of each country. The reader is constantly aware of parallels, but only at the end, when we step back, a global picture emerges, a *vue d'ensemble*. We realize which mechanisms the author wanted to emphasize and where this whole detailed narrative was leading.

The problem with this admirable picture is that it is static, repetitious, and conventional. The wealth of one local knowledge does not help to discover new facts in another environment. It is disappointing to read one history after another, with no room for communication, crossing, imitation, and diffusion.

iii

One way of complicating the parallel narratives and of escaping both Skocpol's apriorism and Blum's redundancy, is to study the connections and crossings between these works. Reference to comparative literature methodologies can be useful here, because literary *comparatisme* assumes that distinct national literatures are always in contact one with another as parts of a vast exchange system. Analogously, the concept of "connected histories" implies individual histories that are multiple and distinct, but connected to and in communication with each other. Researching "connected histories" says Sanjay Subrahmanyam, is much more gratifying than comparing them, less approximative, redundant, and aprioristic.[25] I would suggest, however, that the study of "connections" is not in opposition to, but part of comparative history as a way of tracing borrowings, impositions, transfers, and, occasionally, ancient relationships.

The first obvious connection within the nineteenth-century European elite, peripheral and metropolitan alike, is their shared learned culture. Accounting for some local variations, they all received the same classical education, learned the same modern languages (French and ever more often English) and had the same literary and intellectual points of reference. They even read some of the same journals, such as, for example, the *Revue des Deux Mondes*. It is known for its intercultural vocation, an amazing number of foreign subscriptions, and the top quality of contributors: in the mid-nineteenth century, Italy was covered by Edgar Quinet, Ireland by Ernest Renan, and Poland by Adam Mickiewicz and Cyprien Robert.[26]

Among the modernizers, these intellectual connections were further accentuated. Not only did they share a fascination with political economy, but they all read Adam Smith in the same way, that is, through the mediation of Simonde de Sismondi. The "grandfather of social economics," Sismondi—especially the so-called "second" Sismondi, the critic of too many market mechanisms and proponent of rural harmony—was very influential in European "peripheral" circles.[27] Many modernizing landowners traveled to meet him at his estate near Pescia in Tuscany, where he lived after leaving Switzerland. The University of Vilna, as a testimony of Polish interest, offered him the chair of political economy, which he eventually declined.

Young modernizers' paths often crossed at what I call the *carrefours des idées*. Many met at the new technical universities in Zurich, Geneva, or Paris, but the most important connections were formed in specialized agrarian schools and establishments in France, England, Germany, and Italy, always slightly off the main road. These were the Institut Agronomique in Grignon, where many Poles studied in exile after 1831; the school and model estate run by Mathieu Dombasle in Roville; the Hohenheim model-estate in Württemburg; the Accademia dei Georgofili in Florence; or the Meleto model-estate, school, and factory run by Cosimo Ridolfi. Many modernizers were members or correspondents of learned societies and occasionally met at their meetings. Finally, they traveled, and travel—Lamartine says—is like a translation.

There is yet another self-conscious level of "connection." Peripheral modernizers, Poles, Irish, and Italians, were aware of and sympathetic to each other. They perceived their countries and one another as comparable, and they were actively looking for similarities and for lessons from the other's experience. In the 1830s and 1840s, the Poles were immensely interested in the Irish statesman and modernizer Daniel O'Connell and the implications of his experience for Poland. O'Connell, in turn, was interested in and wrote about Poland; and he died, in 1847, on his way to Southern Italy. Polish historian and politician Joachim Lelewel, compared the Polish constitution of 1791 to the Irish one of 1782; Andrzej Zamoyski traveled to Ireland to study its penitentiary system; Carlo Cattaneo gave his book about Sardinia the title *La Terza Irlanda*; the economist Stanisław Smólka saw the Kingdom of Poland before the 1830 insurrection as "an unfinished economic Piedmont."

iv

The study of connections helps to reveal transfers, translations, and borrowing as well as to highlight similar phenomena that may be products of similar causes, but which are interpreted differently according to their specific context. There exist, however, certain striking resemblances that do not necessarily imply connections and are not perfectly symmetrical in the sense that they are present in some but not in all studied societies (i.e., they are parallel and divergent at the same time). And yet, they are too "good" to be ignored.

At this point, the story of the "normative novel" must be told. The normative novel of a strikingly similar narrative structure was, in the first half of the nineteenth century, widely spread in Ireland and in Poland, but was absent in the Two Sicilies. Whereas in Southern Italy melodramas and novellas reigned, novels were widely published and read in Poland and Ireland, and constituted a formidable vehicle for normative discourse. They offered an almost identical "normative representation" of what is wrong with the rural world and what remedies should be applied. I call "normative" here that representation of a reality (in art or literature) which is produced for a large audience and creates a norm in description and resolution; in our case, it fixes the image of how the rural world is and how should it be. Some very popular writers, such as the Irish Maria Edgeworth and William Carlton and the Polish Józef Korzeniowski and Ignacy Kraszewski, tell the same story.[28]

The action takes place in a typical (Polish or Irish) countryside. Two neighboring landed families, one good and one bad. The good one resides on the property, manages the estate, and implements a gradual and guarded modernization. Economically successful and prudent, the family is well off but is never ostentatious. Simplicity reigns in the old, spacious, hospitable house. There is a respect for traditions (local and national), for the elders, for religion, for family, but also openness to (solid) knowledge. Peasants are treated well in a paternalistic not a democratic way; they have good tenancies, elementary schools, and decent housing. The bad family resides for most of the year in the "foreign" capital (St. Petersburg or London), aping metropolitan *mores* and throwing away lots of money on frivolities (the latest fashions, French novels, and balls). The owner is lazy and insecure, the wife foolish, the children's heads filled with frivolous nonsense. Back home, the property is run by incapable or dishonest agents. The estate lacks infrastructure; it is in disrepair; the yields are very low, the revenues even lower; the owners are heavily indebted; and the peasants reduced to abysmal poverty.

The good proprietor has a daughter, the bad proprietor a son. The young fall in love, and, after overcoming many obstacles, they marry. Redemption and regeneration follow. The son, foolish but with a good heart, is converted to good ways, and through him so is his whole family. It is interesting to notice that regeneration comes through a woman. It is but the first, albeit necessary, step towards a greater regeneration: of the landowning class, of agriculture, of the countryside, and, finally, of the fatherland. These novels carry a deeper normative message to the landowning classes: to till their land well as a way of preparing the people and the country for independence. Well managed land becomes a patriotic statement, a *domaine patriotique*. Prince Leon Sapieha put it explicitly in a letter to Andrzej Zamoyski, his brother-in-law: "The only way of preparing the people for the future independence, is to work the land, your fathers' bequest, your patriotic estate [*ojczysty zagon*]."[29]

The scenarios are similar well beyond the nineteenth-century canon for a rural-life novel, although there doesn't seem to be any direct transfer or borrowing. However it came about, the very fact that the representation of a land-based harmonious social order that could and should be wisely led by the landed class is so similar in Poland and in Ireland confirms that such a project was common to these countries. On the other hand, the absence of such a novel in the Two Sicilies need not imply that the project was substantially different, but rather that the cultural work there was accomplished through a different medium. Of course, both the presence and the absence demand an explanation in light of each other, as a useful means of penetrating the specificity of each historical case. At the same time, in this case the absence/presence is not and should not become the focus of comparison; its useful function has been to remind us that, after all, comparison is not about symmetry.

v

The discussion of normative representation in novels brings us to the question of local reception. Generically speaking, these novels functioned as disseminators of similar values, of land-based projects of economic and social harmony. More specifically, however, we cannot assume that they had the same meaning in the Polish and Irish contexts. And the same is true about all the parameters of comparison; in different cultures, the same terms do not denote the same realities, the same images do not evoke the same reactions, and the "decoding" is culturally specific and unconscious. On the other hand, very often when linguistic parallelism does not exist, analogous phenomena or practices do, without specific terms for them. Thus a researcher engaged in a comparative work must be able to seize the general resemblance and understand the specific context of reception and penetrate the (dead) insiders' point of view, from within the particular culture, while bringing into this local situation a knowledge and observation acquired outside it. In other words, a comparative historian must try to feel and act as an insider but to seek help from an outside disciplinary system to know how we act and feel. How can we do that?

Some fifty years ago, a debate among linguists on the comparative advantages of phonemics and phonetics in understanding and comparing verbal behaviors started spilling over into cultural anthropology, where it became known as the emics versus etics, or insider versus outsider debate.[30] The terms of this debate can be instrumental in an attempt to reconcile the "native point of view," which stresses mental and emotional conditions, with the "objective" point of view, which stresses behavioral and infrastructural conditions and processes involving longer time spans. Emic interprets events according to their particular cultural function; etic characterizes events by spatiotemporal criteria. Often what insiders recognize as emic units, outsiders see as part of a larger, nonlocal, and diachronic regularity. Quite often, emic accounts match up with etic accounts; but when they do not, they may well clash. Let us consider the sensitive example of female circumcision: the emic construction—traditional rite of passage into femininity—contrasts sharply with the etic description of genital mutilation. In this case, emic construction actually prevents the "natives" from seeing their behavior in etic terms.

In recent years, the emic or insider versus the etic or outsider categories have been applied to a variety of methodological distinctions, such as verbal versus nonverbal, private versus public, specific versus universal, subjective versus "scientific," and description versus theory. In his "'From the Native's Point of View,'" one of the texts that most profoundly influenced today's historians, the anthropologist Clifford Geertz conceptualizes this distinction as one between "experience near" and "experience distant."[31] The discipline of history translated it into a tension between a "cultural" approach (from within) and a sociological one (from without), or between "soft" facts (*mentalité*) and hard facts (statistics).

The emic/etic distinction may, of course, lead to a centri-cultural conclusion that historical situations are idiosyncratically incomparable. But I think it is much more useful as a tool in an approach that considers them cross-culturally comparable. Comparative historians must learn how to use this tool, how to access and then to combine the two views, emic and etic, insider's and outsider's. And also how to pass from emic to etic and from etic to emic without asserting a strategic priority of either.

vi

What I want to suggest here is an empirical application of an emic/etic approach according to what Maurice Aymard called a *géométrie variable*, with no strategic priorities accorded a priori and no invariants posed as external and "objective" terms of reference.[32]

I propose to borrow names given and concepts elaborated in one cultural context and transfer them, with the function of interpretative tools, into another cultural context. One culture's emic will become thus another's etic, and vice versa. Such a method offers several opportunities: (1) because in different cultures, the same terms do not denote the same realities, the transfer of a term can help to unlock certain meanings initially hidden to us; (2) because in different cultures, similar groups of phenomena are not equally perceived as such (i.e., as groups) and are not called with a collective name as they may be in another context, naming them with a borrowed term can help uncover their existence; (3) because this method is circular, it allows us to get beyond binary histories and assures a relationship of parity between emic and etic. A few examples of such transferable terms and concepts may help to illustrate the idea.

Praca organiczna or organic labor, was a widely popular emic concept elaborated in Poland in the 1840s, and later became the focus of the modernizers' program after the defeat of the 1863 insurrection. *Praca organiczna* poses the necessity for a deep national regeneration, which must start from an organic work aimed at reconstructing the bases of economy and society (on the land, in the countryside, and on the village level by educating peasants and landowners). An improvement of basic conditions is a pre-condition for a future political mobilization to reclaim independence. The term had a political implication, moderate and gradual; all of Andrzej Zamoyski's work can be locked in this term. When applied to Ireland, *praca organiczna* shows in what sense Daniel O'Connell's program can be interpreted as modernizing, whereas in the Irish perception his work belongs to the "Catholics versus Protestants" emic. *Praca organiczna* can also give a name to the flourishing of economic and agrarian associationism after the defeat of the 1820–1821 revolution in the Two Sicilies.

Vocazioni territoriali, or territorial (local) vocation, was the concept widely used in the Two Sicilies since the 1830s to indicate the necessity to understand what economic activity and social organization of labor is the most proper for a given territory. When applied to the Irish debates on bog-draining, it reveals its unselfconsciously ecological meaning, as it refers really to natural and cultural vocations of the territory.

"Bog-mania" was a term used to describe the rush to drain Irish bogs in the 1830s, when a great number and variety of shareholding companies and credit institutions were formed. When transferred into the Polish context, the concept helps reveal a similar phenomenon, the same maniacal drive to form holdings for large infrastructural works.

Agricola Victor was first used at the time of the passing of Land Acts to define the character of Ireland's modernization, including the political one, which had landownership and agriculture at its very center. What concept could better summarize the peripheral modernizers' project?

Zagroda polskości, or the enclosure of Polishness, was used in 1813–1814 by the poet Kajetan Koźmian in his epic poem *Ziemiaństwo* (*Landowners*). The agricultural estate—home to a landed family—is seen as an enclosure of the national spirit, both the preserver and the hothouse of the future independence. In the Neapolitan context, well-run agricultural estates are often seen as enclosures of civicness, and by extension of the national spirit (in the civic, not ethnic, terms), possibly closer in meaning to the French *domaine patriotique*. But *zagroda polskości* can undoubtedly unlock the patriotic meaning of the Irish post-Famine agrarian mobilization.

Ombra del feudo or the shadow of the manor, a very efficacious term, was elaborated in the Southern Italian context to denote the landed lords' judicial and administrative power and social hegemony. The middle class has always remained adumbrated by, and subaltern to, the titled landowners, well into the twentieth century (*lunga ombra*, the long shadow of the manor). Could not the lasting influence of the Ascendancy be interpreted as an *ombra del feudo*? Can it not explain the "peculiarities" of the Polish case?

Comparison by transfer of concepts helps reveal some characteristics that pertain to the peripheral modernizers' global project, and liberate new meanings in the conventional concept of modernization: these modernizers saw themselves as trustees of national consciousness; they conceived their patriotic role in creating solid economic and educational bases upon which to build citizenship; and they believed that all this was to be done prior to national (or political) liberation, by moderate steps and gradual extension.

Géométrie variable is especially helpful in our case where the question is modernization. Modernization is in itself a powerful etic, a hegemonic concept composed of stable and well-recognized invariants, such as state building, nation making, private property, free market, liberal political institutions, and the like. Explicitly or implicitly, when modernization is concerned, some countries are seen as exemplary. On the other hand, we cannot reject the term "modernization" because it was the term the peripheral reformers referred to in the nineteenth century, and modernization was what they, however critically, sought. It is therefore important to free the concept of modernization of its immobile, exemplary, and aprioristically explanatory character. In the study through transfer, the new context of reception will allow us to reinterpret and alter the object of transfer, reducing the rigid invariants to a supple role of variables. It is hoped that, as Maurice Aymard wrote pleading for less sociologism, "*l'explication ne cesse d'y perdre, et la comparaison d'y gagner.*"[33]

REFERENCES

1. Marc Bloch, "A Contribution Towards a Comparative History of European Societies," in *Land and Work in Medieval Europe: Selected Papers by Marc Bloch* (Berkeley: University of California Press, 1967), p. 49.
2. Hans-Ulrich Wehler, ed., "Einleitung" to *Geschichte und Soziologie* (Cologne 1972), p. 24.
3. Marc Bloch, "Pour une histoire comparée des sociétés européennes," *Revue de synthèse historique* 46 (1928). Cited here as "A Contribution"; Henri Pirenne, "De la méthode comparative en histoire," in *V International Congress of Historical Sciences* (Brussels: Weissenbruch 1923); François Simiand, "Méthode historique et science sociale," *Revue de synthèse historique* (1903), 1–22, 129–157.
4. I think that this is still a valid reflection on these distinctions attempted years ago by William Sewell in "Marc Bloch and the Logic of Comparative History," *History and Theory*, VI: 2 (1967), 208–218.
5. "A Contribution," p. 50–51.
6. Geoffrey Crossick quotes it in reference to comparative historical studies in and of Great Britain. See a thoughtful survey edited by Heinz-Gerhard Haupt, "La storia comparata," *Passato e Presente*, XI: 28 (January-April 1993), 20–51.
7. "A Contribution," pp. 51, 45.
8. Idem, pp. 46–48.
9. Marcel Detienne, *Comparer l'incomparable* (Paris: Seuil, 2000); Carlo Ginzburg, *The Night Battles: Witchcraft and Agrarian Cults in the Sixteenth and Seventeenth Centuries* (Baltimore, MD: Johns Hopkins University Press, 1983).
10. Emile Durkheim, *Rules of Sociological Method*, E.F. Catlin, ed. (Glencoe, IL, 1964), p. 139.
11. I find revealing a survey that Raymond Grew carried out some years ago of manuscripts submitted to *Comparative Studies in Society and History*, a quarterly journal devoted since its inception in 1958 to "*comparatisme*." Grew found that most of the work was being done at what he calls "middle range," theoretically, temporarily, and spatially. Most of the research at that time focused actually on one country and gave full attention only to a single historical case. Raymond Grew, "The Case for Comparing Histories," *American Historical Review* 85: 4 (October 1980), 763–778.
12. Charles Maier, *Recasting Bourgeois Europe: Stabilization in France, Germany and Italy in the Decade After World War I* (Princeton, NJ: Princeton University Press, 1975); Arno Mayer, *The Persistence of the Old Regime: Europe to the Great War* (New York: Pantheon, 1981); David S. Landes and Charles Tilly, eds., *History as Social Science* (Englewood Cliffs, NJ, 1971); Barrington Moore, Jr., *The Social Origins of Dictatorship and Democracy: Lord and Peasant in the Making of the Modern World* (Boston: Beacon, 1966).
13. The advent of quantitative methods signaled a moment of triumph for comparative history: long historical quantitative data series required and facilitated comparisons, of the kind practiced by sociologists, economists, and demographers. See the exhaustive bibliographies cited in Mariuccia Salvati, "Histoire contemporaine et analyse comparative en Italie," *Genèses: Sciences sociales et histoire*, 22 (March 1996), pp. 146–159; Harmut Kaelble, "La récherche européenne en histoire sociale comparative," *Actes de la récherche en Science Sociale*, 106–107 (March 1995), 67–79; Pietro Rossi, ed., *La storia comparata. Approcci e prospettive* (Milano: Saggiatore, 1990).
14. The references here are numerous. See, for example, Peter Kolchin, *Unfree Labor: American Slavery and Russian Serfdom* (Cambridge, MA: Harvard University Press, 1987), Shearer D. Bowman, *Masters and Lords: Mid-Nineteenth-Century U.S. Planters and Prussian Junkers* (New York: Oxford University Press, 1993); Jürgen Kocka, ed., *Europaische Arbeiterbewegungen im 19. Jahrhundert. Deutschland, Oesterreich, England und Frankreich im Vergleich* (Göttingen, 1983); Alan Mitchell, Jürgen Kocka, and Gus

Fagan, eds., *Bourgeois Society in the Nineteenth Century* (Oxford: Berg, 1994); Alberto M. Banti, ed., *Borghesie europee dell'Ottocento* (Venice: Marsilio 1989); Sidney Tarrow, *Between Center and Periphery: Grassroots Politicians in Italy and France* (New Haven, CT: Yale University Press, 1977); J. H. Hall, ed., *States in History* (Oxford: Oxford, 1986); Peter Flora, *State, Economy and Society in Western Europe, 1815–1970* (Frankfurt a.m.: Campus Verlag, 1984); Richard J. Evans, *The Feminists: Women's Emancipation Movements in Europe, America, and Australasia, 1840–1920* (New York: Barnes & Noble, 1987); John Breuilly, *Labour and Liberalism in 19th Century Europe. Essays in Comparative History* (New York: St. Martin's, 1982); Rolf Torstendahl, *Bureaucratization in Northwestern Europe, 1880–1985. Domination and Governance* (London: Routledge, 1990); Peter Baldwin, *The Politics of Social Solidarity: Class Bases of the European Welfare State 1875–1975* (New York: Cambridge University Press, 1990).

15. See a kind of a trajectory from Stein Rokkan, ed., *Comparative Research Across Cultures and Nations* (Paris: Mouton, 1968) to Walter D. Mignolo, *Local Histories/Global Designs: Coloniality, Subaltern Knowledge and Border Thinking* (Princeton, NJ: Princeton University Press, 2000).

16. In a splendid inaugural lecture read at the Oxford University in October 1994 as the first Lord Weidenfeld Professor of European Comparative Literature. Published contemporarily by Clarendon Press as "Qu'est-ce que la littérature comparée?" *Commentaire*, 70 (Summer 1995), 383–393.

17. Michael Werner, "La place relative du champ littéraire dans les cultures nationales" in Michel Espagne and Michael Werner, eds., *Qu'est-ce qu'une littérature national: Approches pour une théorie interculturelle du champ littéraire* (Paris: Edition MSH, 1994), pp. 15–30.

18. Otto Hintze, *Soziologie und Geschichte. Gesammelte Abhandlungen* (Göttingen, 1964), t. II, p. 251; Michel de Certeau, *L'écriture de l'histoire* (Paris 1975), p . See also Tamara K. Hareven, "What Difference Does It Make?" *Social Science History* 20:3 (Fall 1996), 317–344.

19. Michel Trebitsch and Marie-Christine Granjou, eds., *Pour une histoire comparée des intellectuels* (Paris: Ed. Complexe, 1998). See also Christophe Charle, *Les intellectuels en Europe au XIXe siècle. Essai d'histoire comparée* (Paris: Seuil, 1996).

20. As a *curiosum*, in a 1917 study *Ireland and Poland: A Comparison*, Thomas W. Rolleston (London: T. Fisher Unwin) goes to a great effort to argue that parallels in these two countries' history does not mean similarities in their historical destinies.

21. *States and Social Revolutions: A Comparative Analysis of France, Russia and China* (NY: Cambridge University Press, 1979). See also Moore, Jr., *The Social Origins of Dictatorship and Democracy*. A comparative study of a similar construction, where a certain general sociological model holds across different national contexts is *The Rebellious Century 1830–1930* by Charles Tilly, Louise Tilly, and Richard Tilly (Cambridge, MA: Harvard University Press, 1975).

22. Skocpol, *States*, op. cit., p. XI.

23. "A Contribution," op. cit., p. 58.

24. *The End of the Old Order in Rural Europe* (Princeton, NJ: Princeton University Press, 1978). Perry Anderson's remarkable comparative study of *Lineages of the Absolutist State* (London: Verso, 1986) brings out contrasts among nations and/or civilizations.

25. "Connected Histories: Notes Towards a Reconfiguration of Early Modern Eurasia" in V. Lieberman, ed., *Beyond Binary Histories. Re-imagining Eurasia to c. 1830* (Ann Arbor, MI: The University of Michigan Press, 1997), pp. 289–315.

26. Philippe Régnier, "*La Revue des Deux Mondes*" in Espagne and Werner, eds., *Qu'est-ce qu'une littérature nationale?*, op. cit., pp. 289–314.

27. Mark A. Lutz, *Economics for the Common Good: Two Centuries of Social Economic Thought in the Humanistic Tradition* (London and New York: Routledge, 1999), p. 21. Sismondi's *Nouveaux Principes*, the birth-song of the "second Sismondi" were published in 1819, in a revised version in 1927, and only recently translated into English. Jean-Charles-Leonard Simonde de Sismondi, *New Principles of Political Economy*, trans. R. Hyse (New Brunswick and London: Transaction, 1991).

28. See Edgeworth in *Castle Rackrent and Absentee*, Carlton in *Agent*, Korzeniowski in *Kollokacja*, and Kraszewski in *Spekulacja*. I am grateful to Stanisław Barańczak for suggesting that I read Korzeniowski.

29. Cited in Ryszarda Czepulis, *Myśl społeczna twórców Towarzystwa Rolniczego (1842–1861)* (Wrolcaw-Warszawa-Kraków: Ossolineum,1964).

30. For the review of the debate, see Thomas N. Headland, Kenneth L. Pike, and Marvin Harris, eds., *Emics and Etics: The Insider/ Outsider Debate* (Newbery Park: Sage, 1990). I thank Carlo Ginzburg for having led me to emic/etic.

31. "'From the Native's Point of View': On the Nature of Anthropological Understanding" in idem, *Local Knowledge: Further Essays in Interpretive Anthropology* (Boston: Basic, 1983), pp. 55–70.

32. "*De la Méditerranée à l'Asie: Une comparaison nécessaire,*" *Annales ESC*, 1 (January–February 2001), 46.

33. "Causal explanation will be a loser, but comparison will gain." Maurice Aymard, "Histoire et comparaison" in Hartmut Atsma and André Burguière, eds., *Marc Bloch aujourd'hui. Histoire comparée et Sciences sociales* (Paris: Editions de l'EHESS, 1990), p. 278.

11

IS THERE A PRE-HISTORY OF GLOBALIZATION?

David Armitage

"If it is now asked whether we at present live in an *enlightened* age [*aufgeklärten Zeitalter*], the answer is: No, but we do live in an age of *enlightenment* [*Zeitalter der Aufklärung*]."[1] Immanuel Kant's memorable accounting of the unfolding achievements and unfulfilled promises of his own age in his essay "What is Enlightenment?" (1784) might stand as the motto for any consideration of globalization and the writing of history. The difference between an "enlightened age" and an "age of enlightenment" suggests a parallel distinction between a "globalized age" and an "age of globalization," and hence between globalization as a process and globalization as a condition.[2] The process of globalization would be the gradual thickening of connections across national boundaries, their increasing penetration into previously untouched localities, and the emergence of a common set of concerns that define a universal cosmopolitan community. The condition of globalization would be a state of complete transnational integration, encompassing all the people of the world within a single network of economic and cultural connections informed by a common global consciousness. The world is manifestly far from attaining such a condition: farther, surely, than even Kant's Prussia was from enlightenment. That does not mean that there is no process of globalization presently underway; equally it does not mean that that process is necessarily the prelude to the achievement of globalization as a condition.

Like the most optimistic promoters of Enlightenment, globalization's most enthusiastic advocates have assumed both its potential universality and its relative novelty. As the process of worldwide integration and transnational conjunction, globalization (to be worthy of the name) must be all-inclusive and spatially expansive. Anything less than complete global coverage would be only a more generous form of internationalism, transnationality, or even regionalization, on however grand a scale. Because "globalize" can be both a transitive and an intransitive verb, and hence "at once an inexorable material development and a conscious human process,"[3] it implies both an inescapable teleology and a congeries of contingent intentions. Those intentions may be consciously directed towards achieving the condition of globalization; however, like the malign colliding wills that in their "unsocial sociability" [ungesellige Geselligkeit] produce a benign historical trajectory in Kant's vision of a "Universal History with a Cosmopolitan Purpose" (1784), their consequences are likely to be as unintended as they are unforeseeable.[4] The implied character of globalization, like that of Kant's universal history, is teleological: maybe not here, maybe not now, but in an increasing number of locales and with ever gathering velocity.

Globalization's character, like Enlightenment's, derives from its future rather than its past. "The idea of a history of globalization is at first sight a contradiction in terms. Globalization or internationalization has been depicted, for much of the last twenty years, as a condition of the present and the future—a phenomenon without a past."[5] The very novelty of the term "globalization" (and its cognates in other languages, such as the French term mondialisation) encourages the belief that globalization itself must also be quite recent, if not entirely, unprecedented. An unsophisticated nominalist might argue that without the word itself to affirm its existence neither the process nor the condition of globalization could exist. A more subtle nominalist would reply that language is an index of social change: vocabulary mutates and neologism occurs to describe the previously indescribable or undescribed. Either way, the lack of the term "globalization" before the 1980s would indicate that globalization is no more than a generation old, whether as a process of market integration and technological innovation or as the proliferating consciousness of globality itself. To call our era "the age of globalization" distinguishes it from any previous epoch only at the cost of the paradox that what is inclusive and extensive in space must be exclusive and intensive in time.[6]

This temporal foreshortening of the global has not gone unchallenged by historians and historically minded social scientists. The three features that distinguish the boosters' vision of globalization—its teleology, its novelty, and its uniformity—have generated critical counterparts in the forms of aetiology, genealogy, and multiplicity. The search for the historical origins of globalization parallels the examination of its impact of localization by demanding contextual specificity and asking exactly which features, and what definitions, of globalization are at stake.[7] The results of that search have pushed the chronology of globalization ever deeper into the past, well beyond the horizon of the generation now living in the present age of globalization. Most fruitfully, the historical examination of globalization has disaggregated a seemingly homogeneous (and homogenizing) process into a variety of disparate processes that have moved at different speeds across space and time and that appear to be frequently intermittent rather than inevitably linear.

"The chronology of globalisation has generated the most sterile controversy in history today," remarks Felipe Fernández-Armesto dyspeptically.[8] Although we can probably all think of equally apt candidates for that dubious honor, the fertility and the growth of the historical study of globalization give the lie to the assertion that controversy over its chronology is sterile: inconclusive, circular, and frequently Whiggish, perhaps, but hardly sterile. Research on the pre-history of globalization, on the origins, the antecedents, and the analogues of the global integration of the last twenty years, has, on the contrary, been one of the liveliest areas of recent historical inquiry. Fernández-Armesto himself has mischievously suggested pushing back the pre-history of globalization to pre-history itself. "Strong-sense globalisation—worldwide cultural conformity—last happened in the Paleolithic period": the whole of subsequent human history has since been the record of the divergence of humankind from this primal uniformity.[9] The editor of the essay collection that inspired his skepticism proposes instead a four-stage theory of globalization, "categorized as archaic, proto, modern and post-colonial," to encompass a range of phenomena from before the pre-industrial and the pre-national to the post-industrial and post-national eras.[10] This typology is a sign that the field is at least fertile in categories and hence in questions for further inquiry.

The diversity of definitions of globalization determines the variety of globalizations, their origins and trajectories, to be found in the prehistoric—that is, pre-1980—past. For example, if globalization is taken to mean "the integration of international commodity markets" defined by commodity price convergence (as in the work of Kevin

O'Rourke and Jeffrey Williamson), then it "did not begin 5,000 years ago, or even 500 years ago. It began in the early nineteenth century. In that sense, it is a very modern phenomenon."[11] A more expansive definition of globalization backdates its origins by 350 years to the beginnings of a global economy in the sixteenth century. The origins of globalization might only be found at the point where the links in the emergent world economy were joined, specifically at the moment when the silver bullion that was drawn from the Spanish-American empire into China created a link between the Atlantic world and the Asian trade: that is, in Manila in 1571.[12] In this sense, it is an early modern phenomenon.

Versions of this genealogy have a distinguished history, stretching back through Marx's judgment that voyages of Vasco da Gama and Christopher Columbus "opened up fresh ground for the rising bourgeoisie" to Adam Smith's identification of "[t]he discovery of America, and that of a passage to the East Indies by the Cape of Good Hope" as "the two greatest and most important events recorded in the history of mankind" because they marked the origins of a worldwide trading system.[13] The more drastically foreshortened recent histories of globalization compress into the space of little more than a generation developments Smith and Marx traced over half a millennium. As long as there is no agreement about the defining features of globalization (commodity price convergence, intercontinental trading linkages, or the emergence of a "world-system," for example) there is unlikely to be consensus about whether globalization has a pre-history, let alone how long its history may have been.

If, as most definitions of globalization agree, the fact of globalization (however defined) must be accompanied by the consciousness of globality, when did that consciousness emerge? Was it the product of economic convergence or its cause? And did it emerge globally or was it a phenomenon local to particular places and peoples? The most persuasive answers to these questions locate the origins of a consciousness of globality in Europe in the late eighteenth century, as the earlier quotations from Smith and Kant perhaps have already implied. This is not to say that such synchronic conceptions of globality had no antecedents before that time. Cartographers since the early sixteenth century had been able to see the world (almost) whole.[14] Cosmographers in the later sixteenth century had speculated about the potential human habitability of the planet.[15] As early as 1658, the English physician Sir Thomas Browne provided a precocious intimation of time–space compression when he compared his own bedtime in England with that of other peoples in more distant time zones: "The Huntsmen are up in *America*, and they are already past their first sleep in *Persia*."[16] However, a diachronic conception of globality, "the idea that human beings inhabit a unitary and finite global space, move along the same temporal scale of world-historical time and constitute one single collective entity,"[17] was the product of the later eighteenth century.

"The growing call since the midpoint of the century for a new world history testifies to the depth of the experiential shift that can be traced to global interdependence."[18] In these words, Reinhart Koselleck has speculated that world history was the product of the post-war period: that is, of the aftermath of the Seven Years' War of 1756–1763, not of the Six Years' War of 1939–1945, and hence of the late eighteenth century, not the late twentieth century. "Ministers in this country, where every part of the World affects us, in some way or another, should consider the *whole Globe*," wrote the Duke of Newcastle in 1758.[19] He could hardly have known that the conflict would encompass theaters of war as far-flung as the Philippines and Bengal, West Africa and the Plains of Abraham. The fact that it did helped to encourage a wider European public and its leading intellectuals, from Edmund Burke and Adam Smith to the Abbé Raynal and Immanuel Kant, to think globally about history and to think historically about the globe. On the publication of William Robertson's *History of America* in 1777, Burke sent a letter of congratulation to the author exulting at the possibility that the great Enlightenment project of a history of humanity might finally be in sight: "The Great Map of Mankind is unrolld at once; and there is no state or Gradation of barbarism, and no mode of refinement which we have not at the same instant under our View."[20] The decades following the Seven Years' War comprised "the first age of global imperialism" and this stadial view of history was as much the product of that set of conjunctions as it was the result of the intercontinental encounter of European armies and navies.[21] It would take the dismantling of such hierarchical accounts of "barbarism" and refinement before histories of humanity as a global community could be envisaged by Kant (in his "Idea for a Universal History with a Cosmopolitan Intent"), for example.[22]

The history of globalization shows that it repeatedly generated equal and opposite reactions towards deglobalization. This can be shown in the late eighteenth-century transformations of two other global discourses that illustrate the limits of universalism within the history of globalization: the discourses of rights and of international law. Neither was unprecedented, of course: the identification of subjective natural rights as a peculiarly human attribute can be traced back at least to the early seventeenth century and thence to the late middle ages.[23] Likewise, if the antecedents of international law are to be found in either the *jus gentium* or the *jus naturale,* then they extend even farther back to Roman law and to stoic universalism.[24] The modern theory of rights and natural law fashioned by Hugo Grotius in the early seventeenth century had attempted to bridge the gap between the law of nature and the law of nations by deducing a minimalist core of morality for all human beings that was both universally intelligible and necessarily obligatory, even if God himself had not existed.[25] The law of nations had thus been assimilable to the law of nature because it seemed to be universally observed by all rational creatures, at whatever stage of civil development, savage, barbarous, or polite, and without regard to their religious beliefs. As Montesquieu noted in a frequently quoted passage from the opening of *L'Esprit des lois* (1748), "All nations have a right of nations; and even the Iroquois, who eat their prisoners, have one. They send and receive embassies; they know rights of war and peace; the trouble is their right of nations is not founded on true principles."[26] In 1755, the *Encyclopédie* likewise defined "Droit des gens" as "a jurisprudence that natural reason has established among all humans concerning certain matters, and which is observed in all nations": it therefore applied equally to Christians and Muslims, barbarians and infidels.[27]

The subsequent histories of both international law and rights talk have been as discontinuous, reversible, and irregular as those of globalization itself. For example, late eighteenth-century universalism was accompanied by an emergent consensus which held that the scope of the law of nations was restricted to something less than the global scope implied by the law of nature. For example, Robert Ward, the author of the first English-language history of the law of nations argued in 1795 "that what is commonly called the Law of Nations, falls very far short of *universality*; and that, therefore, the Law is not the Law of *all* nations, but only of particular classes of them; and thus there may be a *different* Law of Nations for *different* parts of the globe."[28] According to Ward, the only foundation for an obligatory law of nations was revealed rather than natural religion; the only revealed religion worthy of the name was Christianity; therefore, the only binding law of nations was the law of Christendom. Similarly, in 1798 James Mackintosh concentrated his lectures on the law of nature and nations on "that important branch of it which professes to regulate the relations and intercourse of states, and more especially, both on account of their greater perfection and their more immediate reference to use, the regulations of that intercourse as they are modified by the usages of the civilized nations of Christendom." This was manifestly not the law of "the brutal and helpless barbarism of *Terra del Fuego*,…the mild and voluptuous savages of Otaheite,…the tame, but ancient and immoveable civilization of China,…the meek and servile natives of Hindostan … [or] the gross and incorrigible rudeness of the Ottomans."[29]

Such judgments laid the foundation for a conception of international law as the law of a specifically Christian civilization rather than as the norms of an emergent global society.[30] In the nineteenth century, that law could be extended to non-Christian nations, such as China, Japan, and the Ottoman Empire, but only by means of positive agreements (treaties, trading compacts, and the like) not on the grounds of its universality or its derivation from natural law or natural reason. The consequent standard of civilization became enshrined in nineteenth-century positivist conceptions of European international law, and thence was exported to the extra-European world by such vehicles as the Chinese translation of the American Henry Wheaton's *Elements of International Law* (1836).[31] It is therefore hardly surprising that human rights have also been confounded with imperialism or that public international law itself has been condemned as "Eurocentric," the product of but one self-regulating (and self-regarding) "civilization" among many, but not therefore the only one to be regarded as a legitimate source of international norms.[32] Resistance to rights talk has thus often taken the form of anti-Occidentalism, anti-imperialism, or anti-Americanism. Its dissemination and penetration may be "the products of recent developments—industrialization, urbanization, the communications and information revolutions—that are replicable everywhere, even if they have not occurred everywhere at once."[33] The fact that they have not is no guarantee that they must or ever will, as the various contested histories of globalization repeatedly confirm.

The example of legal discourse is especially revealing because it is from that discourse that the term "international" arose and from it, too, that the reigning contemporary conception of the "transnational." "Whereas 'international' implies a relationship among nations, 'transnational' suggests various types of interactions across national boundaries."[34] Like all such terms of art, "international" and "transnational" are concepts that depend upon broader and more elaborate theories for their analytical precision and utility. Such concepts can migrate from the theories within which they were first located, but they cannot entirely escape their origins. When used to describe a form of history, a set of political relations, or forms of human association, the word "international" functions as a transferred epithet. It has been transferred from jurisprudence to historiography, diplomacy, and politics. "International" was one of the many coinages introduced by Jeremy Bentham to clarify (although just as often to obscure) the conceptual vocabulary of his beknighted contemporaries, like "maximise," "minimise," "terrorist," and "codification," among others.[35] According to Bentham, writing in 1780 in a work first published in 1789, "international law" denoted "that brand of jurisprudence" whose subject is "the mutual transactions of sovereigns as such" rather than the activities of individuals who were subject to "internal" domestic or municipal law.[36]

The extension of forms of regulation and interaction beyond those that could be encompassed within the actions of sovereigns alone demanded a further extension of legal vocabulary to denominate "transnational law." In 1956, the Columbia law professor Philip Jessup took this "to include all law which regulates actions or events that transcend national frontiers. Both public and private international law are included, as are other rules which do not wholly fit into such standard categories."[37] Jessup acknowledged that he had not coined the term, although he may have been the first to endow it with continuing longevity, as a concept whose time had clearly come in the generation after the Second World War, the founding of the United Nations, and the promulgation of the Universal Declaration of Human Rights. Randolph Bourne had nervously celebrated the transcendent multinationalism of the United States in almost Hegelian terms as "the trans-nationality of all the nations" in 1916, and Norman Angell repeatedly applied the term "trans-national" to the conditions of the post-war economy in Europe in 1921, but only in the last half-century does "transnational" seem to have taken root as a term of art across the social sciences and, from thence, to the humanities.[38] In the meantime, the map of law has come to encompass not just international and transnational law, alongside domestic, private, or municipal law, but also "supranational," "global," or "world" law (dealing with the environment or outer space, for example), in addition to the regional law of such supranational organizations as the European Union or intercommunal law, regulating relations between different religious or ethnic groups.[39]

The globalization of law has patently moved at a different speed, along different tracks, from the process of economic globalization. This should hardly be surprising, in light of the discontinuities evident in the history of globalization. Globalization is no more a unitary enterprise than was internationalization before it; multiple tracks towards globalization can be discerned, just as multiple movements of resistance to it have arisen. For example, the early nineteenth-century price commodity convergence, although combined later in the century with an ideology of free trade, the lowering of tariff barriers, and the consequent free movements of capital and labor, could be seen to have run its course by the 1930s as "a backlash against globalization [in the shape of tariff reforms, central banks, and immigration controls] that had been developing progressively since the last third of the nineteenth century...identified globalism with change and sin, and held that moral regeneration required national cultures."[40] Indeed, it was precisely that moment of national reassertion that generated the very term "global," meaning "worldwide" or "universal" in English, as a loan-word from French.[41] Even in its economic form, the process of achieving such a global condition was ephemeral and its pre-conditions had to be constructed afresh for the present moment of globalization.

Even if economic integration had been smoothly unimpeded since the early fifteenth or the early nineteenth century, it would not have been accompanied by the frictionless planetary integration of, say, legal regimes, cultural norms, or religious beliefs. Greater economic convergence undoubtedly had a mutually sustaining relationship with cultural contact, for instance, but that led less readily to a convergence of norms than it did to a collision of competing universalisms, as, for example, in the Macartney embassy's bruising encounter with the Qing emperor in Beijing in 1793, which humiliatingly pitted the mercantile and diplomatic ambitions of the British Empire of George III against the impregnable self-confidence of the Celestial Empire of Qianlong.[42] Such incommensurable universalisms could not be combined or negotiated, leaving economic globalization as just one—far from uncontested or inevitable—alternative among many even today.

There is no single universal process of globalization within which all forms of human interaction move in lockstep towards an inexorably globalized condition. Globalization's histories are multiple and its prehistories just as various. It would be fallacious to seek a single prehistory of globalization, both because it has had many paths and because none of those paths has been unbroken. This makes writing the history of globalization more difficult, but it should not render it impossible as long as we recall that the process can be halted or reversed. To live in an age of globalization is not the same thing as living in a globalized age: after all, there have been processes of globalization before, for example, in the late fifteenth, late eighteenth, and mid-nineteenth centuries, none of which produced a lasting condition of globalization. The historians' contribution to the study of globalization should therefore be to remind us that we may be living amid only the latest (but probably not the last) of globalization's diverse and disconnected pre-histories.

REFERENCES

1. Immanuel Kant, "Beantwortung der Frage: Was ist Aufklärung?" (1784), in Kant, *Schriften zur Anthropologie, Geschichtsphilosophie, Politik und Pädagogik*, Wilhelm Weischedel, ed., 2 vols. (Frankfurt, 1964), I, 59, trans. H. B. Nisbet in Kant, *Political Writings*, Hans Reiss, ed., 2nd ed. (Cambridge, 1991), p. 58.
2. Compare Jean Starobinski, "The Word Civilization," in Starobinski, *Blessings in Disguise: On the Morality of Evil* (Cambridge, MA, 1993), pp. 1–35, on "civilization" as process and condition.
3. Akira Iriye, *Global Community: The Role of International Organizations in the Making of the Contemporary World* (Berkeley, 2002), p. 8.
4. Kant, "Idee zu einer Allgemeinen Geschichte in Weltbürgerliche Absicht" (1784), in Kant, *Schriften zur Anthropologie, Geschichtsphilosophie, Politik und Pädagogik*, Wilhelm Weischedel, ed., vol. I, p. 37, trans. Nisbet in Kant, *Political Writings*, Hans Reiss, ed., p. 44.
5. Emma Rothschild, "Globalization and the Return of History," *Foreign Policy*, 115 (Summer 1999), 107; compare Rothschild, "The Politics of Globalization circa 1773," *The OECD Observer*, 224 (Winter 2001).
6. Bruce Mazlish, "An Introduction to Global History," in Mazlish and Ralph Buultjens, eds., *Conceptualizing Global History* (Boulder, CO, 1993), p. 1: "Ours...is an Age of Globalization."
7. As in the penetrating critique by Frederick Cooper, "What is the Concept of Globalization Good For? An African Historian's Perspective," *African Affairs*, 100 (2001), 189–213.
8. Felipe Fernández-Armesto, review of A. G. Hopkins, ed., *Globalization in World History* (London, 2002), *History Today*, 52: 5 (May 2002), 76.
9. Fernández-Armesto, review of Hopkins, ed., *Globalization in World History*, p. 76; compare Christopher Chase-Dunn and Thomas D. Hall, "Paradigms Bridged: Institutional Materialism and World-Systemic Evolution," in Sing C. Chew and J. David Knottnerus, eds., *Structure, Culture, and History: Recent Issues in Social Theory* (Lanham, MD, 2002), pp. 197–216.
10. A. G. Hopkins, "Introduction: Globalization—An Agenda for Historians," in Hopkins, ed., *Globalization in World History*, p. 3.
11. Kevin H. O'Rourke and Jeffrey G. Williamson, "When Did Globalisation Begin?" *European Review of Economic History*, 6 (2002), 25, 47; compare O'Rourke and Williamson, *Globalization and History: The Evolution of a Nineteenth-Century Atlantic Economy* (Cambridge, MA, 1999); Dani Rodrik, Maurice Obstfeld, Robert C. Feenstra, and Williamson, "Globalization in Perspective," *Journal of Economic Perspectives*, 12 (1998), 1–72.
12. Dennis O. Flynn and Arturo Giráldez, "Born with a Silver Spoon: The Origin of World Trade in 1571," *Journal of World History*, 6 (1995), 201–221; Flynn and Giráldez, "Cycles of Silver: Global Economic Unity through the Mid-Eighteenth Century," *Journal of World History*, 13 (2002), 391–427.

13. Karl Marx and Friedrich Engels, *The Communist Manifesto* (1848), Gareth Stedman Jones, ed. (London, 2002), p. 220; Adam Smith, *An Inquiry into the Nature and Causes of the Wealth of Nations* (1776), R. H. Campbell and A. S. Skinner, eds., 2 vols. (Oxford, 1976), I, p.448, II, p. 626.

14. Thomas Goldstein, "The Renaissance Concept of the Earth in Its Influence upon Copernicus," *Terrae Incognitae*, 4 (1972), 19–51

15. John M. Headley, "The Sixteenth-Century Venetian Celebration of the Earth's Total Habitability: The Issue of the Fully Habitable World for Renaissance Europe," *Journal of World History*, 8 (1997), 1–27.

16. Sir Thomas Browne, *The Garden of Cyrus* (1658), in Browne, *The Major Works*, C. A. Patrides, ed. (Harmondsworth, 1977), p. 387; on "time-space compression" before the Enlightenment see David Harvey, *The Condition of Postmodernity: An Enquiry into the Origins of Cultural Change* (Oxford, 1990), pp. 240–252.

17. Chenxi Tang, "Writing World History: The Emergence of Modern Global Consciousness in the Late Eighteenth Century (1760–1790)" (Ph.D. Dissertation, Columbia University, 2000), 1.

18. Reinhart Koselleck, *Futures Past: On the Semantics of Historical Time*, trans. Keith Tribe (Cambridge, MA, 1985), p. 255.

19. Earl of Newcastle to Earl of Holdernesse, July 25, 1758, British Library Additional Manuscripts 32882, fols. 65–66, quoted in Richard Middleton, *The Bells of Victory: The Pitt-Newcastle Ministry and the Conduct of the Seven Years' War, 1757–1762* (Cambridge, 1985), p. 77; more generally, see H. V. Bowen, "British Conceptions of Global Empire, 1756–83," *Journal of Imperial and Commonwealth History*, 26: 3 (September 1998), 1–27.

20. Edmund Burke to William Robertson, June 9, 1777, in *The Correspondence of Edmund Burke*, III, George H. Guttridge, ed. (Cambridge, 1961), pp. 350–351. On the "Enlightened narrative" that lay behind Burke's vision see Karen O'Brien, *Narratives of Enlightenment: Cosmopolitan History from Voltaire to Gibbon* (Cambridge, 1997); J. G. A. Pocock, *Barbarism and Religion*, II: *Narratives of Civil Government* (Cambridge, 1999).

21. C. A. Bayly, "The First Age of Global Imperialism, c. 1760–1830," *Journal of Imperial and Commonwealth History*, 26 (1998), 28–47.

22. Tang, "Writing World History," Ch. 2, "Anthropological History of Mankind."

23. Brian Tierney, *The Idea of Natural Rights: Studies on Natural Rights, Natural Law, and Church Law, 1150–1625* (Atlanta, 1997).

24. Anthony Pagden, "Stoicism, Cosmopolitanism, and the Legacy of European Imperialism," *Constellations*, 7 (2000), 3–22.

25. Richard Tuck, "The Modern Theory of Natural Law," in Anthony Pagden, ed., *The Languages of Political Theory in Early-Modern Europe* (Cambridge, 1987), pp. 99–119; T. J. Hochstrasser, *Natural Law Theories in the Early Enlightenment* (Cambridge, 2000).

26. Charles-Louis de Secondat, Baron de Montesquieu, *The Spirit of the Laws* (1748), trans. Anne Cohler, Basia Miller, and Harold Stone (Cambridge, 1989), p. 8.

27. *Encyclopédie, ou Dictionnaire raisonné des sciences, des arts et des métiers*, 17 vols. (Paris, 1751–1765), V, p. 126, *s.v.*, "Droit des gens."

28. Robert Ward, *An Enquiry into the Foundation and History of the Law of Nations in Europe, From the Time of the Greeks and Romans, to the Age of Grotius*, 2 vols. (London, 1795), I, p. xiv.

29. James Mackintosh, *A Discourse on the Study of the Law of Nature and Nations, &c.* (London, 1799), p. 25.

30. Martti Koskenniemi, *The Gentle Civilizer of Nations: The Rise and Fall of International Law, 1870–1960* (Cambridge, 2002) provides a magisterial survey of the consequences of this conception.

31. Gerrit W. Gong, *The Standard of "Civilization" in International Society* (Oxford, 1984), pp. 25–35; M. W. Janis, "American Versions of the International Law of Christendom: Kent, Wheaton and the Grotian Tradition," *Netherlands International Law Review*, 39 (1992), 51–59; Lydia H. Liu, "Legislating the Universal: The Circulation of International Law in the Nineteenth Century," in L.H. Liu, ed., *Tokens of Exchange: The Problem of Translation in Global Circulations* (Durham, NC, 1999), pp. 128–129, 136–142, 155–159.

32. Yasuaki Onuma, "When Was the Law of International Society Born—An Inquiry of [sic] the History of International Law from an Intercivilizational Perspective," *Journal of the History of International Law*, 2 (2000), 1–66.

33. Thomas M. Franck, "Are Human Rights Universal?" *Foreign Affairs*, 80 (2001), 198.

34. Akira Iriye, "Internationalizing International History," in Thomas Bender, ed., *Rethinking American History in a Global Age* (Berkeley, 2002), p. 51.

35. Mary P. Mack, *Jeremy Bentham: An Odyssey of Ideas, 1748–1792* (New York, 1963), pp. 191–195.

36. Jeremy Bentham, *An Introduction to the Principles of Morals and Legislation* (1780/89), J. H. Burns and H. L. A. Hart, eds. introd. F. Rosen (Oxford, 1996), pp. 6, 296; M. W. Janis, "Jeremy Bentham and the Fashioning of 'International Law'," *American Journal of International Law*, 78 (1984), 408–410.

37. Philip Jessup, *Transnational Law* (New Haven, CT, 1956), pp. 1–2.

38. Randolph Bourne, "Trans-National America," (1916) in *War and the Intellectuals: Essays by Randolph S. Bourne 1915-1919*, Carl Resek, ed. (New York, 1964) (my thanks to Jona Hansen for this reference); Norman Angell, *The Fruits of Victory: A Sequel to "The Great Illusion"* (London, 1921), pp. 14, 63, 300; *Oxford English Dictionary*, s.v., "transnational."

39. J. W. Head, "Supranational Law: How the Move Toward Multilateral Solutions Is Changing the Character of 'International Law'," *University of Kansas Law Review*, 42 (1994), 606-666; Jost Delbrück, "A More Effective International Law or a New 'World Law'? Some Aspects of the Development of International Law in a Changing Economic System," *Indiana Law Journal*, 68 (1993), 705–725; William Twining, *Globalisation and Legal Theory* (London, 2000), pp. 139–140.

40. Harold James, *The End of Globalization: Lessons from the Great Depression* (Cambridge, MA, 2001), pp. 200–201.

41. *OED, s.v.*, "global," where the citations show an isolated usage in 1892 and then a striking spike in frequency and continuous use in English after 1927.

42. James L. Hevia, *Cherishing Men from Afar: Qing Guest Ritual and the Macartney Embassy of 1793* (Durham, NC, 1995).

CONTRIBUTORS

David Armitage is Professor at Harvard University. He is the author of *The Ideological Origins of the British Empire* (Cambridge: Cambridge University Press, 2000) and the editor of, among other books, *Theories of Empire, 1450–1800* (Aldershot; Brookfield, VT: Ashgate, 1998) and (with Michael Braddick) *The British Atlantic World, 1500–1800* (New York: Palgrave Macmillan, 2002). He is currently working on a study of international thought in the long eighteenth century and on a global history of the Declaration of Independence.

Peter Baldwin is Professor of History at the University of California, Los Angeles, and author of *The Politics of Social Solidarity: Class Bases of the European Welfare State, 1875–1975* (Cambridge: Cambridge University Press, 1990); *Contagion and the State in Europe, 1830–1930* (Cambridge: Cambridge University Press, 1999); and *Disease and Democracy: The State Faces AIDS in the West* (Berkeley: University of California Press, 2005).

Deborah Cohen is Associate Professor of History at Brown University. She is the author of *The War Come Home: Disabled Veterans in Britain and Germany, 1914–1939* (Berkeley: University of California Press, 2001), which was awarded the Allan Sharlin Memorial Award (2002) by the Social Science History Association. She is currently working on a book entitled "Household Gods: The British and their Possessions, 1840s–1950s" (Yale University Press, forthcoming).

Susan Grayzel is Associate Professor of History at the University of Mississippi. She is the author of *Women and the First World War* (Harlow: Longman, 2002) and *Women's Identities At War: Gender, Motherhood, and Politics in Britain and France during the First World*

War (Chapel Hill: University of North Carolina Press, 1999), which won the British Council Prize from the North American Conference on British Studies in 2000.

Nancy L. Green is Directrice d'Études (Professor) at the École des Hautes Études en Sciences Sociales (Paris). She is author of *Ready-to-Wear and Ready-to-Work: A Century of Industry and Immigrants in Paris and New York* (Duke University Press: Durham, 1997); and *Repenser les migrations* (Paris: PUF, 2002).

Heinz-Gerhard Haupt is Professor at the European University Institute (Florence) and Professor of History at the University of Bielefeld. His books include *Nationalismus und Demokratie. Zur Geschichte der Bourgeoisie im Frankreich der Restauration* (Frankfurt a.m.: Fischer, 1974); with Karin Hausen, *Die Pariser Kommune. Erfolg und Scheitern einer Revolution* (Frankfurt a.M: Campus, 1979); *Sozialgeschichte Frankreichs seit 1789* (Frankfurt a.M.: Suhrkamp, 1989); with G. Crossick, *The Petite Bourgeoisie in Europe 1780–1914* (London: Routledge, 1995); with J. Kocka (eds.), *Geschichte und Vergleich. Ansätze und Chancen einer international vergleichenden Geschichtsschreibung* (Frankfurt a.M.: Campus, 1996); *Konsum und Handel. Europa im 19. und 20. Jahrhundert* (Göttingen: Vandenhoeck & Ruprecht, 2003).

Jürgen Kocka is Professor of History at the Freie Universitat Berlin, where he directs the Center for the Comparative History of Europe. Among his publications are the books *Facing Total War: German Society, 1914–1918* (Leamington Spa: Berg, 1984 [1973]; *Unternehmer in der deutschen Industrialisierung* (Göttingen: Vandenhoeck & Ruprecht, 1995); *White Collar Workers in America, 1890–1940: A Social-Political History in International Perspective* (London; Beverly Hills: Sage Publications, 1980 [1977]); *Lohnarbeit und Klassenbildung. Arbeiter und Arbeiterbewegung in Deutschland 1800–1875* (Berlin: J.H.W. Dietz, 1983); with Ute Frevert (eds.), *Bürgertum im 19.Jahrhundert: Deutschland im europäischen Vergleich* (Munich: DTV, 1988); with Allan Mitchell (eds.), *Bourgeois Society in Nineteenth-Century Europe* (Oxford; Providence: Berg, 1993); with H-G Haupt (eds.), *Geschichte und Vergleich. Ansätze und Chancen einer international vergleichenden Geschichtsschreibung* (Frankfurt a.M.: Campus, 1996); *Vereinigungskrise. Zur Geschichte der Gegenwart* (Göttingen: Vandenhoeck & Ruprecht, 1995); *Industrial Culture and Bourgeois Society. Business, Labor and Bureaucracy in Modern Germany* (New York: Berghahn, 1999).

Michael Miller is Professor of History at Syracuse University. He is the author of *The Bon Marché: Bourgeois Culture and the Department Store, 1869–1920* (Princeton: Princeton University Press, 1981) and *Shanghai on the Métro: Spies, Intrigue and the French Between the Wars* (Berkeley: University of California Press, 1994). He is currently writing a book on Europe and the Maritime World in the Twentieth Century.

Maura O'Connor is Associate Professor of History at the University of Cincinnati. She is the author of *The Romance of Italy and the English Political Imagination* (St. Martin's Press: New York, 1998). She is currently working on a book-length study of financial speculation and the London Stock Exchange in the nineteenth century.

Susan Pedersen is Professor of History at Columbia University. Her publications include *Family, Dependence, and the Origins of the Welfare State: Britain and France, 1914–1945* (Cambridge: Cambridge University Press, 1993), which was awarded the Allan Sharlin Memorial Award (1994) by the Social Science History Association; with Peter Mandler, eds., *After the Victorians: Private Conscience and Public Duty in Modern Britain* (London: Routledge, 1994); and *Eleanor Rathbone and the Politics of Conscience* (New Haven: Yale University Press, 2004). She is now working on a study of the mandate system of the League of Nations.

Marta Petrusewicz emigrated from her native Poland in 1969, and has since lived in Italy, Canada and the US. She has taught at the Universita' della Calabria, Harvard, Princeton, and is currently professor of Modern European History at the City University of New York, Hunter College. She has published extensively on economic and social history of Italy and Poland; her most recent book is *Come il Meridione divenne Questione? Rappresentazioni del Sud prima e dopo il 1848* (Soveria Mannelli (Catanzaio): Rubbettino, 1998). She is now at work on a comparative history of the 19th-century European peripheries.

Glenda Sluga is Associate Professor of History at the University of Sydney. She is the author of *The Problem of Trieste and the Italo-Yugoslav Border: Difference, Identity and Sovereignty in Twentieth-century Europe* (Albany: State University of New York, 2001) and co-author of *Gendering European History* (Leicester: Leicester University Press, 2000).

Suggestions for Further Reading

WORKS OF HISTORIOGRAPHIC, METHODOLOGICAL, OR THEORETICAL INTEREST

AHR Forum "Bringing Regionalism Back to History," *American Historical Review* 104: 4 (October 1999), 1156–1220.

Armer, Michael, Allen Day Grimshaw, and the Institute for Comparative Sociology. *Comparative Social Research: Methodological Problems and Strategies*. New York: Wiley, 1973.

Atsma, Hartmut and André Burguière. *Marc Bloch aujourd'hui: Histoire comparée & sciences sociales*. Paris: Editions de l'Ecole des hautes études en sciences sociales, 1990.

Aymard, Maurice. "Histoire et comparaison," in *Marc Bloch aujourd'hui: Histoire comparée & sciences sociales*, edited by Hartmut Atsma and André Burguière. Paris: Editions de l'Ecole des hautes études en sciences sociales, 1990.

Bagby, Philip. *Culture and History: Prolegomena to the Comparative Study of Civilizations*, Berkeley and Los Angeles: University of California Press, 1964.

Baily, Samuel L. "Cross-Cultural Comparison and the Writing of Migration History: Some Thoughts on How to Study Italians in the New World," in *Immigration Reconsidered*, edited by Virginia Yans-McLaughlin. New York: Oxford University Press, 1990.

Benson, Lee. "The Empirical and Statistical Basis for Comparative Analysis of Historical Change," in *Toward a Scientific Study of History: Selected Essays*, edited by Lee Benson. Philadelphia: J.B. Lippincott, 1972.

Bloch, Marc. "Pour une histoire comparée des sociétés européennes," paper delivered at the *Sixth International Congress of Historical Sciences*, Oslo 1928 and printed in *Revue de synthèse historique* 46 (1928), 15–50.

Bloch, Marc. "Toward a Comparative History of European Societies," in *Enterprise and Secular Change: Readings in Economic History*, edited by Frederic C. Lane. London: George Allen and Unwin, 1953.

Bonnell, Victoria E. "The Uses of Theory, Concepts and Comparison in Historical Sociology." *Comparative Studies in Society and History* 22 (April 1980), 155–173.

Breuilly, John, "Introduction: Making Comparisons in History," in J. Breuilly, *Labour and Liberalism in 19th Century Europe: Essays in Comparative History*. New York: St. Martin's, 1991.

Conrad, Christoph and Sebastian Conrad, editors. *Die Nation schreiben. Geschichtswissenschaft im internationalen Vergleich.* Göttingen: Vandenhoeck & Ruprecht, 2002.

Cooper, Frederick. "Race, Ideology, and the Perils of Comparative History." *American Historical Review* 101: 4 (October 1996), 1122-1138.

Cronin, James. "Neither Exceptional nor Peculiar. Towards the Comparative Study of Labor in Advanced Society." *International Review of Social History* 38 (1993), 59-75.

Daum, Werner. "Fallobst oder Steinschlag: Einleitende Überlegungen zum historischen Vergleich," in *Vergleichende Perspektiven—Perspektiven des Vergleichs: Studien zur europäischen Geschichte von der Spätantike bis ins 20. Jahrhundert,* edited by Helga Schnabel-Schüle. Mainz: von Zabern, 1998.

Degler, Carl N. "Comparative History: An Essay Review." *Journal of Southern History,* 31(1968), 425-430.

Detienne, Marcel. *Comparer l'incomparable.* Paris: Editions du Seuil. 2000.

Dumont, Louis. "On the Comparative Understanding of Non-modern Civilizations." *Daedalus* 104 (1975), 153-172.

Eisenberg, Christiane. "The Comparative View in Labour History. Old and New Interpretations of the English and German Labour Movement before 1914." *International Review of Social History* 34 (1989).

Eisenstadt, S.N. "Problems in the Comparative Analysis of Total Societies." *Transactions of the Sixth World Congress of Sociology, Geneva: International Sociological Association* 1 (1966).

Espagne, Michel. "Sur les limites du comparatisme en histoire culturelle." *Genèses* 17 (September 1994): 112-121.

Espagne, Michel and Michael Werner, editors. *Qu'est-ce qu'une littérature nationale? Approches pour une théorie interculturelle du champ littéraire.* Paris: Editions de la Maison des Sciences de l'Homme, 1994.

Etzioni, Amitai and Fred DuBow. *Comparative Perspectives: Theories and Methods.* Boston: Little Brown. 1969.

Fassin, Eric. "Fearful Symmetry: Culturalism and Cultural Comparison after Tocqueville." *French Historical Studies* 19: 2 (Autumn 1995), 451-460.

Flint, John. "Conceptual Translations in Comparative Study: A Review Article." *Comparative Studies in Society and History* 18: 4 (October 1976).

Frederickson, George M. "Comparative History," in *The Past Before Us: Contemporary Historical Writings in the United States,* edited by Michael Kamman. Ithaca, NY: Cornell University Press, 1980.

Frederickson, George M. "From Exceptionalism to Variability: Recent Developments in Cross-National Comparative History." *Journal of American History* 82: 2 (September 1995), 587-604.

Fuchs, Eckhardt and Benedikt Stuchtey, editors. *Across Cultural Borders: Historiography in Global Perspective.* Lanham, MD: Rowman and Littlefield, 2002.

Fumian, Carol. "Le virtù della comparazione." *Meridiana* 4 (1990).

Green, Nancy L. "L'histoire comparative et le champ des études migratoires." *Annales, ESC* 6 (November–December 1990), 1335-1350.

Grew, Raymond. "The Case for Comparing Histories." *American Historical Review,* 85: 4 (October 1980), 763-778.

Grew, Raymond. "The Comparative Weakness of American History." *Journal of Interdisciplinary History* 16 (1985), 87-101.

Guarnari, Carl. "Some Reflections on Comparative and Transnational Histories." NYU-OAH Conference on Internationalizing American History, Florence, Italy, July 6–8, 1998.

Halperin, Charles J. et al. "AHR Forum: Comparative History in Theory and Practice: A Discussion." *American Historical Review,* 87: 1 (February 1982), 123-143.

Hartz, Louis. "American Historiography and Comparative Analysis: Further Reflections." *Comparative Studies in Society and History* 5: 4 (July 1963), 365–377.

Haupt, Heinz-Gerhard. "La lente émergence d'une histoire comparée," in *Passés recomposés: Champs et chantiers de l'histoire*, edited by Jean Boutier and Dominique Julia. Paris: Edition Autrement, 1995.

Haupt, Heinz-Gerhard and Jürgen Kocka. "Historischer Vergleich: Methoden, Aufgaben, Probleme," in *Geschichte und Vergleich: Ansätze und Ergebnisse international vergleichender Geschichtsschreibung*, edited by Heinz-Gerhard Haupt and Jürgen Kocka. Frankfurt; New York: Campus, 1996.

Haupt, Heinz-Gerhard and Jürgen Kocka. *Geschichte und Vergleich: Ansätze und Ergebnisse international vergleichender Geschichtsschreibung*. Frankfurt; New York: Campus, 1996.

Hill, Alette Olin and Boyd H. Hill. "AHR Forum: Marc Bloch and Comparative History." *The American Historical Review* 85: 4 (October 1980), 828–846.

Hintze, Otto and Gerhard Oestreich. *Soziologie und Geschichte; gesammelte Abhandlungen zur Soziologie, Politik und Theorie der Geschichte*. Göttingen: Vandenhoeck & Ruprecht, 1964.

Hradil, Stefan and Stefan Immerfall. *Die westeuropäischen Gesellschaften im Vergleich*. Opladen: Leske + Budrich, 1997.

Immerfall, Stefan. *Einführung in den europäischen Gesellschaftsvergleich*. Passau: Rothe, 1994.

Iriye, Akira. "Internationalizing International History," in *Rethinking American History in a Global Age*, edited by Thomas Bender. Berkeley: University of California Press, 2002.

Jacob, Margaret C. "Science Studies after Social Construction: The Turn Towards the Comparative and the Global," in *Beyond the Cultural Turn: New Directions in the Study of Society and Culture*, edited by Lynn Hunt and Victoria Bonnell. Berkeley; Los Angeles: University of California Press, 1999.

Kaelble, Hartmut. "La récherche européenne en histoire social comparative." *Actes de la récherche en Science Sociale* 106–107 (March 1995), 67–79.

Kaelble, Hartmut. *Der historische Vergleich: Eine Einführung zum 19. und 20. Jahrhundert*. Frankfurt: Campus, 1999.

Kaelble, Hartmut, editor. *Transnationale Öffentlichkeiten und Identitäten im 20. Jahrhundert*. Frankfurt: Campus, 2002.

Kaelble, Hartmut and Jürgen Schriewer, editors, *Diskurse und Entwicklungspfade. Gesellschaftsvergleiche in Geschichts- und Sozialwissenschaften*. Frankfurt a.M.: Campus, 1999.

Kocka, Jürgen. "Comparative Historical Research: German Examples." *International Review of Social History* 38 (1993).

Kocka, Jürgen. "Comparison and Beyond." *History and Theory* 42 (2003), 39–44.

Kolchin, Peter. "Comparing American History." *Reviews in American History (The Promise of American History: Progress and Prospects)* 10: 4 (December 1982), 64–81.

Lamont, Michèle and Laurent Thévenot, editors. *Rethinking Comparative Cultural Sociology. Repertoires of Evaluation in France and the United States*. Cambridge, UK: Cambridge University Press, 2000.

Mahoney, James and Dietrich Rueschemeyer. *Comparative Historical Analysis in the Social Sciences*. Cambridge: Cambridge University Press, 2003.

Matthes, Joachim, editor. *Zwischen den Kulturen?: die Sozialwissenschaften vor dem Problem des Kulturvergleichs*. Göttingen: O. Schwartz, 1992.

Mazlish, Bruce. *Conceptualizing Global History*. Boulder, CO: Westview Press,1993.

McGerr, Michael. "The Price of the 'New Transnational History.'" *American Historical Review* 96: 4 (October 1991), 1056–1067.

McMichael, Philip. "Incorporating Comparison within a World Historical Perspective: An Alternative Comparative Method." *American Sociological Review* 55 (June 1990), 385–397.

Meritt, Richard L. and Stein Rokkan, editors. *Comparing Nations: The Use of Quantitative Data in Cross-National Research.* New Haven, CT: Yale University Press, 1966.

Middell, Matthias. "Kulturtransfer und historische Komparistik. Thesen zu ihrem Verhältnis." *Comparativ* 10 (2000), 7–41.

Mill, John Stuart. "Two Methods of Comparison" (excerpt from *A System of Logic* 1888) in *Comparative Perspectives: Theories And Methods,* Amitai Etzioni and Fred DuBow, editors. Boston: Little Brown, 1969.

Mitchell, Allan. "Caesar's Laurel Crown—The Case for a Comparative Concept: Reply." *The Journal of Modern History* 49: 2 (June 1977), 207–209.

Osterhammel, Jürgen. "Sozialgeschichte im Zivilisationsvergleich: Zu künftigen Möglichkeiten komparativer Geschichtswissenschaft." *Geschichte und Gesellschaft* 22 (1996), 143–164.

Osterhammel, Jürgen. "Transnationale Gesellschaftsgeschichte: Erweiterung oder Alternative?" *Geschichte und Gesellschaft* 27: 3 (2001), 464–479.

Osterhammel, Jürgen. *Geschichtswissenschaft jenseits des Nationalstaats. Studien zu Beziehungsgeschichte und Zivilisationsvergleich.* Göttingen: Vandenhoeck & Ruprecht, 2001.

Paulmann, Johannes. "Internationaler Vergleich und interkultureller Transfer: Zwei Forschungsansätze zur europäischen Geschichte des 18. bis 20. Jahrhunderts." *Historische Zeitschrift* 267: 3 (December 1998): 649–685.

Pirenne, Henri. "De la methode comparative en histoire," in *Compte rendu du Ve Congrès international des sciences historiques, Bruxelles, 1923,* edited by Guillaume Des Marez and François Louis Ganshof. Brussels: M. Weissenbruch, 1923.

Pocock, J.G.A. "The Origins of Study of the Past: A Comparative Approach." *Comparative Studies in Society and History* 4: 2 (January 1962), 209–246.

Przeworski, Adam and Henry Teune. *The Logic of Comparative Social Inquiry.* New York: Wiley-Interscience, 1970.

Ragin, Charles C. *The Comparative Method: Moving beyond Qualitative and Quantitative Strategies.* Berkeley: University of California Press, 1987.

Rokkan, Stein, editor. *Comparative Research across Cultures and Nations.* Paris; The Hague: Mouton, 1968.

Rossi, Pietro, editor. *La storia comparata. Approcci e prospettive.* Milan: Il Saggiatore, 1990.

Rusen, Jorn. "Some Theoretical Approaches to Intercultural Comparative Historiography." *History and Theory* 35: 4 (December 1996), 5–22.

Salvati, Mariuccia. "Histoire contemporaine et analyse comparative en Italie." *Genèses: Sciences sociales et histoire* 22 (March 1996), 146–159.

See, Henri. "Remarques sur l'application de la methode comparative a l'histoire economique et sociale." *Revue de synthèse historique* 36 (1923), 37–46.

Sewell, William H. and Thrupp, Sylvia L. "[Marc Bloch and comparative history]: Comments." *American Historical Review*, 85: 4 (October 1980), 847–853.

Sewell, William H., Jr. "Marc Bloch and the Logic of Comparative History." *History and Theory* 6 (1967), 208–218.

Skocpol, Theda and Margaret Somers. "The Uses of Comparative History in Macrosocial Inquiry." *Comparative Studies in Society and History* 22: 2 (April 1980), 174–197.

Smelser, Neil J. *Comparative Methods in the Social Sciences.* Englewood Cliffs, NJ: Prentice-Hall, 1976.

Spiliotis, Susanna-Sophia. "Das Konzept der Transterritorialität oder Wo findet Gesellschaft statt?" *Geschichte und Gesellschaft* 27: 3 (2001), 480–488.

Steiner, George. "What is comparative literature?" An inaugural lecture delivered before the University of Oxford on 11 October, 1994. Oxford: Clarendon, 1995.

Stoler, Ann L. "Tense and Tender Ties: The Politics of Comparison in North American History and (Post) Colonial Studies." *Journal of American History* (December 2001), 831–864.

Sturmer, Michael. "Caesar's Laurel Crown—the Case for a Comparative Concept." *The Journal of Modern History* 49: 2 (June 1977), 203–207.

Subrahmanyam, Sanjay. "Connected Histories: Toward a Reconfiguration of Early Modern Eurasia," in *Beyond Binary Histories: Re-imagining Eurasia to c. 1830*, edited by V.B. Lieberman. Ann Arbor, MI: University of Michigan Press, 1997.

Swierenga, Robert P. "Computers and Comparative History." *Journal of Interdisciplinary History* 5: 2 (Autumn 1974), 267–286.

Thrupp, Sylvia. "Editorial." *Comparative Studies in Society and History* 1: 1 (October 1958), 1–4.

Thrupp, Sylvia L. "The Role of Comparison in the Development of Economic Theory." *The Journal of Economic History* 17: 4 (December 1957), 554–570.

Tilly, Charles. *Big Structures, Large Processes, Huge Comparisons*. New York: Russell Sage Foundation, 1984.

Tipps, Dean. "Modernization Theory and the Comparative Study of Societies: A Critical Perspective." *Comparative Studies in Society and History* 15: 2 (1973), 199–226.

Triebel, Armin, editor. *Gesellschaften vergleichen. Erträge des Gesellschaftsvergleichs*, vol. I. Berlin: Freie Universität, 1994.

Triebel, Armin, editor. *Die Pragmatik des Gesellschaftsvergleichs. Erträge des Gesellschaftsvergleichs*, vol. II. Leipzig: Leipziger Universitätsverlag, 1997.

Tyrrell, Ian. "American Exceptionalism in an Age of International History." *American Historical Review* 96 (October 1991), 1033–1038.

Vallier, Ivan and David Ernest Apter. *Comparative Methods in Sociology: Essays on Trends and Applications*. Berkeley: University of California Press, 1971.

van den Braembussche, Antoon. "Historical Explanation and Comparative Method: Towards a Theory of the History of Society." *History and Theory* 28 (1989), 1–24.

Walker, Lawrence D. "A Note on Historical Linguistics and Marc Bloch's Comparative Method." *History and Theory* 19: 2 (February 1980) 154–164.

Walton, John. "Standardized Case Comparisons: Observations on Method in Comparative Sociology," in *Comparative Social Research: Methodological Problems and Strategies*, edited by Michael Armer and Allen Day Grimshaw. New York: Wiley, 1973.

Welskopp, Thomas. "Stolpersteine auf dem Königsweg: Methodenkritische Anmerkungen zum internationalen Vergleich in der Gesellschaftsgeschichte." *Archiv für Sozialgeschichte* 35 (1995), 339–367.

Werner, Michael. "La place relative du champ littéraire dans les cultures nationals." *Qu'est-ce qu'une littérature national: Approches pour une théorie interculturelle du champ littéraire*, edited by Michel Espagne and Michael Werner. Paris: Edition MSH, 1994.

Werner, Michael and Bénédicte Zimmermann. "Vergleich, Transfer, Verflechtung. Der Ansatz der Histoire croisée und die Herausforderung des Transnationalen." *Geschichte und Gesellschaft* 28: 4 (2002), 607–636.

Werner, Michael and Bénédicte Zimmermann, "Penser l'histoire croisée: entre empirie et réflexivité." *Annales HSS* (January–February 2003), 7–36.

Wirz, Albert. "Für eine transnationale Gesellschaftsgeschichte." *Geschichte und Gesellschaft* 27: 3 (2001), 489–498.

Woodward, C. Vann, editor. *The Comparative Approach to American History*. New York; London: Basic, 1968.

Zelditch, Morris Jr. "Intelligible Comparisons" in *Comparative Methods in Sociology: Essays on Trends and Applications*, edited by Ivan Vallier and David Ernest Apter. Berkeley: University of California Press, 1971.

WORKS OF COMPARATIVE, CROSS-NATIONAL, OR TRANSNATIONAL INTEREST

Affron, Matthew and Mark Antliff, editors. *Fascist Visions: Art and Ideology in France and Italy.* Princeton, NJ: Princeton University Press, 1997.

Aldrich, Richard J. *The Hidden Hand: Britain, America and Cold War Secret Intelligence.* London: John Murray, 2001.

Allinson, Mark. *Germany and Austria 1814–2000: Modern History for Modern Languages.* London: Arnold, 2002.

Alvarez, Alex. *Governments, Citizens, and Genocide: A Comparative and Interdisciplinary Approach.* Bloomington, IN: Indiana University Press, 2001.

Angerer, Thomas and Jacques Le Rider, editors. *"Ein Frühling, dem kein Sommer folgte?" Französisch-österreichische Kulturtransfers seit 1945.* Vienna: Böhlau, 1999.

Apter, David E. "Radicalization and Embourgeoisement: Some Hypotheses for a Comparative Study of History." *Journal of Interdisciplinary History* 1: 2 (Winter, 1971). 265–303.

August, Thomas G. *The Selling of the Empire: British and French Imperialist Propaganda, 1890–1940* (Contributions in Comparative Colonial Studies no. 19). Westport, CT: Greenwood, 1985.

Aymard, Maurice. "De la Méditerranée à l'Asie: une comparaison nécessaire." *Annales ESC* 56: 1 (January–February 2001), 43–50.

Bade, Klaus J. *Europa in Bewegung: Migration vom späten 18. Jahrhundert bis zur Gegenwart.* Munich: C. H. Beck, 2000.

Baily, Samuel L. *Immigrants in the Lands of Promise: Italians in Buenos Aires and New York City, 1870–1914.* Ithaca, NY: Cornell University Press, 1999.

Baldwin, Peter. *Contagion and the State in Europe, 1830–1930.* New York: Cambridge University Press, 1999.

Baldwin, Peter. *The Politics of Social Solidarity: Class Bases of the European Welfare State, 1875–1975.* New York: Cambridge University Press, 1990.

Balfour, Michael Leonard Graham. *Propaganda in War, 1939–1945: Organisations, Policies, and Publics in Britain and Germany.* London; Boston: Routledge & Kegan Paul, 1979.

Barclay, David E. and Elisabeth Glaser-Schmidt. *Transatlantic Images and Perceptions: Germany and America since 1776* (Publications of the German Historical Institute in Washington, DC). Cambridge, UK; New York: German Historical Institute; Cambridge University Press, 1997.

Barton, H. Arnold. *A Folk Divided: Homeland Swedes and Swedish Americans, 1840–1940,* Acta Universitatis Upsaliensis. Studia Multiethnica Upsaliensia 10. Uppsala. Stockholm: Uppsala University; Distributor Almqvist & Wiksell International, 1994.

Baumgart, Winfried. *Imperialism: The Idea and Reality of British and French Colonial Expansion, 1880–1914.* Rev. ed. New York: Oxford University Press, 1982.

Behrens, C. B. A. *Society, Government and the Enlightenment: the Experiences of Eighteenth-Century France and Prussia.* New York: Harper & Row, 1985.

Bender, Thomas and Carl E. Schorske. *Budapest and New York: Studies in Metropolitan Transformation, 1870–1930.* New York: Russell Sage Foundation, 1994.

Bender, Thomas, editor. *Rethinking American History in a Global Age.* Berkeley: University of California Press, 2002.

Bendix, Reinhard. *Nation-Building and Citizenship.* Berkeley: University of California Press, 1977.

Bendix, Reinhard. *Kings or People: Power and the Mandate to Rule.* Berkeley: University of California Press, 1978.

Benton, Lauren. *Law and Colonial Cultures: Legal Regimes in World History, 1400–1900. Studies in Comparative World History.* New York and Cambridge, UK: Cambridge University Press, 2002.

Berg, Manfred, and Martin H. Geyer, editors. *Two Cultures of Rights: The Quest for Inclusion and Participation in Modern America and Germany*. Washington, DC: Publications of the German Historical Institute, 2002.

Berger, Stefan. *The British Labour Party and the German Social Democrats, 1900–1931*. Oxford: Clarendon, 1994.

Berghoff, H. and R. Möller. "Tired Pioneers and Dynamic Newcomers? A Comparative Essay on English and German Entrepreneurial History, 1870–1914." *Economic History Review* 47 (1994), 262–287.

Best, Heinrich. *Die Männer von Bildung und Besitz. Struktur und Handeln parlamentarischer Führungsgruppen in Deutschland und Frankreich 1848/9*. Düsseldorf: Droste, 1990.

Biddle, Tami Davis. *Rhetoric and Reality in Air Warfare: The Evolution of British and American Ideas about Strategic Bombing, 1914–1945*. Princeton, NJ: Princeton University Press, 2002.

Biernacki, Richard. *The Fabrication of Labor: Germany and Britain, 1640–1914*. Berkeley: University of California Press, 1995.

Birke, Adolf M. and Kurt Kluxen. *Deutscher und britischer Parlamentarismus = British and German parliamentarism*. Munich: Saur, 1985.

Blackbourn, David and Geoff Eley. *The Peculiarities of German History: Bourgeois Society and Politics in Nineteenth-Century Germany*. Oxford: Oxford University Press, 1984.

Bloch, Marc. "A Contribution towards a Comparative History of European Societies," in *Land and Work in Medieval Europe: Selected Papers by Marc Bloch*. Berkeley: University of California Press,1967.

Bloch, Marc. *Mélanges historiques*. Paris: EHESS, 1983.

Bloch, Marc. "Comparaison," [1930], in *Histoire et historiens*. Paris: Armand Colin, 1995.

Blom, Ida. "Gender and Nation in International Comparison." in *Gendered Nations: Nationalisms and Gender Order in the Long Nineteenth Century*, edited by Ida Blom, Karin Hagemann, and Catherine Hall. Oxford; New York: Berg, 2000.

Bock, Hans Manfred, Michel Trebitsch, and Marie-Christine Granjon. *Pour une histoire comparée des intellectuels: textes, collection "Histoire du temps présent."* Brussels: Editions Complexe, 1998.

Boemeke, Manfred, Roger Chickering, and Stig Förster, editors. *Anticipating Total War: The German and American experiences, 1871–1914*. New York: Cambridge University Press. 1999.

Bolt, Christine. *Feminist Ferment. "The Woman Question" in the USA and England, 1870–1940*. London: UCL Press, 1995.

Bonner, Thomas Neville. *Becoming a Physician: Medical Education in Britain, France, Germany and the United States, 1750–1945*. New York: Oxford University Press, 1995.

Bouvier, Pierre. "Différences et analogies," in *France-U.S.A.: Les crises du travail et de la production*, edited by Pierre Bouvier, Olivier Kourchid, and Jean Leroy. Paris: Méridiens Klincksieck, 1988.

Bowman, Shearer Davis. *Masters and Lords: Mid-19th Century U.S. Planters and Prussian Junkers*. New York: Oxford University Press, 1993.

Breuilly, John, editor. *Labour and Liberalism in 19th Century Europe: Essays in Comparative History*. New York: St. Martin's, 1991.

Brewer, John and Eckhart Hellmuth, editors. *Rethinking Leviathan: The Eighteenth-Century State in Britain and Germany*. New York: Oxford University Press, for the German Historical Institute, London, 1999.

Bronstein, Jamie L. *Land Reform and Working-Class Experience in Britain and the United States, 1800–1862*. Stanford, CA: Stanford University Press, 1998.

Brown, Kate. "Gridded Lives: Why Kazakhastan and Montana Are Nearly the Same Place." *American Historical Review* 106 (2001), 17–48.

Brubaker, Rogers. *Citizenship and Nationhood in France and Germany*. Cambridge, MA: Harvard University Press, 1992.

Budde, Gunilla-Friederike. *Auf dem Weg ins Bürgerleben: Kindheit und Erziehung in deutschen und englischen Bürgerfamilien 1840–1914*. Göttingen: Vandenhoeck & Ruprecht, 1994.

Bullock, Nicholas and James Read. *The Movement for Housing Reform in Germany and France, 1840–1914*. Cambridge, UK; New York: Cambridge University Press, 1985.

Burguière, André and Raymond Grew, editors. *The Construction of Minorities: Cases for Comparison across Time and around the World* (The Comparative Studies in Society and History Book Series). Ann Arbor, MI: University of Michigan Press, 2001.

Burton, Antoinette M. *Burdens of History: British Feminists, Indian Women, and Imperial Culture, 1865–1915*. Chapel Hill, NC: University of North Carolina Press, 1994.

Cassinelli, C. W. *Total Revolution: A Comparative Study of Germany under Hitler, the Soviet Union under Stalin, and China under Mao*. Santa Barbara, CA: Clio, 1976.

Charle, Christophe. *La crise des sociétés impériales: Allemagne, France, Grande-Bretagne (1900–1940)* (Essai de histoire social comparé). Paris: Editions de Seuil, 2001.

Chorbajian, Levon and George Shirinian, editors. *Studies in Comparative Genocide*. New York: St. Martin's, 1999.

Cleve, Ingeborg, *Geschmack, Kunst und Konsum. Kulturpolitik als Wirtschaftspolitik in Frankreich und Württemberg, 1805–1845*. Göttingen, Vandenhoeck und Ruprecht, 1996.

Cohen, Deborah. *The War Come Home: Disabled Veterans in Britain and Germany, 1914–1939*. Berkeley: University of California Press, 2001.

Connelly, John. *Captive University: The Sovietization of East German, Czech and Polish Higher Education, 1945–1956*. Chapel Hill, NC: University of North Carolina Press, 2000.

Conrad, Sebastian. *Auf der suche nach der verlorenen Nation: Geschichtsschreibung in West Deutschland und Japan, 1945–1960* (Kritische Studien zur Geschichtswissenschaft, no. 134). Gottingen: Vandenhoeck und Ruprecht, 1999.

Cross, Gary S. *A Quest for Time: The Reduction of Work in Britain and France, 1840–1940*. Berkeley: University of California Press, 1989.

Crouzet, François. *Britain Ascendant. Comparative Studies in Franco-British Economic History*. Cambridge, UK: Cambridge University Press, 1990.

Dienel, Christiane. *Kinderzahl und Staatsräson. Empfängnisverhütung und Bevölkerungspolitik in Deutschland und Frankreich bis 1918*. Münster: Westfälisches Dampfboot, 1995.

Dimitrieva, Katia and Michel Espagne, editors. *Transferts culturels triangulaires France—Allemagne—Russie*. Paris: Editions de la Maison de Sciences de l'Homme, 1996.

Dobbin, Frank. *Forging Industrial Policy: The United States, Britain, and France in the Railway Age*. Cambridge, UK; New York: Cambridge University Press, 1994.

Downs, Laura Lee. *Manufacturing Inequality: Gender Division in the French and British Metalworking Industries, 1914–1939*. Ithaca, NY: Cornell University Press, 1995.

Drescher, Seymour. *Capitalism and Antislavery: British Mobilization in Comparative Perspective*. London: Macmillan, 1986.

Drescher, Seymour. *From Slavery to Freedom: Comparative Studies in the Rise and Fall of Atlantic Slavery*. New York: New York University Press, 1999.

Dunlavy, Colleen A. *Politics and Industrialization: Early Railroads in the United States and Prussia*. Princeton, NJ: Princeton University Press, 1994.

Dunthorn, David. *Britain and the Spanish Anti-Franco Opposition, 1940–1950*. New York: Palgrave, 2000.

Eisenberg, Christiane. *Deutsche und englische Gewerkschaften: Entstehung und Entwicklung bis 1878 im Vergleich*, Kritische Studien zur Geschichtswissenschaft ; Bd. 72. Göttingen: Vandenhoeck & Ruprecht, 1986.

Eley, Geoff. *Forging Democracy: The History of the Left in Europe, 1850–2000*. Oxford: Oxford University Press, 2002.

Ericson, Edward E., III. *Feeding the German Eagle: Soviet Economic Aid to Nazi Germany, 1933–1941*. Westport, CT: Praeger, 1999.

Espagne, Michel. *Bordeaux Baltique. La présence culturelle allemande à Bordeaux aux XVIII et XIX siècles*. Paris: Editions de la maison des sciences de l'homme, 1991.

Espagne, Michel. *Les transferts culturels franco-allemands, perspectives germaniques*. Paris: Presses Universitaires de France, 1999.

Espagne, Michel and Werner Greiling, editors. *Frankreichfreunde. Mittler des französisch-deutschen Kulturtransfers (1750–1850)*. Leipzig: Universitätsverlag, 1996.

Espagne, Michel and Matthias Middell, editors. *Von der Elbe bis an die Seine: Kulturtransfer zwischen Sachsen und Frankreich im 18. Und 19. Jahrhundert*. Leipzig: Universitätsverlag, 1993.

Espagne, Michel and Michael Werner, editors. *Transferts. Les Relations interculturelles dans l'espace franco-allemand (XVIIIe et XIXe siècle)*. Paris: Editions Recherches sur les Civilisations, 1988.

Espagne, Michel, Françoise Lagier, and Michael Werner, editors. *Le maître de langues: Les premiers enseignants d'allemand en France, (1830–1850)*. Paris: Editions de la Maison des Sciences de l'Homme, 1991.

Esping-Andersen, Gøsta. *The Three Worlds of Welfare Capitalism*. Princeton, NJ: Princeton University Press, 1990.

Evans, Richard John. *The Feminists: Women's Emancipation Movements in Europe, America, and Australasia. 1840–1920*. London: Croom Helm; New York: Barnes & Noble, 1977.

Fagge, Roger. *Power, Culture, and Conflict in the Coalfields: West Virginia and South Wales, 1900–1922*. Manchester; New York: Manchester University Press, 1996.

Fahrmeir, Andreas. *Citizens and Aliens: Foreigners and the Law in Britain and the German States, 1789–1870* (Monographs in German History, no. 5). New York: Berghahn, 2000.

Farnie, Douglas A. et al., editors. *Region and Strategy in Britain and Japan: Business in Lancashire and Kansai, 1890–1990* (Routledge International Studies in Business History, no. 7). New York: Routledge, 2000.

Fehrenbach, Heide and Uta G. Poiger, editors. *Transactions, Transgressions, Transformations: American Culture in Western Europe and Japan*. New York: Berghahn, 2000.

Feldman, Gerald and Klaus Tenfelde, editors. *Workers, Owners and Politics in Coal Mining. An International Comparison of Industrial Relations*. New York: St. Martin's, 1990

Finzsch, Norbert and Hermann Wellenreuther, editors. *Visions of the Future in Germany and America* (Germany and the United States of America, Krefeld Historical Symposia). New York: Berg, 2001.

Flora, Peter. *State, Economy and Society in Western Europe, 1815–1870*. 2 vols. Frankfurt: Campus, 1983–1987.

Flora, Peter and A.J. Heidenheimer, editors. *The Development of Welfare States in Europe and America*. New Brunswick, NJ: Transaction, 1981.

François, Etienne and M.C. Hoock-Demarlel, editors. *Marianne—Germania. Deutsch-französischer Kulturtransfer im europäischen Kontext 1789–1914*. Leipzig: Universitätsverlag, 1998.

François, Etienne, Hannes Siegrist, and Jakob Vogel, editors. *Nation und Emotion. Deutschland und Frankreich im Vergleich. 19. und 20. Jahrhundert*. Göttingen: Vandenhoeck & Ruprecht, 1995.

Fredrickson, George M. *White Supremacy: A Comparative Study in American and South African History*. New York: Oxford University Press, 1981.

Fredrickson, George M. "Giving a Comparative Dimension to American History: Problems and Opportunities." *Journal of Interdisciplinary History* 16: 1 (Summer 1985), 107–110.

Fredrickson, George M. *Black Liberation: A Comparative History of Black Ideologies in the United States and South Africa*. New York: Oxford University Press, 1995.

Fredrickson, George M. *The Comparative Imagination: On the History of Racism, Nationalism, and Social Movements*. Berkeley: University of California Press, 1997.

Frémont, Antoine. *La French Line face à la mondialisation de l'espace maritime*. Paris: Anthropos, 1998.

Friedman, Gerald. *State-Making and Labor Movements: France and the United States, 1876–1914*. Ithaca, NY: Cornell University Press, 1998.

Fritz, Bärbel, Brigitte Schultze, and Horst Turk, editors. *Theaterinstitution und Kulturtransfer I: Fremdsprachiges Repertoire am Burgtheater und auf anderen europäischen Bühnen*. Tübingen: Narr, 1997.

Fritz, Martin. *German Steel and Swedish Iron Ore, 1939–1945*. Göteborg: Institute of Economic History of Gothenburg University, 1974.

Fulbrook, Mary. *Piety and Politics: Religion and the Rise of Absolutism in England, Württemberg and Prussia*. Cambridge, UK: Cambridge University Press, 1983.

Fulcher, James. *Labour Movements, Employers, and the State: Conflict and Co-operation in Britain and Sweden*. Oxford, UK; New York: Clarendon; Oxford University Press, 1991.

Gabaccia, Donna R. *Italy's Many Diasporas*. London: UCL Press, 2000.

Gallman, Matthew. *Receiving Erin's Children: Philadelphia, Liverpool, and the Irish Famine Migration, 1845–1855*. Chapel Hill, NC: University of North Carolina Press, 2000.

Gerschenkron, Alexander. *Economic Backwardness in Historical Perspective*. Cambridge, MA: Belknap, 1962.

Geyer, Michael. "Ein Vorbote des Wohlfahrtsstaates: Die Kriegsopferversorgung in Frankreich, Deutschland und Großbritannien nach dem Ersten Weltkrieg." *Geschichte und Gesellschaft* 9 (1983), 230–277.

Ghirardo, Diane Yvonne. *Building New Communities: New Deal America and Fascist Italy*. Princeton, NJ: Princeton University Press, 1989.

Godley, Andrew. *Jewish Immigrant Entrepreneurship in New York and London, 1880–1914*. Basingstoke: Palgrave, 2001.

Gouda, Frances. *Poverty and Political Culture: The Rhetoric of Social Welfare in the Netherlands and France, 1815–1854*. Lanham, MD: Rowman & Littlefield, 1995.

Grayzel, Susan R. *Women's Identities at War: Gender, Motherhood, and Politics in Britain and France during the First World War*. Chapel Hill, NC: University of North Carolina Press, 1999.

Green, Nancy L. "The Comparative Method and Poststructural Structuralism—New Perspectives for Migration Studies." *Journal of American Ethnic Studies*. 13: 4 (Summer 1994), 3–22.

Green, Nancy L. "Modes comparatifs dans le regard de l'Autre: Récits de voyages chez Chateaubriand et Arthur Young," in *De Russie et d'ailleurs: feux croisés sur l'histoire*, edited by Martine Godet, Marc Ferro, Muriel Carduner-Loosfelt, and Hélène Coq-Lossky. Paris: Institut d'études slaves, 1995.

Green, Nancy L. *Ready-to-Wear and Ready-to-Work: A Century of Industry and Immigrants in Paris and New York*. Durham, NC: Duke University Press, 1997.

Green, Nancy L. "The Comparative Gaze: Travelers in France before the Era of Mass Tourism." *French Historical Studies* 25: 3 (Summer 2002), 423–440.

Gregg, Robert. *Inside Out, Outside In: Essays in Comparative History.* New York: St. Martin's, 2000.

Greve, Bent, editor. *Comparative Welfare Systems: The Scandinavian Model in a Period of Change.* New York: St. Martin's, 1996.

Guarneri, Carl J. *America Compared: American History in International Perspective, vol. I.* Boston: Houghton Mifflin, 1997.

Habakkuk, H.J. *American and British Technology in the Nineteenth Century.* Cambridge, UK: Cambridge University Press, 1962.

Hagen, William W. *Germans, Poles, and Jews: The Nationality Conflict in the Prussian East, 1772–1914.* Chicago: University of Chicago Press, 1980.

Harrison, J.F.C. *Quest for the New Moral World: Robert Owen and the Owenities in Britain and America.* New York: Scribner, 1969.

Haydu, Jeffrey. *Between Craft and Class: Skilled Workers and Factory Politics in the United States and Britain, 1890–1922.* Berkeley: University of California Press, 1991.

Hennock, E.P. *British Social Reform and German Precedents: The Case of Social Insurance, 1880–1914.* Oxford: Clarendon, 1987.

Himka, John-Paul. *Socialism in Galicia: The Emergence of Polish Social Democracy and Ukrainian Radicalism, 1860–1890.* Cambridge, MA: Distributed by Harvard University Press for the Harvard Ukrainian Research Institute, 1983.

Hoerder, Dirk and Jörg Nagler. *People in Transit: German Migrations in Comparative Perspective, 1820–1930* (Publications of the German Historical Institute, Washington, DC). Cambridge, UK; New York: German Historical Institute; Cambridge University Press, 1995.

Hollingsworth, J.R. *A Political Economy of Medicine. Great Britain and the United States.* Baltimore, MD: Johns Hopkins University Press, 1986.

Hoover, Arlie J. *God, Germany, and Britain in the Great War: A Study in Clerical Nationalism.* New York: Praeger, 1989.

Hopkins, A. G., editor. *Globalization in World History.* London: Pimlico, 2002.

Hopwood, Derek. *The Russian Presence in Syria and Palestine, 1843–1914; Church and Politics in the Near East.* Oxford: Clarendon, 1969.

Horne, John N. *Labour at War: France and Britain, 1914–1918.* Oxford: Clarendon, 1991

Hughes, Judith M. *Emotion and High Politics: Personal Relations at the Summit in Late Nineteenth-Century Britain and Germany.* Berkeley: University of California Press, 1983.

Hurd, Madeleine. *Public Spheres, Public Mores, and Democracy: Hamburg and Stockholm, 1870–1914* (Social History, Popular Culture, and Politics in Germany). Ann Arbor, MI: University of Michigan Press, 2000.

Jahr, Christoph. *Gewöhnliche Soldaten: Desertion und Deserteure im deutschen und britischen Heer 1914–1918,* Kritische Studien zur Geschichtswissenschaft; Bd. 123. Göttingen: Vandenhoeck & Ruprecht, 1998.

Jeismann, Michael. *Das Vaterland der Feinde: Studien zum nationalen Feindbegriff und Selbstverständnis in Deutschland und Frankreich, 1792–1918,* Sprache und Geschichte; Bd. 19. Stuttgart: Klett-Cotta, 1992.

Jones, Geoffrey. *Merchants to Multinationals: British Trading Companies in the Nineteenth and Twentieth Centuries.* Oxford; New York: Oxford University Press, 2000.

Jordan, Lothar and Bernd Kortländer, editors. *Nationale Grenzen und internationaler Austausch. Studien zum Kultur- und Wissenschaftstransfer in Europa.* Tübingen: Niemeyer, 1995.

Kaelble, Hartmut: *Nachbarn am Rhein: Entfremdung und Annäherung der französischen und deutschen Gesellschaft seit 1880.* Munich: Beck, 1991.

Kaelble, Hartmut and Jürgen Schriewer, editors. *Gesellschaften im Vergleich.* Frankfurt a.M.: Lang, 1999.

Kallis, Aristotle A. *Fascist Ideology: Territory and Expansionism in Italy and Germany, 1922–1945.* New York: Routledge, 2000.

Kaplan, Jeffrey, editor. *Beyond the Mainstream: The Emergence of Religious Pluralism in Finland, Estonia, and Russia* (Studia Historica, no. 63). Helsinki: Suomalaisen Kirjallisuuden Seura, 2000.

Kautsky, John H. *Social Democracy and the Aristocracy: Why Socialist Labor Movements Developed in Some Industrial Countries and Not in Others.* New Brunswick, NJ: Transaction, 2002.

Kelly, Alfred. *The Descent of Darwin: The Popularization of Darwinism in Germany, 1860–1914.* Chapel Hill, NC: University of North Carolina Press, 1981.

Kern, Stephen. *Eyes of Love: The Gaze in English and French Culture, 1840–1900.* New York: New York University Press, 1996.

Kielstra, Paul Michael. *The Politics of Slave Trade Suppression in Britain and France, 1814–48.* New York: St. Martin's, 2000.

Kimeldorf, Howard. *Reds or Rackets? The Making of Radical and Conservative Unions on the Waterfront.* Berkeley: University of California Press, 1988.

Klaus, Alisa. *Every Child a Lion: The Origins of Maternal and Infant Health Policy in the United States and France, 1890–1920.* Ithaca, NY: Cornell University Press, 1993.

Knox, MacGregor. *Common Destiny: Dictatorship, Foreign Policy, and War in Fascist Italy and Nazi Germany.* New York: Cambridge University Press, 2000.

Kocka, Jürgen. *White Collar Workers in America, 1890–1940: A Social–Political History in International Perspective,* trans. Maura Kealey. London; Beverly Hills: Sage, 1980.

Kocka, Jürgen, editor. *Europäische Arbeiterbewegungen im 19. Jahrhundert. Deutschland, Österreich, England und Frankreich im Vergleich.* Göttingen: Vandenhoeck & Ruprecht, 1983.

Kocka, Jürgen and Ute Frevert, editors. *Bürgertum im 19. Jahrhundert: Deutschland im europäischen Vergleich.* 3 vols. Munich: DTV, 1988.

Kocka, Jürgen and Allan Mitchell, editors. *Bourgeois Society in Nineteenth-Century Europe.* Oxford; Providence, RI: Berg, 1993.

Koht, Halvdan. *The American Spirit in Europe: A Survey of Transatlantic Influences* (Publications of the American Institute, University of Oslo). Philadelphia: University of Pennsylvania Press, 1949.

Kolchin, Peter. *Unfree Labor: American Slavery and Russian Serfdom.* Cambridge, MA: Belknap Press of Harvard University Press, 1987.

Krejcí, Jaroslav and Anna Krejcová. *Great Revolutions Compared: The Outline of a Theory.* 2nd ed. New York: Harvester Wheatsheaf, 1994.

Kulawik, Teresa. *Wohlfahrtsstaat und Mutterschaft: Schweden und Deutschland 1870–1912* (Politik der Geschlechtsverhältnisse, no. 13). Frankfurt: Campus, 1999.

Lahiri, Shompa. *Indians in Britain: Anglo-Indian Encounters, Race and Identity 1880–1930* (The Colonial Legacy in Britain, no. 1). Portland, OR: Frank Cass, 2000.

Laslett, John H. M. *Colliers Across the Sea: A Comparative Study of Class Formation in Scotland and the American Midwest, 1830–1924* (The Working Class in American History). Champaign, IL: University of Illinois Press, 2000.

Lehmann, Hartmut, Hermann Wellenreuther, and Renate Wilson, editors. *In Search of Peace and Prosperity: New German Settlements in Eighteenth-Century Europe and America.* Assisted by John B. Frantz and Carola Wessel. University Park, PA: Pennsylvania State University Press, 2000.

Liedtke, Rainer. *Jewish Welfare in Hamburg and Manchester, c. 1850–1914* (Oxford Historical Monographs). New York: Clarendon, 1998.

Lieven, Dominic. *The Aristocracy in Europe, 1815–1914.* New York: Columbia University Press, 1992.

Liu, Tien-Lung. *The Chameleon State: Global Culture and Policy Shifts in Britain and Germany, 1914–1933.* Oxford and Providence, RI: Berghahn, 1999.

Locke, Robert R. *The End of the Practical Man: Entrepreneurship and Higher Education in Germany, France, and Great Britain, 1880–1940* (Industrial development and the social fabric; vol. 7). Greenwich, CT: JAI, 1984.

Loubère, Leo A. *The Red and the White: A History of Wine in France and Italy in the Nineteenth Century.* Albany, NY: State University of New York Press, 1978.

Low, D. A. *Britain and Indian Nationalism: the Imprint of Ambiguity, 1929–1942.* New York: Cambridge University Press, 1997.

Lustick, Ian. *Unsettled States, Disputed Lands: Britain and Ireland, France and Algeria, Israel and the West Bank-Gaza* (The Wilder House Series in Politics, History, and Culture). Ithaca, NY: Cornell University Press, 1993.

Magee, Gary Bryan. *Productivity and Performance in the Paper Industry: Labour, Capital, and Technology in Britain and America, 1860–1914* (Cambridge Studies in Modern Economic History, no. 4). New York: Cambridge University Press, 1997.

Maier, Charles S. *Recasting Bourgeois Europe: Stabilization in France, Germany, and Italy in the Decade after World War I.* Princeton, NJ: Princeton University Press, 1975.

Mandel, Maud S. *In the Aftermath of Genocide: Armenians and Jews in 20th-Century France.* Durham, NC: Duke University Press, 2003.

Max, Stanley M. *The United States, Great Britain, and the Sovietization of Hungary, 1945-1948* (East European monographs ; no. 177). Boulder, CO; New York: Columbia University Press, 1985.

Mayer, Arno. *The Persistence of the Old Regime: Europe to the Great War.* New York: Pantheon, 1981.

Mayne, A.J.C. *The Imagined Slum: Newspaper Representation in Three Cities, 1870–1914.* Leicester; New York: Leicester University Press; St. Martin's Press, 1993.

McClellan, Woodford D. *Revolutionary Exiles: the Russians in the First International and the Paris Commune.* London; Totowa, NJ: F. Cass, 1979.

McClelland, Charles E. *The German Historians and England; a Study in Nineteenth-Century Views.* Cambridge, UK: University Press, 1971.

McLeod, Hugh. *Piety and Poverty: Working-Class Religion in Berlin, London, and New York, 1870–1914.* (Europe Past and Present series.) New York: Holmes & Meier, 1996.

McMurray, Jonathan S. *Distant Ties: Germany, the Ottoman Empire, and the Construction of the Baghdad Railway.* Westport, CT: Praeger, 2001.

Meyer, Donald B. *Sex and Power: The Rise of Women in America, Russia, Sweden, and Italy.* Middletown, CT: Wesleyan University Press, 1987.

Michie, R. C. *The London and New York Stock Exchanges, 1850–1914.* London; Boston: Allen & Unwin. 1987.

Middell, Matthias, editor. *Transfer und Vergleich.* Leipzig: Leipziger Universitätsverlag, 2000.

Miller, Wilbur R. *Cops and Bobbies: Police Authority in New York and London*, 1830–1870. Chicago: University of Chicago Press, 1977.

Mitchell, Allan. *The Great Train Race: Railways and the Franco-German Rivalry, 1815–1914.* New York: Berghahn, 2000.

Mohun, Arwen P. *Steam Laundries: Gender, Technology, and Work in the United States and Great Britain, 1880–1940.* (Johns Hopkins Studies in the History of Technology, new series, no. 25.) Baltimore: Johns Hopkins University Press, 1999.

Mommsen, Wolfgang J., editor. *The Emergence of the Welfare State in Britain and Germany, 1850–1950.* London: Croom Helm on behalf of the German Historical Institute, 1981.

Mommsen, Wolfgang J., Hans-Gerhard Husung, and German Historical Institute in London. *The Development of Trade Unionism in Great Britain and Germany, 1880–1914.* London; Boston: German Historical Institute; Allen & Unwin, 1985.

Monaco, Paul. *Cinema and Society: France and Germany during the Twenties.* New York: Elsevier, 1976.

Müller, Frank Lorenz. *Britain and the German Question: Perceptions of Nationalism and Political Reform, 1830–63.* New York: Palgrave, 2002.

Nolte, Ernst. *Three Faces of Fascism; Action Française, Italian fascism, National Socialism.* Translation by Leila Vennewitz. London: Weidenfeld and Nicolson, 1965.

Obolenskaia, Svetlana Valerianovna. *Franko-Prusskaia voina i obshchestvennoe mnenie Germanii i Rossii.* Moscow: Nauka, 1977.

O'Brien, Patrick Karl and Çaglar Keyder. *Economic Growth in Britain and France, 1780–1914: Two Paths to the Twentieth Century.* London; Boston: Allen & Unwin, 1978.

Oertzen, Christine von. *Teilzeitarbeit und die Lust zum Zuverdienen: Geschlechterpolitik und gesellschaftlicher Wandel in Westdeutschland 1948–1969.* Göttingen: Vandenhoeck & Ruprecht, 1999.

O'Rourke, Kevin H. and Jeffrey G. Williamson. *Globalization and History: the Evolution of a Nineteenth-Century Atlantic Economy.* Cambridge, MA: MIT Press, 1999.

Oz-Salzberger, Fania. *Translating the Enlightenment: Scottish Civic Discourse in Eighteenth-Century Germany.* Oxford; New York: Clarendon; Oxford University Press, 1995.

Panayi, Panikos, editor. *Germans in Britain since 1500.* Rio Grande, OH: Hambledon, 1996.

Palmer, R.R. *The Age of the Democratic Revolution: a Political History of Europe and America. 1760–1800.* 2 vols. Princeton, NJ: Princeton University Press, 1959.

Pancaldi, Giuliano. *Darwin in Italy: Science across Cultural Frontiers.* Bloomington, IN: Indiana University Press, 1991.

Paulmann, Johannes. "Interkultureller Transfer zwischen Deutschland und Großbritannien im 19. Jahrhundert," in *Aneignung und Abwehr. Interkultureller Transfer zwischen Deutschland und Großbritannien im 19. Jahrhundert,* edited by Rudolf Muhs, Johannes Paulmann, and Willibald Stein. Bodenheim: Philo Verlag, 1998.

Paulmann, Johannes and Martin H. Geyer, editors. *The Mechanics of Internationalism: Culture, Society and Politics from the 1840s to the First World War,* Oxford: Oxford University Press, 2001.

Payne, Stanley G. *Fascism, Comparison and Definition.* Madison, WI: University of Wisconsin Press, 1980.

Pedersen, Susan. *Family, Dependence, and the Origins of the Welfare State: Britain and France, 1914–1945.* Cambridge, UK; New York: Cambridge University Press, 1993.

Portes, Jacques. *Fascination and Misgivings: The United States in French Opinion, 1870–1914.* Translated by Elborg Forster. New York: Cambridge University Press, 2000.

Prinz, Michael. *Brot und Dividende: Konsumervereine in Deutschland und England vor 1914,* Kritische Studien zur Geschichtswissenschaft; Bd. 112. Göttingen: Vandehoeck & Ruprecht, 1996.

Prothero, I. J. *Radical Artisans in England and France, 1830–1870.* Cambridge, UK; New York: Cambridge University Press, 1997.

Puhle, Hans-Jürgen. *Politische Agrarbewegungen in kapitalistischen Industriegesellschaften: Deutschland, USA und Frankreich im 20. Jahrhundert.* (Kritische Studien zur Geschichtswissenschaft, vol. 16.) Göttingen: Vandehoeck and Ruprecht, 1975

Raeff, Marc. *Russia Abroad: A Cultural History of the Russian Emigration, 1919–1939.* New York: Oxford University Press, 1990.

Reimann, Aribert. *Der große Krieg der Sprachen. Untersuchungen zur historischen Semantik in Deutschland und England zur Zeit des Ersten Weltkrieges.* Essen: Klartext Verlag, 2000.

Ringer, Fritz K. *Fields of Knowledge. French Academic Culture in Comparative Perspective, 1890–1920.* Cambridge, UK: Cambridge University Press, 1992.

Ritter, Gerhard Albert. *Der Sozialstaat: Entstehung und Entwicklung im internationalen Vergleich.* Munich: R. Oldenbourg. 1991.

Ritter, Gerhard Albert. *Deutscher und Britischer Parlamentarismus. Ein verfassungsgeschichtlicher Vergleich.* Tübingen, 1962.

Robertson, Andrew W. *The Language of Democracy: Political Rhetoric in the United States and Britain, 1790–1900.* Ithaca, NY: Cornell University Press, 1995.

Rodgers, Daniel T. *Atlantic Crossings: Social Politics in a Progressive Age.* Cambridge, MA: Belknap Press of Harvard University Press, 1998.

Rolleston, T. W. *Ireland and Poland, a Comparison.* London: Unwin Ltd., 1917.

Romani, Roberto. *National Character and Public Spirit in Britain and France, 1750–1914.* New York: Cambridge University Press, 2002.

Rose, Mary B. *Firms, Networks and Business Values: The British and American Cotton Industries since 1750* (Cambridge Studies in Modern Economic History, no. 8). New York: Cambridge University Press, 2000.

Ruble, Blair A. *Second Metropolis: Pragmatic Pluralism in Gilded Age Chicago, Silver Age Moscow, and Meiji Osaka.* New York: Cambridge University Press. Washington, DC: Woodrow Wilson Center, 2001.

Rudé, George F. E. *The Crowd in History: A Study of Popular Disturbances in France and England, 1730–1848* (New Dimensions in History; Essays in Comparative History). New York: Wiley. 1964.

Ruggie, Mary. *The State and Working Women: A Comparative Study of Britain and Sweden.* Princeton, NJ: Princeton University Press, 1984.

Runeby, Nils. *Den nya världen och den gamla. Amerikabild och emigrationsuppfattning i Sverige 1820–1860,* Studia historica Upsaliensia 30. Stockholm: Läromedelsförlaget (Svenska Bokförlaget), 1969.

Ruotsila, Markku. *British and American Anticommunism before the Cold War* (CASS Series: Cold War History, no. 3). Portland, OR: Frank Cass, 2001.

Rupp, Leila. *Worlds of Women: The Making of an International Women's Movement.* Princeton: Princeton University Press, 1997.

Rupp, Leila J. *Mobilizing Women for War: German and American Propaganda, 1939–1945.* Princeton, NJ: Princeton University Press, 1978.

Sahlins, Peter. *Boundaries: The Making of France and Spain in the Pyrenees.* Berkeley: University of California Press, 1989.

Scase, Richard. *Social Democracy in Capitalist Society: Working-Class Politics in Britain and Sweden.* London; Totowa, NJ: Croom Helm; Rowman and Littlefield, 1977.

Schalenberg, Marc, editor. *Kulturtransfer im 19. Jahrhundert.* Berlin : Centre Marc Bloch, 1998.

Schapiro, J. Salwyn. *Liberalism and the Challenge of Fascism: Social Forces in England and France, (1815–1870).* New York: Octagon, 1964.

Schmale, Wolfgang. *Historische Komparatistik und Kulturtransfer. Europageschichtliche Perspektiven für die Landesgeschichte.* Bochum: Winkler. 1998.

Scholliers, Peter, editor. *Real Wages in 19th and 20th Century Europe. Historical and Comparative Perspectives.* Oxford: Berg, 1989.

Seidman, Michael. *Workers against Work: Labor in Paris and Barcelona during the Popular Fronts.* Berkeley: University of California Press, 1991.

Serrier, Thomas. *Entre Allemagne et Pologne. Nations et identités frontalières, 1848–1914.* Paris: Belin, 2002.

Siegrist, Hannes, editor. *Bürgerliche Berufe. Zur Sozialgeschichte der freien und akademischen Berufe im internationalen Vergleich.* Göttingen: Vandenhoeck & Ruprecht, 1988.

Siegrist, Hannes. *Advokat, Bürger und Staat. Eine vergleichende Geschichte der Rechtsanwälte in Deutschland, Italien und der Schweiz (18.–20.Jh.).* Frankfurt a.M.: V. Klostermann, 1996.

Silverman, Victor. *Imagining Internationalism in American and British Labor, 1939–1949.* Urbana and Chicago: University of Illinois Press, 2000.

Skocpol, Theda. *States and Social Revolutions: A Comparative Analysis of France, Russia, and China*. Cambridge, UK; New York: Cambridge University Press, 1979.

Smith, Dennis. *Conflict and Compromise: Class Formation in English Society, 1830–1914: A Comparative Study of Birmingham and Sheffield*. London; Boston: Routledge and Kegan Paul, 1982.

Stavrakis, Peter J. *Moscow and Greek Communism, 1944–1949*. Ithaca, NY: Cornell University Press, 1989.

Steffen, Jerome O. *Comparative Frontiers, a Proposal for Studying the American West*. Norman, OK: University of Oklahoma Press, 1980.

Steinberg, Jonathan. *All or Nothing: The Axis and the Holocaust, 1941–1943*. London: Routledge, 1990.

Steinmo, Sven. *Taxation and Democracy: Swedish, British, and American Approaches to Financing the Modern State*. New Haven, CT: Yale University Press, 1993.

Stuchtey, Benedikt and Peter Wende, editors. *British and German Historiography 1750–1950: Traditions, Perceptions, and Transfers*. (Studies of the German Historical Institute London) New York: Oxford University Press, 2000.

Sutcliffe, Anthony. *Towards the Planned City: Germany, Britain, the United States, and France, 1780–1914*. New York: St. Martin's, 1981.

Szostak, Rick. *The Role of Transportation in the Industrial Revolution: A Comparison of England and France*. Montreal; Buffalo: McGill-Queen's University Press, 1991.

Tacke, Charlotte. *Denkmal im sozialen Raum: Nationale Symbole in Deutschland und Frankreich im 19. Jahrhundert,* Kritische Studien zur Geschichtswissenschaft; Bd. 108. Göttingen: Vandenhoeck & Ruprecht, 1995.

Tarrow, Sidney G. *Between Center and Periphery: Grassroots Politicians in Italy and France*. New Haven, CT: Yale University Press. 1977.

Todorova, Maria. *Imagining the Balkans*. New York: Oxford University Press, 1997.

Tolliday, Steven, and Jonathan Zeitlin. *Shop Floor Bargaining and the State: Historical and Comparative Perspectives*. Cambridge, UK; New York: Cambridge University Press, 1985.

Topp, Michael Miller. *Those without a Country: The Political Culture of Italian American Syndicalists*. (Critical American Studies Series.) Minneapolis, MN: University of Minnesota Press, 2001.

Torstendahl, Rolf, editor. *State Policy and Gender System in the Two German States and Sweden, 1945–1989* (Opuscula Historica Upsaliensia, no. 23). Uppsala: University of Uppsala, 1999.

Torstendahl, Rolf. *Bureaucratisation in Northwestern Europe, 1880–1950. Domination and Governance*. London: Routledge, 1991.

Trebitsch, Michel and Marie-Christine Granjou, editors. *Pour une histoire comparée des intellectuals*. Paris: Editions Complexe, 1998.

Turgeon, Laurier, editor. *Transferts culturels et métissages. Amerique—Europe XVIe—XXe siécle*. Paris: L'Harmattan, 1996.

Vichniac, Judith Eisenberg. *The Management of Labor: The British and French Iron and Steel Industries. 1860–1918*. Greenwich, Conn.: JAI Press, 1990.

Vogel, Jakob. *Nationen im Gleichschritt: der Kult der "Nation in Waffen" in Deutschland und Frankreich. 1871–1914,* Kritische Studien zur Geschichtswissenschaft; Bd. 118. Göttingen: Vandenhoeck & Ruprecht. 1997.

Volmer, Annett. *Presse und Frankophonie im 18. Jahrhundert. Studien zur französischsprachigen Presse in Thüringen, Kursachsen und Russland*. Leipzig: Universitätsverlag, 2000.

Walton, John. *Reluctant Rebels: Comparative Studies of Revolution and Underdevelopment*. New York: Columbia University Press, 1984.

Weber, William. *Music and the Middle Class: The Social Structure of Concert Life in London, Paris, and Vienna*. London: Croom Helm, 1975.

White, Nicola. *Reconstructing Italian Fashion: America and the Development of the Italian Fashion Industry.* New York: Berg, 2000.

Winter, J. M. and Jean-Louis Robert. *Capital Cities at War: Paris, London, Berlin, 1914–1919.* Cambridge, UK; New York: Cambridge University Press, 1997.

Wrench, John and John Solomos, editors. *Racism and Migration in Western Europe.* New York: Berg, 1993.

Zimmermann, Bénédicte, Claude Didry, and Peter Wagner. *Le travail et la nation: histoire croisée de la France et de l'Allemagne.* Paris: Maison des sciences de l'homme, 1999.

INDEX